EARLY BUDDHIST NARRATIVE ART

Illustrations of the Life of the Buddha from Central Asia to China, Korea and Japan

D1553131

Patricia E. Karetzky

University Press of America, ® Inc.
Lanham • New York • Oxford

Copyright © 2000 by
University Press of America,® Inc.
4720 Boston Way
Lanham, Maryland 20706

12 Hid's Copse Rd.
Cumnor Hill, Oxford OX2 9JJ

Library of Congress Cataloging-in-Publication Data

Karetzky, Patricia Eichenbaum.
Early buddhist narrative art : illustrations of the life of the
Buddha from Central Asia to China, Korea, and Japan /
Patricia E. Karetzky.
p.   cm.
Includes bibliographical references and index.
1.   Gautama Buddha—Art. 2. Art, Buddhist—Asia,
Central. 3. Narrative art—Asia, Central. 4. Art, Buddhist —
East Asia. 5. Narrative art—East Asia. I. Title.
N8193.2.K37   2000   704.9'4894363—dc21   00-025210 CIP

ISBN 0-7618-1670-4 (cloth: alk. ppr.)
ISBN 0-7618-1671-2 (pbk: alk. ppr.)

⊖™The paper used in this publication meets the minimum
requirements of American National Standard for Information
Sciences—Permanence of Paper for Printed Library Materials,
ANSI Z39.48—1984

THIS BOOK IS DEDICATED TO
SAHM DOHERTY SEFTON
MY INSPIRATION AND SUPPORT THROUGH A LIFETIME

CONTENTS

Sincere thanks to Duan Wenjie, Director of the Dunhuang Research
Institute; Wang Shiping, Curator, Shaanxi Province Historical
Museum, Xian; Zhou Yue, Vice-President of Education, Shaanxi
Province Historical Museum, Xian; Zhang Fang, Chief Curator Shaanxi
Provincial Museum, Xian; Yang Ziusha, Sichuan Provincial Museum,
Chengdu; and in general to the Shanghai Museum of Art; Xinjiang
Autonomous Region Province Museum, Urumqi; Gansu Provincial
Museum, Lanzhou; Ding Liang, Patrick Coleman, Chief Librarian
Metropolitan Museum of Art Library, and Maria Paguoarlo. With deep
appreciation Alexander Soper and C.T. Hsia.

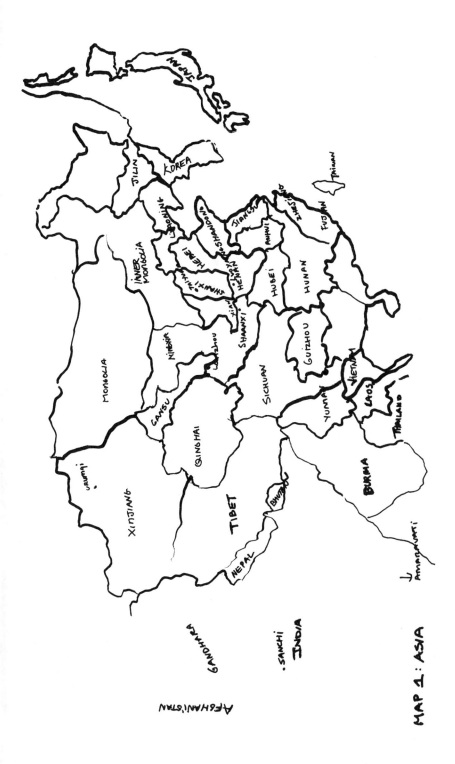

MAP 1 : ASIA

INTRODUCTION

The Buddha was born in the northeastern part of India, around the sixth century B.C.E. By the time of the Common Era, Buddhist doctrine had spread south to the island of Sri Lanka (Ceylon). With the opening of the silk route, monks, missionaries, and merchants traveled from one oasis city to another bringing the Buddhist teachings eastward. In this way Buddhism traveled the land routes from India through Central Asia to northern China, Korea, and Japan. A few centuries later sea routes skirting the coasts of the subcontinent and Southeast Asia led to south China. The Buddhism that was transported east around the time of Common Era had already evolved into an aggregate of religious sects with a variety of icons and complex iconography. In addition to the earliest forms of Buddhism that centered on the life and teachings of the historic Buddha, a later development of the religion, which focused on an ever-increasing pantheon of deities, was also transported. This study is dedicated to tracing the transmission of the earlier images of the historic Buddha and the narrative cycle based on his life to the multifarious cultures of Central Asia and the Far East.

The life of the Buddha was transmitted in four modes—the original oral form of the teachings; a later pictorial tradition; a subsequent body of scriptures; and finally, an illustrated scriptural format. Although related by the common theme of the life of the Buddha that they portray, these formats existed as independent modes of expression in India and may be distinguished from each other by the particular way in which they narrate the biography. In India the pictorial tradition, which evolved separately from the scriptural one, was formative in determining the artistic programs of ancient architectural monuments. It was not until the Common Era that the teachings were cast in written form. Somewhat later, the format of the illustrated scripture evolved as the result of the merging of the pictorial and textual traditions.

This study has several foci of inquiry. In general this is an analysis of the evolution of a pictorial narrative in Chinese Central Asia, China, and Japan.¹ Scenes of the life of the Buddha are independently viewed within their own cultural milieu. Contrasts in the visual presentation of the biography are drawn to highlight alterations made by the various cultures. In addition stylistic and iconographical analysis can sometimes determine which mode of narration was adopted at the various sites, and consideration of the details of the narrative scenes may establish the particular sect and text that served as the basis for the illustrations. There is also an appreciation of the role of the events in the iconographical context in which they appear. Finally, there is an overview of the importance of the pictorial narratives in Buddhist art and iconography.

The chronological period under investigation begins with the earliest Buddhist art in India up until the Guptan era (fourth to seventh century) when the production of Buddhist art suffered a decline. In Central Asia the period of inquiry ends with the eighth century Arab conquests. Though at some sites Buddhist art continued to be produced, it was categorically a far later form of Buddhism, which excluded the kind of narratives under analysis in this study. The examination of Buddhist biographical portrayals in China does not go past the Tang dynasty (627-905) when there was a great falling off of artistic production in mid-ninth century due to an imperial proscription of Buddhism. Although Buddhism was quickly reinstated, artistic output did not achieve the level it had attained prior to the persecution. Moreover, narratives of the Buddha's life were no longer an important theme in art, though in later eras the subject was occasionally represented.² In Japan Buddhist narratives enjoyed an uninterrupted development and consideration of its art extends to the sixteenth century.

Prior to undertaking an analysis of the ways in which the various cultures adopted the pictorial biography, it is necessary to survey its development in India. By addressing the major issues of Buddhism and the evolution of its art and scriptural canon, such an introduction provides a background for analyzing the adaptation and evolution of pictorial narratives in Central Asia, Korea and Japan.

BUDDHA AND HIS DOCTRINE

The Buddha was born in the foothills of the Himalayas, in Nepal, around the sixth century B.C.E. His doctrine, the result of enlightenment reached during deep meditation, is encapsulated in the Four Truths, or four realizations. The first is that all life is suffering; the second, that the cause of suffering is attachment; third, to end suffering attachments must be severed; and lastly, the means to achieve non-attachment is by following the Eight-fold (Middle) Path. After his enlightenment he preached as he traveled from town to town, gradually gathering about him a group of disciples and lay followers.

The Buddhist creed assimilated many contemporary indigenous beliefs. The doctrine of *karma* (eternal cycle of rebirths) for example, is essential to an understanding of the teaching. One's *atman* (soul) transposes through eons of rebirths, the quality of these reincarnations being determined by actions of the past. Buddhism never disputes the existence of the native gods—Indra, Brahma, Agni, and others. Even the model of an ascetic meditating in the woods was common to contemporary religious practice. Traditionally, a man, having fulfilled his familial obligations, might leave home to study with the sage-like ascetics who had renounced worldly pleasure for a life of spiritual retreat far from society.

Naturally, there are many fundamental differences between Buddhism and the indigenous religious traditions. The Buddha's insight during the fateful night of meditation when he reached enlightenment revealed that not only was this particular life, as we know it, filled with the pains of old age, sickness, and death, but the doctrine of karma implied endless life cycles filled with pain. Indeed, the relation between suffering and attachment stated in the second truth may be understood as the very desire to live and to be reborn. Thus Buddhists reject the cycle of reincarnation for the goal of non-birth. To achieve this state one must live the Middle Path, a life that differs dramatically from that of the Brahmin ascetic who traditionally practiced self-mortification to achieve spiritual understanding. For the Buddha the path of austerities was as fruitless as the life of pleasure shunned by the ascetics, when the self is subject to sensations whether pleasure or pain, it is distracted from the goal of achieving eternity without pain. As for the indigenous gods, since they were subject to the laws of karma themselves, they were of little help in the quest for enlightenment. Only self-discipline, meditation, and a careful cutting off of attachments result in enlightenment. Thus the Eight-fold Path stresses the non-acquisition of evil karma in the formulation of a moral and meditative code of behavior: right livelihood, right actions, right words, right view, right intentions and effort, right mindfulness and right concentration.

Disciples imitated the life of the Buddha by leaving home, giving up all possessions, shaving their heads, wearing the simple garb of a monk, and destroying their personal identities. Living as mendicants, they practiced meditation and listened to the teachings of the Buddha. Lay followers, unable to break their ties with society and family, supported the monastic community and thereby achieved spiritual benefit with the hope that in a future reincarnation full renunciation would be possible.

At first the Buddha and his followers formed an itinerant band, begging their meals and preaching in the towns of northeastern India. Soon, however, lay devotees donated shelters for the monks during the monsoon season, when travel was nearly impossible. At first, these were gardens but gradually they developed into monastic centers, where the faithful gathered to hear the word of the Buddha, either directly or from an eminent monk.

Tradition asserts that the Buddha lived for eighty years. Growing terminally ill, he retreated to a forest grove, bid his followers farewell, and passed away. Since he had destroyed all attachments, he was no longer subject to the laws of karma and is said to have achieved his final *nirvana* (extinction). The Buddha left instructions that the lay followers bury him, so that funeral matters need not concern his disciples, the monks. After the traditional cremation, the bodily remains were to be buried under a mound of earth, like those of kings and heroes. However, a squabble broke out among the lay devotees as to whom the sacred ashes would be entrusted. The battle was peacefully resolved by the intervention of a wise ascetic, the brahmin Drona, who divided the ashes equally. The eight clans returned home, where each interred their share and built a mound over it. The brahmin Drona kept the scrapings from the vessel he used to apportion the remains and thus also had a relic to inter. The honorific structure, known as a *stupa*, constituted a reliquary containing the remains of the Buddha that was buried in the ground and covered with a mound of earth.

The religious practices of primal Buddhism took the form of the *Triratna* (Three Jewels): respecting the person of the Buddha; revering the *dharma* (his words); and supporting the *sangha* (monastic community). Followers made pilgrimages to the places important to

Buddha during his lifetime and to the sites of his remains—the eight stupas. Gradually, some of these places became holy centers where monastic complexes developed. There the faithful could hear sermons based on the Buddha's tenets and the recitation of the events of his life, which became an important aspect of the teachings. Spiritual credit was earned by the faithful for any support given to the Buddhist community, whether for sustaining the monks and monasteries, having the holy tenets recited, dedicating images or erecting monuments.

The most famous Indian ruler to espouse Buddhism was Ashoka, the third emperor of the Mauryan dynasty (r. 272-231 B.C.E.). Converted after the carnage of a battle waged to enlarge his empire, Ashoka vigorously embraced the teachings. Because of his patronage, the cult of the stupa developed quickly. It is said that he had the stupas opened to redistribute the relics, and built 84,000 new stupas throughout his empire to spread the practice of Buddhism. Newly conquered territories were encouraged to take up the religion. Ashoka also visited pilgrimage sites and supported the monastic community. In an effort to disseminate the doctrine beyond the confines of his own empire, he sent emissaries to the known world. Sri Lankan annals record the arrival of Ashoka's ambassadors as well as the gifts of a tooth relic and a grafting of the tree of wisdom under which the founder sat when he achieved enlightenment. It should be mentioned that Ashoka also generously supported other religious sects. Ashoka was seen as the ideal Buddhist ruler, unifying his realm with the worship of the Buddha, constructing monuments on a large scale, sending emissaries to other countries, while achieving the unity of his people under one dominant faith and winning everlasting fame.

EARLY BUDDHIST ART

The first appearance of Buddhist art is tied to the architectural structure of the stupa to which it was inextricably linked for hundreds of years. The evolution of the decoration of the stupa began with the traditional Indian commemorative act of placing fresh garlands and flowers. Then a railing surrounding the structure protected the hallowed area; it had four gateways oriented to the four directions.[3] By the time of Ashoka, bricks, a sacred building material since ancient Indian altar construction, covered the mound to prevent erosion of its surface. Later, lime stucco decoration and polychrome were applied over the bricks in designs that imitated fresh floral decor. It appears that the first area to be decorated was the gateway, though regional variants abound. Bharhut, for example, one of the earliest monuments ascribed to the second century B.C.E., has carved stone reliefs adorning the railing of the stupa. Although the stupa no longer exists, remnants of its railing are in the Indian Museum in Calcutta and elsewhere. These sections of the railing (comprising crossbars, roundels, and coping stone) and a gateway (with uprights and architraves) bear deeply incised designs. Carved on these architectural elements are such purely auspicious images as lotus flowers, vases filled with vines, trees, plants and animals as well as narrative scenes and portraits of donors. The Buddha does not appear in anthropomorphic form; symbols associated with the events in his life—the tree under which he sat during enlightenment, the wheel, which represents his sermons, and the stupa, which stands for his death—indicated his presence.[4] Judging by a fragment from a section of the railing of the Bharhut stupa now preserved in the National Museum of Delhi, the monument itself may have been decorated only with garlands and handprints.

The monument of Bharhut, whose railing provides some of the earliest evidence for narrative, already displays several story-telling techniques. In roundels, the continuous format is used to relate a *jataka* or a story from life experiences of the previous incarnations or life the Buddha.[5] The climactic event of the episode, is large and placed at center, as in the conception (FIGURE 1). Distributed along the periphery are the narrative details and secondary events. On the pillars of the gateway, several of the vertical panels also bear narrative themes, though the action is not yet continuously linked chronologically or thematically from one scene to the next. For example, the scene of Mara, god of death and desire, in his heaven utilizes vertical panels filled with standing deities in the heavens. On the far left of the lowest panel, sits Mara. Along the architectural element of the architrave, the processional format is used. The story unfolds along the horizontal and moves laterally. In addition to the few extant examples, there must have been many more such narratives from this early stage that have been lost.

The stone-carving technique employed at Bharhut and elsewhere was imported. Both the technical skill and the concern for monumental and long lasting edifices were not characteristic of pre-Buddhist India. The clearest sources for the new medium were the ancient stone-carving cultures of the Iranian plateau and the Hellenistic world which was brought into contact when Alexander the Great invaded of India in 326 B. C.E.

By the time of the building of Sanchi stupa, ascribed to the first century C.E. story telling techniques were greatly enhanced. Long complex narratives unfold along the horizontal lintels of the gateways, and the story is read much like that of a scroll, as in the defeat of Mara (FIGURE 2). Scurrying to the right are the vanquished demon warriors of the god of love and death. The rectangular format found on the supporting pillars uses the continuous method seen in the Bharhut panels, but now the vertical compositions of the uprights depict several sequential episodes. For example at the top of one pillar are two panels. The one at the top portrays the conception of the Buddha, below is the return home to the city of Kapilavastu after the birth. (FIGURE 3) Although the actions are not always continued from one panel to another, they share a unity of time and space.

The anthropomorphic image of the Buddha first appears around the time of the first century of the Common Era. The evidence to establish the time and place of the first such images is still lacking and the subject is the source of numerous scholarly debates. What can be stated with certainty is that there were two regional styles—one in the northwest clearly dependent on Western prototypes; the other, located further south, evolved directly from native images. At first the image of the Buddha was of natural proportions in relation both to the setting and to the other narrative figures. It seems likely that these first icons of the Buddha as a man simply replaced the symbols previously used to indicate his presence—footprints, throne, umbrella, wheel, tree, stupa. Much later they became larger, independent icons.

At the time when these dramatic changes were taking place in Buddhist art, around the first century of the Common Era, the northwest territory was under foreign dominion. The Kushans, a semi-nomadic horde identified as a people living on the frontiers of the Chinese empire, moved west. Gradually the Kushans entered India, taking over several profitable stations in international trade, for north India was an important sector on the western end of the silk routes that linked China to the West. As a result, the Kushan culture was a hybrid one. In addition to the Indian civilization that they adopted, they were subject to heterogeneous foreign influences emanating from the trade routes. With the Kushan King Kanishka (whose dates are contested but range from 78 to 144) Buddhism found another royal patron. Seeing himself as the contemporary Ashoka, Kanishka undertook the sponsorship of Buddhism in the same manner as his predecessor— making pilgrimages, building grand monuments, and holding a huge convocation. Prodigious patrons, the Kushans built numerous monasteries and temples that were discovered in northwestern India, Pakistan, and Afghanistan. With the invasion of the Kushans, the appearance of Buddhist art changed radically.

The predominance of Kushan art comprises the decorations that were placed on the exterior of stupas of northwest India, or Gandhara. Most are stone reliefs. In these there is a clear dependence on Hellenistic narrative traditions that were available due to continuous contact with the West on the silk roads. In these north Indian biographical scenes, figures conform to many of the standards of Western art: the scenes are arranged chronologically for the first time and read in a horizontal fashion. Each scene has a single episode of action that is formally divided from the other scenes, often by architectural members such as columns or pilasters. Within the panel, all the figures are the same size, and the classical unity of time, character, and place is observed in each unit. The figures stand on a shallow stage, slightly overlapping each other. (FIGURE 4) Sometimes characters or architectural forms are placed on a diagonal to give the appearance of spatial recession. In their physical attributes and costume, Gandharan figures closely resemble Western prototypes. This is especially true of the Buddha, who has a striking resemblance to the Apollo Belvedere, with a heroic head and muscular athletic body posed in the controposto stance. The noble head bears a neat chignon at the crown. Carefully modeled planes of the face articulate the bony structure and its muscular covering in conformance with the western ideal of beauty. It was this hybrid image forged in the Gandharan regions during the Kushan era that traveled east with the doctrine.

With the end of the Kushan occupation (ca. fourth century), the Indian artistic tradition re-emerges and overrides Western style art in India. Interest in narrative radically declines. The heroic athletic figure of the Buddha gives way to a fleshier, more rounded yogic body, placed in a more rigid stance. The face has nearly geometric-shape features to convey the perfection of divine physiognomy, defying the classical laws of naturalistic representation.

EARLY BUDDHIST SUTRAS

When the Kushans took control of north India they ended the nearly five hundred-year oral tradition by commissioning written versions of the *sutras* (scriptures). Being foreigners the Kushans were not bound by the ancient tradition that eschewed written transmission of the doctrine. Moreover, the Kushans were influenced by the great epic myths of the western world. Thus the life of the Buddha was cast in dramatic form, the heroic story unfolding in chronological order from birth to later life. Like the myths of Hercules, the biography expanded to include such new themes as combative martial arts contests and dramatic confrontations, like the youthful archery contest or attack of Mara on the eve of the Buddha's enlightenment. Unlike the closed canon of revealed texts of the Judeo-Christian religions, the Buddhist scriptures were never formally codified into a sacred core of teachings. Thus scriptures number in the thousands, awesome in their scope and diversity. Of the many scriptures committed to writing during the Kushan era, (in Sanskrit, the Indian religious language; Prakrit, its Kushan counterpart; and Kharoshti, a Kushan language) few are extant.[6] This is because the oral tradition that flourished in the post-Kushan age overwhelmed the newly introduced historical interest that might have preserved texts or historical documents. Often, it is only by external evidence that events or texts can be ascribed dates.[7]

The earliest written commissions of the scriptures are in the Pali language of Sri Lanka. These are largely ascribed to the first century B.C.E. These scriptures do not relate the life of the Buddha in chronological fashion. Rather, the sequence of the sermons depends on numerical groupings, disciplinary laws, and other classifications. Emphasis is on the enlightenment and post-enlightenment events.[8] Far outnumbering these are the Chinese renderings. Although the original texts in Sanskrit or other languages are, for the most part, lost, Chinese translations not only survive (sometimes in multiple versions) but also record the date and the monk responsible for the translation. Owing to the reverence for both history and writing in China, as soon as a monk arrived from the west with sutras, he arranged for the translation of the scriptures into Chinese. Usually the western monk working with a Chinese counterpart made a rough translation, after which a third scribe cast it into polished literary form.

Chinese scriptures have been considered to be of only limited value in transmitting the original texts, for in the earliest stage the Chinese relied on the borrowing of words, expressions, and concepts from their own religious traditions. In this way the Taoist or other ideological concepts naturally associated with the term compromised the accuracy of the Buddhist term. For some terms no equivalent was found, for others erroneous associations inevitably were made. Gradually over the centuries a Chinese Buddhist vocabulary evolved and more reliable translations achieved. This was accomplished through the consistent borrowing of terms, which eventually took on specific Buddhist connotations. Sometimes a phonetic loan system was used: terms lacking equivalent phrases in Chinese were sounded out with characters, imitating the foreign pronunciation. Such a set of characters had no meaning in Chinese. Soon these terms became part of a Buddhist vocabulary. But however much improved the skills in rendering Buddhist terms, translations still reflect Chinese values, employ familiar idioms, and include native details and ideas.

SCRIPTURES OF THE LIFE OF THE BUDDHA

Narratives of the life of the Buddha were just one of the many types of scripture. Judging by the numerous texts preserved in Chinese and other languages, there must have been a great output of texts. For this study of the life of the Buddha several texts were consulted. These are categorized into narratives of the early life of the Buddha and those that tell of the later events. The point of division is the first sermon, for several of the early texts end with this episode. The second group is generally concerned with the events after enlightenment, focusing primarily on the *parinirvana* (death cycle). The oldest biographical text is the *Xiuxing benqi jing* (XXBJ) translated in 197 C.E. by Gu Dali and Kang Mengzeng.[9] This sutra is brief; it ends before the first sermon, is relatively straightforward in its telling of the story, and there are few supernatural details. The *Taizu ruying benqi jing* (TRBJ), translated by Zhi Qian in the third century, extends the life to include a shortened treatment of the first sermon and a few of the first conversions.[10] Some supernormal embellishments appear in the descriptions of the nature of the Buddha with his Ten Powers and in the inclusion of divine attendants participating in the important events. Although the third scripture, the *Guoqu xianzai yingguo jing* (GXYJ) translated in 435-443 C.E. by Gunabhadra, is similar in the scope of events, the narrative details are greatly expanded.[11] There is also a group of biographical scriptures that are categorized as Mahayanist, for these include a plethora of supernatural details—for example, ten thousand celestials attend each event—but more importantly their definition of the Buddha nature is distinctive.[12]

Three of the narrative texts are affiliated with a specific school of Buddhism. First, the *Lalitavistara* is associated with the Sarvastivadin School. Dharmaraksha made the earliest Chinese translation, the *Foshuo puyao jing*, in 308 C.E.[13] Djanakuta, a priest of north India at the end of the sixth century made a later Chinese translation by the title *Abhinishkramana sutra—Fobenjing*. In the nineteenth century Samuel Beal rendered this scripture into English.[14] This version ends long before the death, with the conversions of the famous disciple Sariputra. Second, the *Mahavastu*, ascribed to the early centuries of the Common Era, is identified with the Lokkattaravadin School of the Mahasanghikas. This is the unique case where a version is extant in Sanskrit but apparently no translation of it in Chinese survives.[15] For centuries the *Buddhacarita*, the third text, was attributed to Asvaghosha, a poet in the court of King Kanishka, and thus ascribed to the end of the first to the mid-second century. The style of this scripture is radically different. Simplified in its narration, the story is told with a minimum of detail. Using a Chinese version by Dharmaraksha of 414-421, Samuel Beal translated the scripture into English, at the end of the nineteenth century.[16] His contemporary, E.B. Cowell, also made a translation into English but his was based on a Sanskrit text.[17] The latter version is a simple narrative that includes the death and funeral.

Conspicuously absent from the early Chinese texts are the events of the later life of the Buddha. These narratives are found elsewhere. For example they appear in the Pali *Vinaya*, or transcription of monastic rules, and in the *Sutras*, a collection of sermons.[18] In addition there is a relatively large group of Chinese translations of texts entitled *Mahaparinirvana sutra* that tell the last days and death.[19] Among this group are recensions that have been categorized as Mahayanist and pre-Mahayanist; of the latter, the earliest is by Fa Xian, the famous fourth-century Chinese monk who traveled to India and wrote a travel diary of his experiences.

One must ascertain one's priorities in dealing with this rich scriptural tradition. For this study, interest is directed to the earliest versions of the pictorial biography and the scriptures on which they are based. Also analyzed are the changes these narratives undergo in time. As this study is not an exegesis on Buddhist narrative texts, relevant sections are compared with the illustrations. In this analysis of how the story of the Buddha is transmitted from India through Central Asia to China, Korea and Japan, cultural differences, historical forces, and the evolution of Buddhism and its art are important themes. The relative homogeneity of the material is astonishing. In examples of art from disparate parts of the Asian world that span centuries, there is essential agreement in the content and iconographical details. Despite the lack of a canonical tradition that informs the transmission and illustration of the texts, there is still a basic conformity. Perhaps a good story is best left intact.

THE GROWTH OF MAHAYANA BUDDHISM

Divergence in the oral transmission of Buddhism was addressed in great councils held to codify the renditions. The first was held after the death of Buddha, the second in the time of Ashoka. This second council recognized eighteen sects of Buddhism. These different factions continued to increase.

By the time of the Common Era, when the eastward transmission of the doctrine began, Buddhism had undergone several astonishing changes. In addition to the radical developments such as the commission of written scriptures and their translation into local languages, new religious elements appear. The factional differences between the various sects and their regional practices are very complex. Even the identification of individual sects by their adherence to certain beliefs that distinguish them as belonging to one school or the other, upon close examination, is confounding.

Nonetheless, from a general point of view the aggregate of Mahayanist sects adhere to several special beliefs. First, the uniqueness of the historic Buddha is challenged by the presence of a great number of such beings. Not only are there Seven Buddhas of the Past, or Twenty-four, depending on the various traditions, there are Buddhas of the future, of Infinite Light, of Healing. In the Mahayanist doctrine a Buddha rules a paradise that offers eternal afterlife. In addition there are innumerable celestial helpers, or bodhisattvas—divine beings who have evolved to the highest spiritual stage and are ready to enter *nirvana* but postpone their own salvation to help others achieve it.

xxiii

Early Buddhist devotees emulated the life of the Buddha and his disciples; the monk ideal of an *arhat* was the goal of religious practice. Only through self-discipline and great effort could success be achieved. For the later school, salvation was possible through the intercession of the new pantheon of deities; their ideal was based on the selfless bodhisattva.[20] The Mahayanists criticized their predecessors for selfishly attending only to their own spiritual progress, while the Mahayanists espoused universal salvation. Mahayanists named themselves greater vehicle and applied the derogatory term Hinayana, meaning lesser vehicle, to their antecessors. Though widely used in the past, the term Hinayana is no longer acceptable. Similarly the term Theravada Buddhism (Way of the Elders) often used to distinguish the earlier phase, is more accurately applied to the kind of Buddhism practiced in Sri Lanka and Southeast Asia. For this reason the terms pre-Mahayana and Mahayana will be used here.

The fate of the biography of the historic Buddha is inextricably linked to developments in Buddhist iconographic and religious practices. When the new deities of the Mahayanist pantheon dedicated to attaining universal salvation became important, the popularity of Shakyamuni Buddha waned. When interest in the historic Buddha diminished, so did the narration of his life. However, it should be said that the role played by the historic Buddha was still an important one. There is a concerted effort by Mahayanist syncretists to place their works in the continuum of the development of Buddhist thought, not in the light of a new religion. Several texts accomplish this by including a synoptic treatment of the life of the Buddha as a transitional introduction to the Mahayanist scriptures. For example, the *Mahayana Samparigraha shastra*, attributed to Asanga of the fourth century, begins with a list of the important events including:

> *The dwelling in Tushita Heavens as a bodhisattva, Birth,*
> *Education, Leaving home to practice austerities, the Desire*
> *to leave the world, Attaining full Enlightenment, Turning*
> *the Wheel of the Law and the Parinirvana.*[21]

The *Mahayana Shradaddhotpada Shastra*, attributed by some to Asvaghosa of the Kushan era under King Kanishka and the first sutra translated into Chinese by Paramartha in 553, offers:

> *Descent from Tushita Heavens, Entering the womb,*
> *Dwelling in the womb, Birth, and the remaining four—the*
> *Great Departure, Enlightenment, First Sermon and*
> *Parinirvana.*[22]

Other important Mahayanist sutras, like the *Lotus sutra*, are treated as a sermon delivered by the historic Buddha. In fact, many Mahayanist scriptures, seeking to align themselves in the ancient scriptural tradition, assert that Buddha preached at the level of his audience during his lifetime. The sutras from the earlier life correspond to the "so called" lesser vehicle or "Hinayana" texts, while Mahayanist texts delivered at the end of his life are the sermons of a more complete truth. Several of these "last sermons" are titled the *Mahaparinirvana sutra* and deal with the narrative of his death as well as the "higher level" sermons. Thus the figure of Shakyamuni remains important in Mahayanist thought, and the details of his historic existence are not forgotten.

Images of the Mahayanist school are truly expansive. Whether the appearance of the Buddha achieves colossal size in actuality or only in relation to the scale of his attendants, he is clearly superhuman. The iconographic implication of the over-life-size icon is of course dramatic: no longer normal in scale, the Buddha transcends the human experience and its limitations. Perhaps these juxtapositions were meant to recall colossal scale sculptures of the Buddha carved out of the living rock; these could measure as much as 55 meters, as for example, the one at Bamiyan in Afghanistan.[23] But it should be pointed out that the large scale Buddha image is common to both schools of Buddhism.

Mahayanist iconography presents multiple images of the Buddha, asserting the prevalence of such beings. The most famous is the Twin Buddha Miracle from the *Lotus sutra*: while preaching to an audience, Buddha ascends to the sky, duplicates himself, and carries on a conversation with his twin.[24] Also prevalent is the theme of the thousand Dhyana Buddhas, reproducing Buddha images innumerable times in any given space. There also is the vision of an everlasting paradise filled with celestial beings. Both in the art and in the literature the grand and awesome aspect of these divinities, their capabilities and divine compassion are stressed. But in Mahayanist art Shakyamuni far from disappears; here, as in the scriptures, he shares the stage with other prominent Buddhas and bodhisattvas. With the exception of attributes, posture, and, when applicable, settings, it is virtually impossible to distinguish one Buddha from another, for they are identical. As for scenes of the life of the Buddha, though at times these were overwhelmed by Mahayanist imagery, they continued to be a source of artistic expression for the faithful. Moreover, just as the life was epitomized in Mahayana texts, the images were reduced to a few important events in the art.

ART TRANSMITTED EAST

Many different kinds of Buddhist art in a variety of formats and materials must have been transported east to provide local artists with models to copy. Chinese monks who traveled to the west and returned to China reportedly brought back with them small portable images as well as scriptures. In all probability there were also illustrated scriptures, as will be shown. Over time little of the portable art survived. The most widespread monument associated with the Buddha in India, the stupa, did not evolve in China; rather the pagoda or tower acted as a reliquary celebrating the remains of the Buddha. It was not until the end of the sixth century that these were decorated, in a limited way, with biographical narratives.

Most of the early artistic evidence that remains can be found in the cave-chapels carved into the mountains that skirt the Silk Road through Central Asia and Northern China. These caves and the ritual forms of worship associated with them are closely based on Indian prototypes. The idea, iconography, and basic design of the cave-chapel are Indian in origin. Visiting the cave is a metaphor for a journey leading to spiritual rebirth. From the brightly-lit outdoor exterior of a classical cave, one travels to a columned portico or to an anteroom that leads to a rear chamber; each room is progressively darker. At the back of the cave is the icon, dimly lit and shrouded in mystery. Painting or sculptures or some combination of both cover every surface of the cave's walls. The large surfaces of the walls provide the artist with a format for narrative depictions, which for the most part took the form of murals. At first the paintings imitate rather closely the western models, in time local preferences seep into the images altering both their appearance and content.

ENDNOTES

1. In the last few years several art historians have addressed the question of what constitutes narrative art in Asia. The argument is not really applicable here, as the story of the life of the Buddha is a narrative epic illustrated on Buddhist monuments. For the question of narrative see: Vidya Dehejia, "On the Modes of Visual Narration in Early Buddhist Art," *Art Bulletin,* vol. 73.3 (1990): 111-115 and *Discourse in Early Buddhist Art: Visual Narratives of India* (New Delhi: Munshiram Manoharlal Publ. 1997); J. Murray, "Buddhism and Early Narrative Illustration in China," *Archives of Asia Art* vol. 48 (1995): 17-31; and Hsio Hsio-Yen Shih, "Readings and Re-readings of Narrative in Dunhuang Murals," *Artibus Asiae* vol. LIII, no. 1-2 (1993): 59-88.
2. P. Karetzky, "The Recently Discovered Chin Dynasty Murals Illustrating the Life of the Buddha at Yen-Shang-ssu, Shansi," *Artibus Asiae* vol. XLII.4 (1980): 245-259.
3. The stupa is a very complex cosmological symbol, for an extended discussion of its meaning, see: *The Stupa and its Religious and Historical Architectural Significance,* A. Dellapiccola, ed. (Wiesbaden: Franz Steiner Verlag,1980): 12-38 and A. Snodgrass, *The Symbolism of the Stupa* (Ithaca: *Cornell Southeast Asia Program,* 1985).
4. There is a general disagreement as to the use of these symbols and the anthropomorphic images on early Buddhist structures. See Susan Huntington, "Early Buddhist Art and the Theory of Aniconism," *Art Journal,* vol. 49 (Winter 1990) no. 4: 401-8; Susan Huntington, "Aniconism and the Multivalence of Emblems: Another Look," *Ars Orientalis* vol. 22 (1992): 111-156; Vidya Dehejia, "Aniconism and the Multivalence of Emblems," *Ars Orientalis* vol. 21(1991): 45-66; and Vidya Dehejia, *"Rejoinder" Ars Orientalis* vol. 22 (1992): 157.
5. Many of these are tales of his incarnation as an elephant, monkey king, golden stag, etc.
6 Richard Saloman, *Ancient Buddhist Scrolls From Gandhara* (Univ. of Washington, Press, 1999): 6 ff.
7. Including the date of the life of the Buddha, which is generally reconstructed by references in the texts according to how many years have elapsed since his passing away.
8. Andre Bareau, *Recherches sur la Biographie du Buddha dans les Sutrapitaka et les Vinayapitaka Anciens,* 3 vols. (Paris, 1963) is the most admirable comparative study of the ancient texts. See also Andre Bareau, "La Legende de la Jeunesse du Buddha dans les Vinayapitaka anciens," *Oriens* vol. 9 (1962): 16ff.

9. The Chinese scriptures appear in printed form as part of a complete transcription of the *Tripitika* or Buddha canon, the edition edited by B. Nanjio, *Daizokyo*, printed in the Tokyo during the Taisho era (1912-1926) is used here; this *sutra* appears in vol. III, no. 184: 461.

10. TRBJ appears in *Daizokyo*, vol. III, no. 185: 471 ff.

11. GXYJ appears in *Daizokyo*, vol. IV, no. 189: 622.

12. N. Dutt, *Mahayana Buddhism* (Delhi, 1977). This book concerns the evolution of Mahayana Buddhism and its concepts of the nature of the Buddha.

13. The *Puyaojing* appears in *Daizokyo* vol. IV, no. 186: 491 ff.

14. *Abhinishkramana Sutra*, translated into Chinese by Djnanakuta, *Foben jing*, ca. sixth century, was translated into English by Samuel Beal, *The Romantic Legend of Sakya Buddha* (1875, reprint Delhi: Motilal Banarsidass, 1985).

15. The *Mahavastu* survives in a Tibetan version translated by Eduard Foucaux into French (Paris, 1880).

16. Samuel Beal, *Fo Shwo Hing Zan Jing, Sacred Books of the East*, vol. XIX (Oxford, 1883).

17. E. B. Cowell, *Buddhist Mahayana Texts, Sacred Books of the East*, vol. XLIX, (1894, reprint NY, 1969).

18. Bareau 1963.

19. It is interesting, if not confusing that several versions of the *Mahaparinirvana sutra* preserved in Chinese translations are of the earlier Hinayana tradition. See B. Nanjio, *A Catalogue of the Chinese Translation of the Buddhist Tripitaka* (Oxford, 1883, reprint San Francisco, 1975). Three such versions were translated in the fourth century by Fa Xian (317-420) see p. 41-42, no. 118 and no. 120; and no. 119, no. 552. The Mahayanist renderings date as early as the fifth century; see no. 113-117 and later, with the exception of a text translated by Dharmaraksha in the third century; see no. 116.

20. This is a curious term in Buddhism for it has several other meanings. Before the Buddha achieves enlightenment, he is also called by the term bodhisattva. Thus during his life as a prince and in other previous lifetimes he is referred to by this term.

21. Paramartha translated it by 563 C.E.; it is reprinted in the Japanese Tripitika of Nanjio, no. 1183. Translations of this sutra were also made by Buddhasanta in 531 C.E.; Nanjio, no. 1184; and Xuan Zang in 648-649 C.E., Nanjio, no. 1247. These references to the Chinese sutras and the groupings of eight come from S. Mochizuki, *Bukkyodaijiten* (Tokyo, 1960) 10 vols., vol. V: 4215.

22. Mochizuki 1960, vol. V: 4215. This sutra was attributed to Ashvaghosa, according to Edward Soothill, *A Dictionary of Chinese Buddhist Terms* (London: Kegan Paul, et. al. Co., 1934): 84b, without sufficient evidence.

Translations into Chinese were made by Paramartha in 553 C.E., and Siksananda in 679-700 C.E.

23. Described by Xuan Zang, *in Siyuki,* translated into English by Samuel Beal, *Records of the Western World* (London, 1882, reprint, NY, Paragon Books, 1968): 50-51. This is described as a Hinayanist site, belonging to the Lokottaravadins; the sculpture is described as golden and measuring 140-150 feet. For the extant sculptures, see Talbot Rice, *Ancients Arts of Central Asia* (N.Y., 1965): 162-164, pl. 149.

24. See *The Lotus Sutra*, translated by Leon Hurvitz, *Scripture of the Lotus Blossom of the Fine Dharma* (NY: Columbia Univ., 1976).

THE LIFE OF THE BUDDHA

according to the *Xiuxing benqi jing* (XXBJ) translated in 197 C.E. by Gu Dali and Kang Mengzeng.

The bodhisattva transformed himself and by riding a white elephant entered his mother's womb. It was the eighth day of fourth month when the queen had just finished bathing and perfuming herself and put on fresh garments. Feeling as relaxed as a young girl, she fell asleep and dreamed she saw a white elephant being ridden in the sky. A brilliant light filled the earth and she heard the sound of musical instruments and singing. Flowers were scattered everywhere and the air was scented with fragrant incense. (The bodhisattva) hovered over her. Then, all at once, everything disappeared, and she woke with a start. The king asked and she told him her dream. They called for the master of reading omens and he interpreted it: "This dream betokens good fortune for the king. A holy spirit has descended into the (queen's) womb and has brought about this dream. He who will be born in your household will become either a supreme ruler who will possess the flying wheel (Chakravartin) or he will leave home to 'seek the Way,' attain Buddhahood, and bring release to the ten directions." The king was overjoyed and the queen sang a song. . . .The queen thought, "I no longer want to hear the sounds of the vulgar world, I will hasten to live in the mountains and forests in pure and solitary meditation". . . . On the seventh day of the fourth month Maya neared the Lumbini garden whose flowers were all in bloom. The stars were out. She grasped hold of the branch of a tree, and the babe issued forth from her right flank and came down to the ground, took seven steps, raised his hand and declared: "Above and below the heavens, only I am lord. The three realms are all sorrowful; it is I who am to bring them peace." Heaven and earth greatly shook; there was a brilliant light throughout the trilicosmos. Brahma and the Four Guardian Kings with their own divine retinues and the various (divine creatures) gandharvas, asuras, nagas and yakshas looked on as they came nearer to him.

The two dragon king brothers, Kala and Akala welcomed the prince. They rained warm water on his left and cool water on his right. Indra and Brahma wrapped him up in heavenly cloths. From the heavens fragrant flowers fell like rain; the music of strumming lutes and drums was heard; and the fragrant, rich and dense vapors of burning incense filled the skies.

To the accompaniment of (celestial) music, Maya embraced the crown prince and rode (home) in a chariot that was drawn by yoked dragons with flying streamers. On their way back to the palace, the king heard of the crown prince's birth and his heart was full of joy. He danced and leaped in happiness. Then with a group of a hundred officials he came out to greet them.

They were (still) outside the city, at the place on the side of the road near the temples venerated by the state, when the brahmin soothsayers said: "It is fitting that the future heir should worship the (state) icons." So they carried him into the temple. All of the images fell down in prostration. The brahmins gathered together and said: "The heir is really a marvelous spirit, he who has such majestic virtue (must) be the reincarnation of a compassionate divine spirit." Some called him crown prince; others called him god of gods. They returned to the palace. Heaven rained down thirty-two auspicious signs.

There was a sage by the name of Asita who lived in the fragrant mountains. In the middle of the night he felt the earth shake greatly and he saw a constant brilliant light. In the mountains a flower called the *udumbra* fell, this flower miraculously produced lion kings who descended to earth and roared so loud that they could be heard for over 40 li[1].... Asita thought, "In the world there is a Buddha, I must respond to this good omen!...So he flew to Kapilavastu....Then the ladies-in-waiting wrapped the child up and brought him out so that he could receive Asita's blessing. Asita then excitedly arose and prostrated himself at the baby's feet. Asita, a man of such fierce strength -- equal to that of a hundred men, embraced the child and his body quivered. He saw the thirty-two *lakshana* (signs of beauty)....and spoke: "Now is born a great sage who will rid the world of its various calamities. I only grieve that I myself am so unlucky. In a week my life will end, and I will not see his spiritual transformation or (hear) his preaching the law that will rain on the world."

The king understood well the importance of the lakshana. He ordered palaces built in locations appropriate to each of the four seasons--spring, fall, winter and summer. In front of these palaces rows of sweet fruit trees were planted and in the orchard a bathing pond....The king selected five hundred ladies to engage in ceremonial preparations; they were elegant and poised. They took care of the crown prince.

On the same day that the prince was born the 84,000 elders all bore male children. The 84,000 stable horses all bore colts; one was unique: his coat was all white, and his mane was like precious pearls; because of this they named him "special soaring," Kanthanka. In the stable 84,000 white elephants were born, the hair and tusks of one of these white elephants were like white pearls, his mouth had six tusks. For this reason they named him Precious, the white elephant. The groom of the white horse was named Chandaka.

Seven days after the birth of the Buddha, his mother died. Because she had cherished heavenly teachings and diligently acquired virtue, she was born in one of the Thirty-three Heavens of Tushita where she was immediately honored . . . .

The crown prince lived in the palace but was unhappy . . . .The king asked the ladies if the prince was happy, to which the women responded: "Together we attend him and try to amuse him. We don't miss any occasion to watch him because we see he is not happy." The king was depressed and summoned his advisors (asking): "(Do you remember) Asita's words 'He will inevitably achieve the Way (Buddhahood)'? How can we make the crown prince stay home?" (They answered:) "Educate him! Give him books and these will (help) to control his thoughts." Thus, attended by a hundred servants, they arrived at the teacher's gate. Hearing the heir apparent approach, the teacher came out to welcome him. The prince inquired, "What kind of man is this?" A minister answered: "He is the chief educator of the state." The prince asked (the teacher): "In which of all of the sixty-four kinds of books do you find the word Jammu (tree) explained?" And he proceeded to enumerate all of the kinds of books. "Now which book will you use to educate me?" The brahmin was flabbergasted and answered, "You, crown prince have just described sixty-four books that you already know, but I only use two books to teach people." So (the prince) returned home....

Then with his various retainers he returned to the palace. It was his seventeenth year and the increase in his marvelous talents was obvious; but he was depressed and read books until late in the night. He was never happy, constantly thinking about leaving home. The king asked his servants: "What does the prince say?" They answered him: "With each day, he grows more despondent; he is never happy." The king was in despair, and summoned his various advisors saying: "The heir apparent is depressed. What should we about it?" One subject suggested, "Let him learn calvary!" Another said: "He should learn archery and charioteering." While a third recommended: "He should study law and how to govern the realm." They were deliberating on the various possibilities when another subject spoke up, saying: "The heir apparent is already grown up, it is fitting that he should be married and settle down....There was a petty king named Shanxue, who had a daughter named Yashodhara who was upstanding and virginal. Various rulers from the eight kingdoms had unsuccessfully sought her hand in marriage. Shanxue reported that his daughter would leave in a week's time to find the most courageous victor of martial arts in the kingdom (to marry). On the appointed day, Yashodhara, followed by five hundred ladies in waiting, went to ascend the kingdom's gates. There the skilled performers from all the neighboring countries gathered like clouds....The king said: "Go and tell the crown prince that in order to get married, he should now display some special skills."

Then the crown prince with Yuda, Devadatta, Nanda and 500 others took up their ceremonial instruments and weapons for the archery and other contests of skills. But when they tried to go out the city gates, they found that earlier an elephant had gotten stuck in the gate. They decided (to make this a test) to see who was the strongest. Devadatta was the first to go out; he saw the elephant blocking the gates and tried to expel it with one blow, but when he grasped it, it died. Nanda found it and dragged it to the side of the road. Later the heir apparent came and asked his servant who had killed the elephant. "Devadatta slayed it," he was told. "Then who moved it?" "Nanda did." The bodhisattva felt great compassion, he slowly came in front of it, placed his hand on the elephant, lifted it and pitched it outside the city walls, simultaneously causing the elephant to be revived and revitalized.

Devadatta arrived at the arena. He beat all the strong men (in the contests); none could match him. He disgraced everyone, even those who were known for their ferocity and strength. The king asked his servant, "Who was victorious?" The servant answered, "Devadatta." The king told Nanda, you and Devadatta have a two man-wrestling contest. Nanda pinned him in the first take down, and Devadatta stumbled. Stupefied, they (had to) pour water on him and made him rest. The king again inquired who won and the servant responded: "Nanda won." The king told Nanda to test himself against the heir apparent. But Nanda told the king that he was no match for the prince. He paid his respects and withdrew.

Next was the archery contest. They put up the iron drums, placing seven drums at a distance of ten li. The renowned archers shot their arrows but they could not reach the first drum. Devadatta shot his arrow and it penetrated the middle of the first two drums....The crown prince shot his arrow and it pierced all seven drums and entered the ground with such force that a spring burst forth.

Shanxue majestically provided an escort for his daughter to go to the prince's palace. The serving girls followed. In all 20,000 women read to him at night and made pleasant music to distance him from the sounds of the world. But the prince was lost in thought and did not consider this as happiness. He rejected the (women) (wanting) only to quietly cultivate the Way to carry the masses across the sea of sorrow. The king asked the servants if the prince welcomed his bride when she arrived, and if he was pleased by what she said. The servant answered the king, "He has sad thoughts and is not happy."

Then the prince told the king he wanted to go traveling . . . .The heir went out the eastern gate of the city. At the time the chief head of the deities Lord Indra wanted to hasten the prince's departure from the palace so that he could save (the world) from the fires of the ten poisons by raining on them and quenching them. So the deity (Indra) transformed himself into an old man squatting by the side of the road. He had white hair and loose teeth; his skin hung slack and his face was wrinkled; his flesh was dissipated. He was hunchbacked with withered limbs and crooked joints. His eyes teared; his nose dripped; and he was drooling; and he (suffered from) other such manifestations of old age. When he took a breath, he wheezed; the color of his body was sallow; his head and entire body shook. He emitted a foul smelling gas as he lay down. The heir asked what kind of person was this and the heavenly spirit awoke his servant to answer "An old man." "And who becomes old?" The other answered: "A man is old when his years are mature, his form has changed and his color faded. His spirit is diminished and his vitality is exhausted. Eating does not impede this transformation. His bones begin to separate. He sits down, getting up only when necessary. His eyesight has grown dim; his ears grown deaf. He no longer gets around and becomes forgetful. They say (his life) has suddenly come to a sad end and that his remaining years are few. This is what they call old age." The prince sighed, saying: "(All) people born in this world know the grief of old age. Stupid people covet physical pleasure, (but) how can one be happy, (knowing that) animals born in the spring, by the autumn fall dead and in winter decay. Old age approaches like lightning. (The prince's) body grew still and he spoke calmly: "Old age is when one's color fades, a malady for which there is no cure. ..."

Utterly depressed the prince turned his carriage around and went home. His great grief made him despondent....Several years passed and the prince wanted to foray out (into the world) again. The king issued a proclamation throughout the realm that the heir was going out and all disreputable and unclean persons were forbidden to be out on the road. The prince went out the southern gate. Indra transformed himself into a sick man by the side of the road. His body was emaciated but his stomach distended. His body was flaccid. He coughed and vomited. The one hundred evils that produce illness caused the nine apertures (of the body) to break down and drip. He was filthy from having leaked on himself. His eyes were no longer clear and he had grown deaf. He groaned and cried out loud. His hands and feet groped at the emptiness. He called out to his (dead) parents as his grieving wife attended to him. The prince asked: "What kind of person is this?" His servant answered: "This here is a sick man." The prince asked: "Who gets sick?" and he was told: "People are made of the four principal (elements) earth, water, air and fire. There are 101 major diseases, which combining with the (different elements) simultaneously develop and spread into the 404 illnesses. This man must have suffered the extremes of cold, heat, hunger, over-eating, thirst or over-drinking. Now because of this disease he has lost his stability and tosses about aimlessly. The prince sighed: "I always lived in a place surrounded by riches and treasures, eating with a jaded appetite. (Now) I will separate my heart from lust, from the debauchery of the five senses. If one cannot know oneself, this also is a sickness, How is it different?" Then he spoke in rhyme: "The body is so fragile! (Comprised of) of the four elements. The nine apertures are (prone) to disease, and so there is the grief of old age and sickness. Even if one is born in heaven, there is no constancy; and men suffer the hardship of old age and illness. Looking at the body, it is like a puddle of rainwater. In this world how can anyone be happy?"

So the prince turned his carriage around and went back home, his mind consumed with grief. Several years passed and again the prince wanted to sojourn (outside of the palace)....The prince left by the western gate. Indra transformed himself into a dead man who was being carried out of the city (for cremation). Members of his family followed the cart crying and calling out, "Why have you forsaken us, leaving us forever?" The prince asked: "What's happening?" His servant answered: "This is a dead man." "What is it like to be dead?" He explained: "To be dead that is to be finished. The spirit leaves (the body) and that's it. The four great elements scatter, the spirit-soul is unsettled. When the breath leaves, every (function) ceases. Fire destroys the body and then it gets cold. First wind comes, then fire. The soul leaves, and that's that. The body becomes stiff and straight. It no longer has any faculty by which to know anything. After a period of a few days, the flesh decays, the blood flows out, the belly swells, the bones rot. Nothing can be preserved. The body has worms, and the worms turn and eat it. The muscles, veins, and belly disintegrate. The bones disjoint and dissolve. The skull is detached (and rolls) to another place. The spine, ribs, shoulders, arms, stomach, shinbone, feet and toes each separate and disperse. Flying birds and crawling animals wrangle with each other to eat it. Heavenly dragons, souls, spirits, emperors, princes, men wealthy or poor, honorable or mean, none can escape this grief!" The prince heaved a long sigh and said in verse: "I have seen (the visions of) old age, sickness and death. . . . People are born without a permanent dwelling. My body will also end up like this. The body is a mortal thing. The spirit is without form. Even if commanded, the dead cannot return to life. Whether under the threat of pain or punishment, (life) is still lost....One suffers pain and pleasure, then the body dies and the spirit is lost. Not in the sky nor sea, nor among the mountains or rocks is there any place on earth where one can escape or prevent being caught by death."

The prince turned his carriage around and returned to the palace. His grievous thoughts amassed. Now with (the knowledge of) the suffering of old age, sickness and death, a bitter sadness occupied his thoughts....Again he wanted to leave the city. The god (Indra) transformed himself into an ascetic at the gate, dressed in that manner and (carrying a) begging bowl. He walked peacefully and with care, his eyes not gazing far ahead. The heir asked his servant. "What kind of man is this?" The servant answered, "This is a brahmin ascetic. The way to being an ascetic is to forsake your family and wife, discard love and desire, cut off the six passionate feelings, protect and guard nothing and obtain a single mindedness. Then the 10,000 depravities are diminished and that's it. That is the way of a single heart. We call him a sramana, a true man. Sounds and colors cannot seduce him. High position cannot make him submit. He is as difficult to move as the ground. . . .The prince said: "This is excellent. Who is not cheered by this?"

The heir turned his carriage around and returned home. He was so depressed. Then the king summoned his advisors to join in discussion to come up with some plan that would prevent the prince from leaving the palace to study the path of religion. One minister suggested that it was fitting that the prince oversee the farmer's ploughing to end this kind of thinking. Thus it was the prince followed a servant up to the fields to (find) the farmer with his plough yoked with oxen. He was instructed on how to oversee the work. The prince sat under a Jambu (a rose apple) tree and watched them till the land to break the new soil and how the worms came out of it. Indra caused the oxen to toil, raising feelings (of compassion) in the prince's heart. The worms came thickly falling out (of the newly turned soil) and the birds swooped down to peck and swallow them. Then the frogs pursued them and ate them. From their holes snakes came out and swallowed the frogs....The young prince witnessed the living creatures devouring each other and his merciful heart was grieved and wounded. (As he sat) under the tree he attained the first degree of meditation. The sun's rays were strong and bright, and the tree (under which he sat) had a crooked branch that provided shade for his body (despite the movement of the sun).

The heir returned to the palace with solemn thoughts, thinking on the purity of the way. He saw that it was not fitting to live at home, that he should dwell in the mountains and forests. (He wanted) to study how to purify the spirit and practice meditation. When it came to his twenty-ninth year, on the seventh day of the fourth month, he swore an oath to leave home. During the middle of the night, when the stars were shining, the various deities on the edges of the sky exhorted him. . .The devas told the heir that he should leave. Fearing any delay, they summoned (the god) Wusuma and they entered the palace. Within the realm everyone was asleep, then (the gods) Nandi and Brahma transformed the palace making it exactly like a tomb. Yashodhara and the ladies in the harem appeared as dead people, their bones dislocated, their skulls displaced in another location, their bellies were distended, and gave off a foul odor. From their bodies blood and pus flowed, and other such (unseemly) things. The prince saw that the palace had become a tomb: owls, foxes, wolves, and other animals flew and prowled through it. He saw this scene as if it were a magical illusion, an apparition, a dream or an echo. (He saw) how everything returns to nothingness and it is stupid to try and prevent it.

Then he called Chandaka quickly ordering his horse be saddled. Chandaka said: "It is not yet dawn, why have the horse saddled?" The prince told Chandaka in verse: "Now I am not happy in the world, Chandaka do not delay my achieving my basic desire to escape the three sufferings of the world.". . .The bodhisattva himself went and patted the horse's back and said in verse: "In life death lasts a long time. I must mount and ride you now, you are my special escort for my departure. When I achieve the way, I will not forget you." Kanthaka stood still. (Nandi) thought to himself, "Now if his hooves strike the ground, others will be aware of our movement." So (he caused) four spirits to carry the horses' hoofs, not letting them touch the ground. When the horse wanted to cry out, he caused the sound to be heard far away by having the spirits scatter the sounds into nothingness. Riding the horse, the prince left the city gates. Then devas, dragon spirits, Indra, Brahma, and the Four Guardian Kings joyfully followed forming a canopy in the sky. The city goddess appeared, kowtowed and said: "You, Siddhartha, protect my state. Under heaven we enjoy prosperity and happiness, the people are at peace. Why do you abandon me?" The prince answered in verse: "In life death lasts a long time. The spirit is incarnated along the five paths. I have found my basic desire, open the gate to nirvana." As the city gate opened itself, out he flew.

At dawn he had gone 480 li and come to Animo country (Han calls it Changman) when he alit his horse. After taking off his luxurious clothing, adornments and jeweled turban, he was finished with Chandaka, and told him: "You (may) lead the horse home, go up to King Suddodhana and thank him for (me)." Chandaka said: "I should now follow you and attend to your needs, I cannot return alone. (I'll) untie the horse and let (him) go. In the mountains there are often evil snakes, tigers, wolves and lions. Who will provide the food for you to eat, water to drink and a bed on which to repose? How can I follow you? I want be with you and share your life." Kanthaka kneeled deeply, cried and licked his foot; he would not drink any water nor eat any grass. He cried and his tears flowed as he paced to and fro. The prince spoke, in verse: "Bodies that (were once) strong become diseased. The vitality that was plentiful diminishes in old age. One loses one's life in death and is far away. How can anyone be happy in the world?" Chandaka, piteously weeping, bowed down to his foot, and in a resigned manner led the horse home.

They were about 40 li outside of the city gates when Kanthaka cried out. His sounds were heard in the kingdom. Throughout the realm everyone said that the heir had come home and the spirits of the people in the kingdom were lifted. They came out to greet him, but they saw only Chandaka leading the riderless horse. Yashodhara saw them and came down from the palace. She embraced the horse, bent her arm about his neck and cried; (their tears) intermingled. The king saw Yashodhara weeping. Five men who were inside (the palace) were also sad. Restraining himself, the king told them saying: "My son went off to study by himself." When the state ministers and people saw the king and Yashodhara sobbing, they were also sad and distressed. . . .The king summoned his ministers and said: "I have a son who has rejected me to go into the mountains. Have the officials send five men to pursue him. They should be cautious and not come home without him."

The prince, having separated himself from the vulgar world was very happy. Peacefully he entered a city. When the people of that realm gazed upon the prince, they were happy and not oppressed. The prince had left behind sad thoughts and now hardship and pain (of separation) were far away. He was thinking that he wanted to shave his head but he left in such a hurry he did not bring any implements to do so when Indra brought him a knife. Heavenly spirits caught the shorn locks and departed. Continuing on by himself the prince went forth and the people of the realm followed, watching him until he had left the state. . . . Later he thought: "Now I should exchange my luxurious clothes to be a commoner. All of these material possessions are dangerous. Then he saw a hunter wearing plain clothes. The prince thought, "These are a real man's clothes, clothing for the (path to) compassionate salvation." He explained his intention to the hunter, how he wanted to exchange clothes with him. Then holding his gold embroidered clothes he exchanged them for the (hunter's) garment. . . .

Following this he entered the mountains. As the bodhisattva made his way, his clothes emitted an auspicious light that illuminated the mountain forest. There were several ascetics (who lived in the forest). (Among them were) Ayalan and Jyalan, who having studied for several years, reached the fourth stage of meditation and the five understandings. Seeing the bright light, they grew afraid of its portent and went out to see it. From a distance they recognized Siddhartha who had left home. They greeted him, "Good, come Siddha then sit on this bed. (You) may (drink from) the ice cold streams and eat these beautiful fruits." Then they spoke in verse: " The sun king rises on the mountaintop, and his intelligence illuminates all living things. Look at him. His is the way of highest virtue, without equal, without peer." To this the bodhisattva said: "Even though you have cultivated the four meditations, you do not have supreme intelligence. The center of the way is one's self, it does not dwell in worship of false gods. When you practice the commonly called truth, you spend long nights seeking Brahma's Heaven. As a result you do not learn the (true) way, and turn the wheel to fall into life and death (again)."

Thus the bodhisattva walked (away). Compassionately, he considered the multitudes being born, growing old and transmitting ignorance, not able to avoid the pain of sickness or death. He wanted to understand (this pain) and reject it. . . .

Walking on he arrived at the Tzuna River whose course was peaceful and straight with many fruit groves. . . .The bodhisattva sat under the *(pi) shaba* tree and then directed all his thoughts on seeking the way of highest truth. The devas sent down sweet dew, but the bodhisattva did not accept one drop. He vowed to himself that he would only eat one seed and one kernel of rice a day. In order to unify his spirit, he sat upright for six years. His body became emaciated; his bones protruded the skin. His tender spirit was peaceful and silent. With a single mind, his inner thoughts (grew) peaceful. . . .For six years he sat like this. Then Indra (concerned for his wellbeing) instructed two women to prepare a meal for the bodhisattva. . . .The two women respectfully offered it to the bodhisattva. The bodhisattva thought first I want to wash up, afterwards I will take the gruel. He went to the side of the flowing stream and washed his body. When he was finished he tried to get out of the water (but was too weak). Devas touched the tree branches which bent allowing him to come out. Then the two women presented the milk gruel and he took it. (Soon) his vitality and strength were replenished. He spoke his wish (to the women) for their prosperity without limit. . . .He finished eating, washed his hands, and rinsed his mouth. . . . Then 500 blue birds came flying down. Singing, they circled him three times and left. . . . He then walked across the pool of the blind dragon, who was so overjoyed he leapt up and said in verse: "Excellent! I see Siddhartha, coming tonight to save all living things, offering them the supreme sweet dew. When he walks on the ground, it deeply shakes. The creatures are happy and naturally cry out. He passes exactly as the Buddhas (of the Past). I have no doubt. Now I harbor no rage, the angry demons prostrate (themselves). Now the Buddha shines, aware of the many living (yet still) asleep.

The bodhisattva walked on and saw from afar that the marsh in the mountain forest was level. Everywhere he gazed were pure fresh grass and soft leaves. . . .There was a grove with trees that were tall and especially beautiful . . . .This was fortunate. . . .He saw a grass cutter and asked him: "What is your Name?" "My name is Auspicious Omen." "Now cut (some) auspicious grass, lay it out for me . . . .

Then the bodhisattva sat on the seat and made three vows to not move until he achieved Buddhahood. There he peacefully entered meditation, rejecting thoughts of pain and pleasure.

As he sat in meditation . . . Mara was in his palace and became aware of a brilliant light emanating from the spot between the eyebrows of the bodhisattva. Mara grew greatly frightened, his heart was not at peace. He saw the bodhisattva already seated under the tree, cleansed of desire, in pure thought and (Mara) grew annoyed. He tried to eat, but the food had no sweetness, the drum music had no rhythm. He thought: "If he achieves the way, inevitably it will be a great victory over me. I want to destroy his chance of achieving the way. Mara's son Sumati came forward and exhorted his father saying: "The bodhisattva has practiced purity, the three worlds are without his peer. In this way his spirit has progressed, the 100,000 gods in Brahma's heaven all revere him. This is not something either gods or men can stop. No action, neither good nor evil, can destroy his meditation." Mara did not listen to him.

Mara's three daughters divined his (thoughts). One was called Loving Sex; the other was called Constant Pleasure, the third was called Great Gratification. (They said) "Father do not grieve! We ourselves will go and destroy the bodhisattva's concentration. It is not necessary for you, father, to toil." Dressed in the jeweled heavenly clothes of the five hundred jade maidens, they came to the bodhisattva. They played lute music and sang, lewdly wanting to arouse his desire and confuse his thoughts of the way. The three girls said: "The righteousness and virtue you have (accumulated) is heavy, the gods all revere you, you have nurtured (these) yourself thus the gods have given you us. We enjoy purity; our years are full, we want to bed you at night and rise with you in the morning, to be on your right and left." The bodhisattva answered them: "In the past you have (earned) some good fortune and received the bodies of goddesses, but you won't keep them forever; and when you behave so lewdly, even though your bodies are beautiful, your hearts are depraved. You are like stinking jars filled with filth. You will destroy yourselves. How will this be the result? Even though (you have had) good fortune, it is difficult to keep it for a long time. (These actions of yours) are lewd and evil. When you die, you will return to the source, your good fortune will be exhausted then retribution will come, and you will fall into the three evil paths and receive the bodies of animals from which escape will be very difficult. . ." As the bodhisattva spoke, they became old hags, their heads grew white, their teeth fell out, their eyes grew dim and they became stooped over. With a cane they took enfeebled steps and returned (home).

When Mara saw his three daughters returning to his palace transformed into old hags his vexation greatly increased. He summoned his demon army. All 180,000 came down from heaven and surrounded the bodhisattva. They transformed themselves into lions, bears, horned oxen, tigers, elephants, dragons, oxen, horses, dogs, pigs, monkeys and apes. Their appearance was indescribable. There were snake-headed men. . . Some had six eyes, others one neck and many heads with teeth, fangs, claws and talons. They lifted mountains and spit fire as thunder and lightning surrounded him on all sides. They were armed with halberds and swords. The bodhisattva's compassionate heart was neither excited nor afraid, not one hair of his head moved. The rays of light (emanating from) his countenance increased, the demon army could not get near. Mara then came forward, saying: "Oh bodhisattva of compassionate nature, I ask you to tell me what is it you seek seated under the tree? Is it pleasurable in the forest among these poisonous animals? Clouds arise and a fearful darkness spreads (throughout the skies). The god Mara has surrounded you and you are not disturbed. . . . You should become Cakravartin. The Seven Jewels will naturally come from the four quarters. That which you will receive has no equal among the five senses. This place has no "way"! Get up and enter the palace. (Or else) I will completely swallow (you up in) a cauldron of fire. You have rejected the state like spitting, is there nothing you covet? . . . ."

The bodhisattva spoke: "Mara you want to make me flee, but I promised myself (to fulfill my destiny). Now the, blessed earth, (knows) what it's like to be a Buddha and who shall be victor. In the past I was incarnated and sincerely gave (to others) . . . I once meditated, received Dipamkara Buddha's blessing and prediction I would be Shakyamuni Buddha. My angry and fearful thoughts are exhausted sitting in this place. Meditation inevitably will destroy your army. . . " The bodhisattva then with the power of his wisdom, touched the earth with his hand (saying): "The (earth) knows me." At that moment the earth greatly shook everywhere and Mara and his troops fell over. Mara's army scattered. Loosing their advantage, they were routed. In confusion they fled and crouched on the ground. . . .

---

[1] A *li* is a Chinese measure of distance equal to a third of a mile.

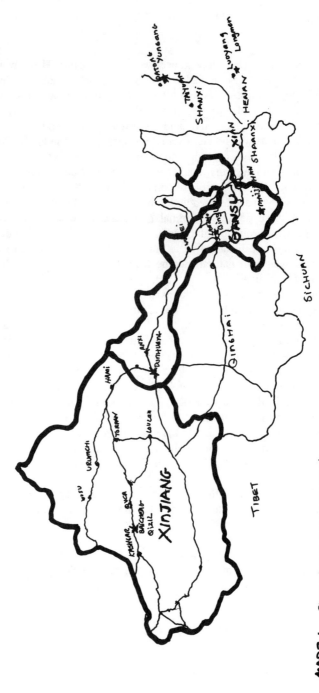

MAP 2 : SILK ROUTE CAVE SITES ★

CHAPTER 1

THE PICTORIAL BIOGRAPHY OF THE BUDDHA IN CHINESE CENTRAL ASIA—XINJIANG

The area formerly known as Chinese Central Asia, sometimes as Chinese Turkistan, and now as modern Xinjiang, was of critical importance in the transmission of Buddhism to the Far East. Consisting of uninhabitable desert surrounded by forbidding mountains, this area, which encompasses the Taklamakan, the Lop, and Gobi Deserts, is bordered on the north by the Tian Shan Mountains, in the west by the Pamirs, and in the south by the Tibetan Kun Lun range. Several trade routes linking the West, India, and China began in the east at Dunhuang. A northern route skirted the foothills of the Tian Shan Mountains and passed through major oasis cities at Turfan, Quca, Kashgar, Bokhara, and Merv before merging with the southern route. The southern route began at Dunhuang with centers at Miran, Khotan, Yarkland, and Balkh. At Merv the route led westward through Hamadan and Palmyra, terminating at either Antioch or Tyre before entering the Mediterranean Sea.

BUDDHISTS AND BUDDHIST ART IN XINJIANG

Traveling along the dangerous highways, merchant caravans and monks carrying sacred images and texts, transported Buddhism eastward. Because of the rich trade, towns and villages on the route became oasis cities or independent city states.[1] Some had an allegiance to the Kushans,[2] for Kanishka's conquest extended to Khotan; those further east were within the Chinese sphere of influence since the Han dynasty.[3] Although much of the evidence of the traffic in ideas, arts, and technology in this area is lost, some records of its existence and influence survive in China, where ancient documents were treasured and preserved. Chinese records of Buddhist missionaries reaching China in the mid-second century attest to the fact that the caravan routes became important places of intercourse. Several such westerners originating from various geographical locations left their mark on Chinese history, like the Parthian An Shigao who arrived in 148 C.E. and died in 170. The Central Asian Zhu Shufu with the Kushan Zhi Zhao, established one of the first monasteries in Luoyang in 170. Another Kushan, Zhi Jian, who arrived in 223 and died in 253, is famous as a prolific translator of the sutras into Chinese.[4]

Evidence of the proliferation of Buddhism throughout the Central Asian oasis states is provided by the testimonies of Chinese monk travelers who recorded their visits to the many temples and monasteries along the Silk Road. In their travelogues they described the communities they encountered as to their cultural, economic, and topographic situations, and the Buddhist sects' temples, important icons, and population of resident monks. From these accounts it is evident that both pre-Mahayanist and Mahayana Buddhism were introduced into Central Asia. Because there were several such traveler-historians—Fa Xian, in the early fifth century, Song Yun in the second decade of the sixth century, and Xuan Zang, who traveled in the later part of the seventh—a comparative history of these Buddhist centers is possible. The names by which the ancient travelers identified the sites of Central Asia are different from the modern ones, but a picture of the environment may be reconstructed from their diaries. For example Fa Xian described Wu-i in Shenshen or Loulan as belonging to the Hinayana sect, with about four thousand priests. His next stop, Khotan, in contrast, was Mahayanist, supporting fourteen great monasteries and several lesser ones, and a great temple with over three thousand monks. Yarkland also espoused the "great vehicle."[5] Although Song Yun in his journal dated to 518, extensively described Khotan and its Buddhist king, he did not identify the school of Buddhism practiced there.[6] In contrast, in Xuan Zang's account, Wu-i, also called Okini, is distinguished as Hinayana, more specifically Sarvastivadin:[7]

> There are about one hundred convents (sangaramas) in this country, with five thousand and more disciples. These belong to the Little Vehicle of the school of the Sarvastivadas. Their doctrine (teaching of the Sutras) and their rules of discipline (principles of the Vinaya) are like those of India, and those who read them use the same (originals). . . .[8]

These Buddhists are categorized as pre-Mahayanists and differ in several important ways from the later Mahayana school. Pre-Mahayanists revered the historic Buddha and stressed salvation through self-discipline and meditation while the later school believed in numerous Buddhas and other divinities capable of aiding the devout in their spiritual development. Important in the Kushan era (second to fourth century), Sarvastivadins were associated with Kushan King Kanishka. Their canon, the *Abhidharma*, was fixed at the Fourth Council at Kashmir held during his reign.[9] One of the texts associated with them, the *Lalitavistara,* narrates the life of the Buddha Shakyamuni in exhaustive detail with innumerable divine particulars. Several translations of the *Lalitavistara* were made into Chinese and one into Tibetan; these have been rendered into English and French.[10] This text establishes Sarvastivadin interest in the biographical narrative of Shakyamuni Buddha and accord can be established between the text and illustrations at Sarvastivadin sites.

Active patrons of Buddhist art, Sarvastivadins established major centers of worship in Kushan sites in Gandhara (Peshawar, Shravasti), Mathura and western Kashmir. Unfortunately so far no excavated sites in Kushana have definitively been associated with specific sects. Amaravati has also been identified as a site where the Sarvastivadins were active. Located in the southeast on the Krishna River in Andhra Pradesh, Amaravati (second BCE to third century CE) has a profusion of bas-reliefs that decorated the stupa with depictions of biographical scenes of the life of the Buddha. Correspondences with the art of Xinjiang (in particular with the site of Qizil) exist in the choice of scenes, the particularities of their representation as well as certain iconographical conventions. These similarities are attributable to the fact that this site was also affiliated with the Sarvastivadins and the importance of the *Lalitavistara* scripture in the illustrations.[11]

Nagarjunakonda, not far from Amaravati, was heavily influenced by its art and thus shares many similarities.   In sum, the architectural monuments at Qizil, Kushan India and Amaravati present extensive narrative illustrations of the biography of Shakyamuni that share many of the iconographical details and narrative formats in common. Belonging to the same sect is no doubt the reason for the strong agreement among them. Analysis of the art from Qizil allows for an appreciation of its sectarian affiliation and the range of iconographical images associated with it. It is apparent that scenes of the life of the Buddha play a large role in Sarvastivadin art. However it is important to note the presence of large-scale images at the site of Qizil as well, for others have asserted that the anthropomorphic image of the Buddha and its oversize versions were the result of the development of Mahayanism.[12]

Physical evidence of the flourishing of both schools of Buddhism (Mahayana and pre-Mahayana) is found in the archaeological remains of the sites on the Silk Road. Excavations made in the early decades of the twentieth century supply further proof of the vast areas that accepted Buddhism. At the opening of the twentieth century a number of international archaeological campaigns exploring the area discovered dozens of Buddhist monuments and cave-chapels cut into the mountains skirting the trade routes and in the oasis cities that supported them. Expeditions were led by Baron Oldenberg for Russia, Aurel Stein for England, Paul Pelliot for France, Albert Grunweld and Albert Le Coq for Germany, and a Japanese campaign organized by Prince Otani.[13] As a result of their efforts, Buddhist artifacts from these ancient sites fill national museums around the world. Analysis of their finds reveals that the site around Quca, with the exception of Qumtura, was pre-Mahayanist, while establishments along the northern route at Khotan and Turfan were Mahayanist, which is in basic agreement with the Chinese travelers' testimony.[14]

Archaeological activities of the twentieth century have also unearthed copies of scriptures translated into local languages. Stein found texts of the *Buddhacarita, Prajnaparamitra,* and *Saddharmapundarika* (or *Lotus sutra*) in Khadalik[15] and Le Coq unearthed Asvaghosa's *Cycles, Kapanamanditikia,* and other sutras written in Kharosti script and Turkistanic Brahmic at Qizil.[16] It has been ascertained that by the third century the Kharosti script was in use in the Central Asian states from Khotan to Kroraina (Loulan) in the Lopnor Region, while at Quca,

Tocharian was in use.[17] Translating the sutras into numerous native languages naturally facilitated the spread of Buddhism. Although predominantly Buddhist, Chinese Central Asia also supported Manichaeanism and Nestorian Christianity which thrived until the Islamic invasions of the ninth century.[18]

Just as the scriptures were translated into native languages, the artistic material also underwent changes to accommodate native tastes and preferences. This is most apparent in the painting of individuals' facial features, skin color and costume. Architectural and decorative details differ as well. But more subtle effects in the rendering of the divine visions of the celestial and the message they bring are also observable.

PERSIAN INFLUENCE

Persian art and religion had a formative influence on the art of Chinese Central Asia. The Sassanians (200-635) conquered the western Iranian plateau and annexed the Kushan realm of Gandhara (comprising northern India and Afghanistan),[19] extending their control at least as far as Quca. The organization of the interior space of the Buddhist cave-chapels, with their flanking aisles and icons nearer the middle of the room, the barrel vaults, and domes supported by squinches are similar to the Persian Zoroastrian fire temples built by the Parthians and Sassanians.[20] As for iconographical emblems, Soper has established a clear correspondence between Sassanian prototypes and the bodhisattvas' crowns and drapery style of fluttering scarves.[21] The Buddha, shown in Sassanian style with flames emitting from the shoulders, is frequently seen on the central zone of the barrel vault ceiling, for example in Caves 8 and 38. So, too, the rayed halo of Sassanian kings and divinities is used for the Buddha in Cave 69 and elsewhere.[22] An orb surrounded by an outer ring of pearls that depicts the sun and stars strongly resembles the Sassanian pearled roundel.[23] In addition, the artists of Qizil have adopted the lumpish triangles that represent mountain forms in the landscape settings of hunt scenes on such Sassanian vessels as the vase in the National Collection, Teheran, and used them for scenery in the small-scale scenes on the ceilings of the cave temples.[24] Sassanian art is also important in iconographical innovations; in particular the image of the seated Maitreya, Buddha of the Future, frequently is placed in a lunette in the fore hall. The prototype for the bodhisattva waiting in heaven for his time to be reborn evolves out of Gandharan Sassanian images. Rosenfield has pointed out that the cross-ankled princely figure seated in a palatial setting with flanking auditors found at Shotorak, Afghanistan is a prototype for the image of the paradise of Maitreya.[25] The composition is, in fact, remarkably similar to the painting of a Zoroastrian god in a setting of a trabeated arched balcony on the ceiling of a grotto of a Sassanian tomb, Dokhtar-i-Noshirwan, near the Buddhist caves of Bamiyan, in Afghanistan.[26] Two attendants rendered in profile flank the winged disc of Ahura Mazda, god of light. The formulaic icon of a central deity housed in a trabeated arch is also present in Bamiyan's Buddhist caves.[27]

Manicheanism, an unorthodox Sassanian religion with great similarities to Zoroastrianism, prospered in the area.   After their leader's execution (ca. 272-75) the Manicheans were persecuted and forced to move east. The district of Tocharistan in Khorastan in the area of Balkh was their eastern center.   At Karakhoja (the ancient Khotcho) near Turpan, Le Coq found evidence of Persian influence in a necropolis with many domed Manichean tombs and a city of temples.[28] In the substrata of a modern building, the remains of murals show a Manichean priest surrounded by monks and nuns dressed in their characteristic monastic white robes (ruin K).[29] A number of Manichean texts were also found in Khocho and have been ascribed to the eighth to ninth centuries. One hymnbook has both Soghdian and Persian texts; several others that were found are illustrated.[30] Stein's excavations in Yarkhoto also uncovered the remains of Manichean shrines.[31] This is evidence that the Persian religion continued to be practiced in Central Asia. In summary, Sassanian influence spread from Persia to Afghanistan and northern India to Central Asia, reaching as far east as Turfan and Quca.

OTHER ARTISTIC SOURCES

The most notable artistic source for Buddhist caves of Chinese Central Asia is Gandhara, in particular Afghanistan, notably the site of Bamiyan (ca. third to seventh centuries) where several caves are carved from the nearby Hindu Kush Mountains. The site was under Kushan rule until the fourth to fifth century when the Sassanids took control. For this reason monuments dedicated to Buddhism and Zoroastrianism are present. The Indian monastic architectural prototypes of the *vihara* (monastery) and *chaitya* (stupa hall) were both utilized as were the domed and *laternendecke* type ceilings and fore hall, all of which became important in Xinjiang. The finds nearby at Kakrak and Foladi suggest that there were numerous locations with similar architectural and painting styles. There must have been others that did not survive.[32] The direct source for the cave with square central pillar and ambulatory path is less clear. It seems probable that this form developed out of the Indian chaitya hall with its stupa and ambulatory path, but the modifications resulted in a dramatic change—a square pillar replaces the stupa at the rear of the cave chapel. The room is now square and the ambulatory takes the form of two walled aisles that lead to the rear chamber. Also the interiors are organized and painted in a similar fashion.[33] Although little Gandharan painting has survived, the remains at Bamiyan and elsewhere demonstrate that there were a variety of styles and themes. One type clearly derived from the naturalism of the classic tradition; such images as the Dioscuri and a skeleton in the painted grotto of Tapa-i-shotor in Hadda reveal the impact of the west.[34] Other caves show a clear relationship to the native Indian Guptan style. Those at Dilbarjin-qazan have such images as the gods Shiva and Parvati seated on the bull Nandi.

Although at first glance the Xinjiang material seems related to that of the Ajanta caves, in the Western Deccan of India (second centuries B.C.E. to fifth century C.E.). Significant differences in the structural characteristics of the caves as well as the concept and style of narrative painting suggest that the Deccani caves were not a formative influence. The caves at Ajanta differ in their formal columned porticos and the chaitya halls with a stupa in an apse at the end of the narrow hall. At Ajanta there are no domes or central square piers. The square viharas have flat ceilings with painted designs that imitate wooden coffers, while the oblong chaitya halls have ribbed barrel vaults that are sometimes adorned with painting. Biographical scenes at Ajanta are fewer in comparison to the profusion of jatakas and the theme of the thousand Buddhas. When narratives of the life of the Buddha occur, they are without individual frames, and defy any kind of hieratic organization, appearing on the wall or architectural surfaces in defiance of chronological or iconographic import. Moreover, Ajanta depictions differ greatly in the luxuriant jungle-like scenery with its lush vivid green vegetation and brightly colored fauna and the strangely skewered treatment of the rocks and architecture. Clearly related to some of the figure painting of Chinese Central Asia are the physical grace and idealized beauty of the figures at Ajanta. There is a real appreciation of a body's curvaceous forms rendered naturalistically with the effective use of shadow and highlighting. But these stylistic characteristics are attributable to the generic Guptan-era aesthetic (fourth to seventh century) that spread eastwards.

THE EVOLUTION OF NARRATIVE TECHNIQUES IN CHINESE CENTRAL ASIA

True narratives are relatively rare in Chinese Central Asia. In viewing the artistic remains, most of which were found in Buddhist cave temples, it soon becomes clear that although Buddhism was widely practiced, evidence of narratives of the historic Buddha's life is extremely limited. Fragments of biographical narratives appear only at a few sites. In addition to these, several jatakas may be cited.[35] By and large, the commission of larger-scale icons overshadowed interest in the biographical depictions, with some notable exceptions.

One partial explanation for the dearth of narratives is the growing prevalence of a medium that was cheaper, more readily available, and easier to model, that is, stucco and lime plaster. The new material was employed since the Kushan era, predominantly in the northeastern area of Gandhara, Afghanistan, and in Central Asia. In these areas where there was a shortage of stone, the use of stucco prevailed, for it eliminated the need to travel to quarry stone, transport it back to the site, and train workmen to laboriously chip out intricate patterns. However, there were clear limitations to the material, mainly elaborate detail was impossible and stucco was best used for moderate-scale sculpture with little need of delicate articulation. Being friable, it was prone to breakage.

Although it appears that no extensive narrative cycles were attempted in stucco, despite the fragility and difficulty of modeling details, narratives were executed in the new material. At Hadda, Afghanistan the story is told in the most extreme abbreviation. The great departure, a lunette-shaped fragment now in the Musée Guimet in Paris, has only three half figures—the prince, his wife, and the groom; and the farewell scene has but two—the prince embracing his horse.[36] Other locales like Tumshuq, a monastic complex on the northern silk route ascribed to the fourth to fifth centuries, have remnants of figures that suggest biographical depictions. For example, at the monastery of Toqquz Sarai, a number of demonic heads were discovered. It is tempting to imagine these as well as the small Buddha seated in *bhumisparsa mudra*, a hand gesture associated with the temptation and attack of Mara, as part of a scene of that story. So, too, the princely figure riding an elephant from Grand Temple B, and several emaciated torsos, allude to a lost narrative.[37] Mahayanist sites around Khotan, like Rawak and Kara Shahr near Turfan, yielded only icons of the Buddha and his attendants made of stucco or mud covered with lime plaster.[38] Although the lack of sculptural evidence may be attributed to the limitations of the new material in articulating the detailed stories of the life of the Buddha, such is clearly not the case with the medium of painting. Most examples of Buddhist narrative derive from the murals in pre-Mahayanist cave-chapels. But here too, biographical illustrations are far less numerous than the iconic images.

The fact is that narrative art all but disappears. With few exceptions, narratives in this region no longer play the primary role they did in India. The scenes are now severely diminished in number, size, and place of importance in relation to the icons of the Buddha. Thus stories here, for the most part, appear in reduced size, with a limited number of characters, minimal setting, and little detail. Typically, small-scale attendant figures are shown flanking or in the general area of an icon of the Buddha, reminding the devout of one biographical episode or another. It is clear from the presentation of the images that the ancient didactic function of the biographical narratives, once intended to introduce and educate the faithful to the doctrine of the Buddha, had changed. The faithful were no longer enjoined to model their life after that of the Buddha. Perhaps because the narratives expanding on the Buddha's unique qualities cast him more and more as a divine, not human figure, it no longer seemed possible to emulate his life. Or perhaps the foreign origin and distant date of existence of his historical identity seemed remote and so the narrative of his life became less important. One thing is certain—by this time, large-scale icons of the Buddha, made for the practice of *bhakti* (devout worship), dominate the interiors of the cave-chapels.

Comparison of extant Buddhist narratives at the various sites reveals several contrasting stages in the evolution of narrative. These stylistic and iconographic changes gradually evolved; in general they resemble the decline of sculptural narratives in India. There are three major formats.

I. TYPE ONE. At this stage narrative is a major element of decor on the walls of the main cella of the cave-chapel. These scenes, contained in large rectangular frames, sometimes laid out in multiple registers on the main walls of the caves, tell the complete life of the Buddha in chronological order. Each scene is independently conceived with its own cast of characters, scenery, and props. Continuity between the scenes is thematic not compositional, and the scenes are read horizontally. In this first format the Buddha may be shown in normal scale in relation to the accessory figures or larger than life size.

II. TYPE TWO. Here one or more scenes in relatively large scale occupy a major area of the wall. Sometimes contained in lunette-shaped frames over the door wall, this type more often appears on the rear wall. The narrative details are extremely abbreviated.

III. TYPE THREE. The third type is nearly miniature in scale. Narratives combine to form a decorative pattern, generally a lozenge design, covering the vaulted barrel ceiling of the main room.

Sometimes these three types of narratives appear together in a single cave, sometimes not; they are not mutually exclusive.

CAVES OF XINJIANG

Thirteen sites with Buddhist cave-chapels have been found in modern Xinjiang province: Qizil, located 60 kilometers west of the county town of Quca, in Baicheng county, has 236 caves. Qizilgaha, with 46 caves, is not more than 10 kilometers away. There are 52 caves in Simsim, 40 kilometers to the northeast of Quca town; 34 in Mazabohe, and 72 in Qumutura (Kumutula) located 30 kilometers northwest of Quca. In addition there are caves in Bezeklik, Tuohulakaiken, and Tuhelak. Only remnants of caves are found in Taitail, Wenbash, Shengjinko, Yarl Lake, and Tutugo. For Chinese scholars, the period of activity began in the third century, reached a peak in the fourth, and continued until the fourteenth, though Islam began to replace Buddhism as early as the seventh century.

1. THE THOUSAND CAVES AT QIZIL (MING-ÖI)

Located south of the Tian Shan Mountains in Baicheng County, modern Xinjiang, Qizil's 236 caves are carved out of the mountain bluffs bordering the Muzart River. According to Chinese scholars the site was active as early as the third century and continued to be constructed until the Tang.[39] Chinese records in the fourth-century account of the *History of Jin,* in a text known as the *Bhiksunipratimoksa,* attributed to the fourth-century Chinese monk Tao An, and in several biographies of famous monks like Kumarajiva, who trained at Quca in the fourth century, establish its prominence as a Buddhist site.[40] Its importance during the Tang dynasty is reflected in the lengthy account given in Xuan Zang 's seventh-century travel diary. In addition to noting the mineral richness of the soil, the kindness of the people, the beauty of their silk and embroidery, and the slaughter and destruction of a nearby town by the Turks, he describes their practice of Buddhism and mentions the caves:

> *There are about one hundred converts (sangharamas) in this country, with five thousand and more disciples. These belong to the Little Vehicle of the school of the Sarvastivadas. . . . About 40 li to the north of this desert city there are two convents close together on the slope of a mountain, but separated by a stream of water, both named Chau-hu-li, being situated east and west of one another, and accordingly called. (Here there is) a statue of Buddha, richly adorned and carved with skill surpassing that of men. The occupants of the convents are pure and truthful, diligent in the discharge of their duties. . . . Outside the western gate of the chief city, on the right and left side of the road, there are two erect figures of Buddha, about 90 feet high. . . . [41]*

The site of Qizil today attests to the accuracy of the Chinese pilgrim's report; there are a series of gorges along the riverbanks carved with caves. Although the German archaeologists methodically ravaged the caves, many are still intact and relatively well preserved. These are a startling contrast to other Buddhist cave sites in Xinjiang like Qaraqizil, Qumtura, or Bezeklik, which today are not nearly so rich in paintings. Because of the poverty of narrative material in the region, the rich finds at Qizil are a great surprise. Indeed, the caves from this site contain two important and rare examples of a complete narrative cycle of the life of the Buddha.

The main archaeological activity at Qizil was accomplished by several German expeditions. Grunwedel led the first campaign; Le Coq led a later one. Having primary access to the material, the Germans became expert on the dating and stylistic analysis of the various kinds of painting. They described two major styles of painting on the basis of pictorial characteristics. In general the first style, as outlined by Grunwedel, was clearly dependent on Indian Gandharan bas-reliefs and was ascribed to the fifth to sixth centuries. The second, a century later in date, was more strongly influenced by Iran and China.[42] Waldschmidt characterized the first style primarily by its elegant linearity, plastic modeling of forms through line, and with highlighting and shading rendered by tones darker or lighter than the dominant hue.[43] The whole, giving a harmonious effect, was based on the so-called Indo-Iranian (Sassanian) prototypes of Gandhara.

The second style is closer to Iranian-style painting. Here contour and shading are more obvious, with contrasting colors resulting in a less unified design. The line of the second style is less descriptive and fluid, appearing schematic and ornamental in the drawing of the human figures and their drapery. In contrast to the natural portrayal of characters in the first style which uses reasonable coloring, the second seems unconcerned with such effects, and the figures have gray, green, blue, or red complexions and similarly toned body hair. A sub-group of the second style, actually a development of the first, is distinguished by the dominant role of shading—wide bands of color are applied in defiance of natural effects. Landscape elements are also treated differently. In the first, there is a concern for naturalistic effects and an accurate portrayal of the various forms; in the second, trees are uniform and monotonous. The conical mountains, common to both, have interior modeling to suggest volume and texture in the first style, while in the second these lines, if present, are repetitious. Dividing the scenes of the first style are trees or decorative bands; the backgrounds, whether continuous or independent, share the same coloring and provide visual continuity. In the second style, no formal divisions are made between scenes and there is an alternation of background color.

More recently, Hartel has reaffirmed the stylistic analysis of his predecessors, stressing the importance of evidence found in the Cave of the Painters. This unique cave has several paintings of artists and an inscription ascribed to the year 500.[44]   Although American scholars acknowledge the two styles, their dates have been disputed.[45] A later third style influenced by the contemporary Chinese Tang dynasty was also identified.

Currently Chinese and Japanese scholars have been publishing a great deal on the Xinjiang caves.[46] These new studies challenge the German dating.   In general, much earlier periods of activity are ascribed, based on the inscription found in Cave 224 dating to the Han and others dating to the Tang.[47] Their analysis of the caves is based on the presence of architectural features: the square central pier, ambulatory, laternendecke roof, the relative large size of the rooms, and features in the monks' rooms.[48]

For this study, three categories of mural decoration in the caves are proposed: caves with narratives as their main decor, caves with narratives as secondary decor, and caves with narratives as a minor theme.

I. Caves with Narratives as the Main Decor

1. Cave 76 The Peacock Cave (Pfaüenhöhle)
The name of the Peacock Cave (Pfauenhöhle) derives from the bird feathers that once adorned the dome ceiling of the main room. Because this cave was one of the earliest and the most beautiful at Qizil, the Germans dismantled, removed, and reconstructed it in the Museum for Ethnology in Berlin.   Unfortunately an Allied bombing raid subsequently destroyed the murals during World War II.[49] Nothing is left but fragments of the murals and the descriptions, drawings, and photos that were made by the German expedition.   Yet the extraordinary pictorial biography, attributable to an early date of execution, can be reconstructed. The Chinese ascribe this cave to the second period (395 to 465) partly because of the central square pier with surrounding ambulatory path in the main room.[50] The pier may have been structurally necessitated by the weakness of the stone from which the cave was carved, but it is also a symbolic allusion to the cosmic Mount Sumeru. The cosmic pillar, present also in the stupas of India, links heaven and earth. This mystical significance is reflected in its décor—each face of the cave's pier has a seated Buddha surrounded by a group of figures; the whole may represent the Buddhas of the Four Directions.   Scenes from the life of the Buddha were an important

decorative theme. Painted at eye level on the side walls of the fore hall and main chamber, the scenes were contained in square frames and arranged into several registers.[51] Placed thusly, the scenes could be read in the same manner as those that adorned the stupa—during ritual circumambulation.

ANTECHAMBER

The side walls of the antechamber once bore large scenes of the temptation and first sermon.

MAIN CHAMBER

The first two registers on the left side wall seem to be an epitomized version of the life cycle. Twelve scenes were extant at the time of the German excavation. Only the scenes of greatest import are illustrated: the birth and seven steps, four encounters, temptation, Mara's attack, first sermon, visit of Indra, and various preaching scenes as well as the death cycle. Of these only the first four paintings survived. (FIGURE 6) The secondary scenes differ from those seen in India. It is possible that the Indian cycle, more important for the pilgrimage sites in India than for the events that transpired in those locations[52] was less relevant on this side of the world.

1. The birth presents the miraculous way in which the young baby is born from his mother's side. The child, issuing forth from her right flank, exits her body in the same manner in which he entered it. In this way both the conception and birth were immaculate, without the aid of any human agent.[53]

> *Maya was taking a walk; she neared the Lumbini Garden whose flowers were all in bloom. The stars were all out. Then Maya grasped hold of the branch of a tree, and the babe issued forth from her right flank and came down to the ground.* [54]

Maya is in the traditional pose: her right hand grasps a bough of a tree in the Lumbini Garden, her left arm rests on her hip.[55] (FIGURE 6a) Maya is naked but for a diaphanous dhoti, the heavy jewels adorning her body and thick strands of pearls in her hair. Unfortunately, due to damage in the area to the left, there is no evidence of the baby emerging forth from her flank. Only the lower section of the body of the kneeling king of the gods, Indra, who received the child, remains.

All that is left of the god of creation Brahma, who stood behind him, is a tall topknot and halo. To the right of Maya was Mahaprajapati, her sister, who following Maya's death soon after childbirth, raised the baby. Delicate line renders the curvaceous forms of the body whose three-dimensionality is most convincing despite the lack of highlighting and shading. Maya's ample form is balletically posed in controposto. Her face has highly arched eyebrows, a small nose and full rich lips.

Though lacking a formal separation, the first steps are drawn as an independent scene on the right. The naked babe, standing the full height of the panel, has a tall ushnisa or cranial protrusion, one of the distinguishing marks of a Buddha, and a halo. Walking to the right, he holds his right hand in *abhaya mudra* (right hand facing out, fingers pointing up); the left hand is extended down, palm facing out. Footprints clearly indicate the extraordinary event of his walking immediately following his birth. The seven steps enacted the Vedic ritual of taking possession of the universe, the cardinal directions, heaven, earth and nadir.[56] This is undoubtedly the moment of the great declaration of the newborn from the *Lalitavistara: "In the entire world I am the very chief; from this day forth my births are finished"*[57]

Or the XXBJ:

> *Among the gods and men I am the most revered, the most victorious. I have been born and died innumerable times. This one (life) is my last. In this life I will be the salvation of men and gods.*[58]

At Qizil the two nativity events are shown in one panel like examples from the later Kushan era. When such combinations of scenes occur, it signifies the first stage in the growing lack of interest in narratives. At the height of narrative development in Kushan art, each scene was afforded its own panel and artistic dramatization. It was only later that the birth and seven steps were coupled. In the Gandharan examples however, the two events were shown in a single scene: the baby issued from his mother's side and in the foreground, took his first steps; while in the Peacock Cave, the scenes, though sharing the same composition, are quite distinct. As at Amaravati, the figural disposition, rather than architectural members, suggests the division between the scenes.[59]

2. The four encounters, which appear next, related the young prince's
first experience of the sad limitations of the human condition - old age,
sickness, and death. They take the narrative form of a series of four
trips outside the confines of the palace. On each excursion he
encountered a vision on the road — an old man, a sick man, and a dead
man.

> *Nandihara (the god Indra) . . . assumed the form of an old man
> squatting by the side of the road. He had white hair and loose
> teeth. His wrinkled skin hung away from his face, his flesh was
> dissipated. He was hunchbacked, his limbs and joints were
> withered and crooked. His eyes were tearful, his nose was
> dripping, and spittle dribbled from his mouth. As he took a breath
> he wheezed. The color of his body was sallow and his entire body,
> head, and hands shook. He emitted evil humors. The crown prince
> asked what kind of person is this. The god awoke the servant who
> answered "an old man."[60]*

On the next sortie he meets a sick man:

> *His body was emaciated, his stomach distended, he could not
> swallow. His bones were disjointed and separated from his flesh.
> His skin was sallow. When he lifted himself, he shook. He could
> not support himself (without) two crutches under his armpits.*

Leaving the palace for the third time, he encounters a dead man:

> *When the prince left by the western gate, Indra transformed himself
> into a dead man who was being carried out of the city (for
> cremation). His family members followed the cart crying and
> calling out. [61]*

On the last trip the prince sees an ascetic:

> *Again he wanted to leave the city, the god (Indra) transformed
> himself into an ascetic at the gate, dressed in that manner and
> (carrying a) begging bowl. Peacefully walking with care, he kept
> his gaze far ahead.[62]*

It is this last experience, which introduced him to the traditional path of
conventional spiritual practices. Combining the four exits into one

scene was probably necessitated by the monotony of the narration for the pictorial representation differed only in the detail of which individual was encountered on the outing. Similar attempts to economically portray this event are also found in Gandhara in present day Afghanistan.[63] In general there is a scarcity of extant representations of the scenes in the northwest region, which is curious, for the event is doctrinally important; it occurs twice at Qizil. On the left of the Peacock cave mural the prince rides in his chariot drawn by his white horse; attending him, Chandaka, his groom, holds a parasol over his head. Indra, the Vedic deity of the sky, is in the mid-ground. (FIGURE 6b) (In the scriptures, it is Indra who magically brings about these encounters.[64]) To the right are three of the visions: in the upper area a dead man lies on a palette borne by four mourners. In the mid-ground is the old man, a stooped semi-nude, thin figure, balding with a fringe of white hair, and leaning on a staff. The sick man is in the lower right corner, an emaciated reclining figure propped up on one elbow; the mural has suffered damage in the area above his head. The emotional content of the Qizil scene is rich, the prince's face, still in good repair, has refined features, with an aquiline nose, full lips, and delicate mustache. His melancholy response is conveyed by the inclination of his head to one side, a gesture of sympathy. Gazing directly at the old man, he raises his left eyebrow. His eyelids are slightly lowered. This composition, with the prince on the left and the visions on the right, is similar to the Gandharan examples, but here the emotional content is far more pronounced. This dramatization of mood though gestures and expression is however seen in the art of other regions of India, particularly in the southeast at Amaravati and Nagarjunakonda as well in the west in the murals of Ajanta (fifth century). In fact the Peacock cave painting has much in common with two versions at Nagarjunakonda,[65] in one the prince, riding in his chariot facing left, encounters the corpse held aloft by bearers in the upper left. Damage to the lower area prevents further comparison but the similarity in composition is unmistakable.

3. The next scene shows the evening of the enlightenment. The prince, following the four exists, left home to be an ascetic. Having followed the traditional spiritual path for six years, he abandons the practice of austerities in the forest and sits in meditation. Mara, deity of death and desire, seeing the youth seated in concentration, decides to prevent him

from attainting his goal. At the center of the scene of the temptation the young ascetic is shown with a cranial protrusion, semi-nude, and emaciated, his skeletal structure protruding beneath the skin. His hands sit in his lap in *dhyana mudra*, one on top of another face up. (FIGURE 6c) A narrow scarf winds round his shoulders. Behind him a huge halo illuminates his body like the rising sun. This extraordinary manner of depicting the starved bodhisattva is seen in Gandharan compositions and concurs with the textual descriptions of his emaciated state. His pitiful appearance after having practiced austerities with the Brahmin ascetics in the forest for six years is described in the *Lalitavistara*:

> *Thus it was his skin became wrinkled, his body attenuated and his eyes hollow as an old man's; whilst his limbs were unable to support him as he moved, and all who beheld him were filled with a strange feeling of awe and reverence at the sight of the penance he was thus enduring. . . .*[66]

Or: "*He sat upright for six years; his body became emaciated; the bones protruded through the skin. . .*"[67] A few icons of the skeletal Buddha are found in Gandhara, though showing the emaciated figure in a narrative was fairly rare. It is sometimes found in Pakistan and at the site of Shotorak in Afghanistan.[68] The relative infrequence with which it is portrayed is probably due to its being such a gruesome image. At Qizil Mara stands with his son on the left, both handsome men, they are bedecked in jewels and a crown, wearing a dhoti and scarf. They too have halos, but these are quite small in comparison with the Buddha's.

The temptation of Mara was a three-pronged attack on the meditating bodhisattva on the night of his enlightenment. As the bodhisattva sat in contemplation under the bodhi tree, the god of death and desire grew unhappy in his heaven. Mara was fearful if the bodhisattva were successful in destroying his bonds of *karma* and escaped the Wheel of Causation of life, death, and rebirth, all would follow his lead and his kingdom would be empty. First he sent his beautiful daughters to tempt the bodhisattva with sensual thoughts. Since they were ignored, Mara tried to persuade the bodhisattva to give up his pursuit, reap the fruits of his long spiritual labor, and become a god in the heavens. In light of these failures, he called upon his demonic warriors who, armed with weapons of all kinds, descended on the bodhisattva and threatened him with destruction. These attacks failed and, with the rising sun, the forces of Mara scattered, and the bodhisattva achieved the illumination of a Buddha.

Here at Qizil, on the left, near the seated bodhisattva, one of Mara's daughters, a beautiful woman in transparent silk garments and bedecked with adornments, stands in a pose of languorous grace, in three-quarters rear view, her curvaceous rump facing the viewer. In a provocative manner, her hand jauntily rests on her hip. Cascading down her back, her luxuriant hair is caught in a twist of pearls. Her face, in profile, looks up longingly at the Buddha. As in Gandhara, the action is synoptically portrayed--Mara's daughters' seduction on the left, their defeat on the right. Transformed into three white-haired old hags, the daughters still wear their opulent jewels, but now their haggard bodies are decorously covered with garments. Turning to look back at the seated figure, the sisters are anguished in their newly fallen state, which is reflected in their bent over postures; one turns to the right to escape. This too is a literal illustration of the scriptures. But there is no extant depiction of the gruesome transformation of the goddesses in India. As is the case with the starved bodhisattva, showing suffering and physical deformation was eschewed in traditional Indian art. The closest parallel to the Qizil representation of the transformation of Mara's daughters is found at Nagarjunakonda and Amaravati where the events are also synoptically told—the seduction to the left, the defeat on the right. Here the transformed daughters are shown in gestures of reverence, there are no portrayals of their misshapen state, but the female figure closest to the Buddha has the same posture: the left hand, bent at the elbow, reaches up to the face, other rests on the hip.[69]

4. The adjacent scene on the right is the attack of Mara's army. At center is the seated Buddha, with flames emitting from his shoulders, in addition to his halo and body mandorla. To the left is Mara, a princely crowned figure. (FIGURE 6d) As the text explains, he tries to tempt the bodhisattva, telling him to stop meditating and reap the benefits of his long spiritual practices. To the right, Mara wears battle dress—a scaled cuirass. His son Sumati, standing behind him, restrains him from personally striking the Buddha. Armed monsters attack in the upper area. In the upper left one demon bears an ax and another, a three-headed figure, holds a large rock over his head, both are about to strike. Behind them is a hairy, fanged demon with a pitchfork; in the sky demons blow clouds of black smoke and strike a drum rendering the

texts description of Mara's summoning up dark clouds, violent winds, thunder and lightning. The climax is in the foreground with the earth spirit, who emerges from the ground and attests to the incalculable merit the bodhisattva acquired through uncountable births during which the greatest compassion and self-sacrifice were manifest, earning him the right to achieve enlightenment. To the right are a poisonous snake and a fallen soldier. Here too, exact parallels with Gandharan steles exist in the drawing of the restraint of Mara, the particular demonic types, their assault weapons, the earth spirit's giving witness, and the fallen soldier; only in Qizil the vanquished warrior is not at center but moved to the right.

5. The Visit of the god Indra was not preserved. This event was extremely popular in Gandhara, no doubt due to the tradition that it took place in the northwest territories.[70] Its popularity at Amaravati and Nagarjunakonda is not so easily explained.[71] Its importance, as others in which the Vedic deities were given a role, was to attest to both the acceptance of the native gods by Buddhism and to the endorsement by the ancient deities of the new religion.

6. This once was an illustration of the miracle that converted the Kasyapa brothers at Uruvilva: Buddha stood among the Brahmins, ejecting water from his feet and flames from his shoulders. Once again there is a strict concordance with the *Lalitavistara* text: "*He could make water or fire come out of his body.*"[72] This scene may be identified as an illustration of what is generically termed the Miracle of Shravasti,[73] named after the place where the marvels were performed. Here, Buddha was shown in human scale. The miracle of Pairs, as it is also known, was a subject favored by the Sarvastivadins as it occurs at several sites in Gandhara associated with them.[74] The miracle is rendered at Amaravati as well, where the flames radiate from the shoulders.[75]

7-12. Lastly several episodes of the *parinirvana* cycle were told beginning with the farewell to the disciples and followers. These are no longer extant, only drawings by Grunwedel represent what was once painted on the walls. In typical Gandharan style, twin sala trees framed the scene and two large size tree deities looked down from their leafy perches, only one of which was observed in the drawing. (FIGURE 7)

In another scene drawn by Grunwedel the reclining Buddha was at center with a mourning monk at the feet and a haloed divinity by the head. The next scene was completely destroyed; it may have been the wrapping of the corpse. The final farewell of the disciple Kasyapa, who opens the jeweled coffin to say goodbye, is preserved in a line sketch. (FIGURE 8)

Undoubtedly additional narratives were painted on the other side walls as they are in Cave 110 (Stepped cave, the TreppenHöhle) at Qizil. Considering these, some conjectures can be made about the destroyed murals. Scenes of the youth—the athletic competitions, first meditation, and marriage, or of the pre-enlightenment events—the great departure, change of clothes with the hunter, and cutting of the hair, or post-enlightenment scenes—first meal, gift of four bowls, meeting with the ascetics—may have been depicted.

CONCLUSIONS

In summation, the pictorial biography found in the Peacock Cave is illustrated in true Gandharan style. Although comparable contemporary paintings are unfortunately no longer extant in India, the reliance on Gandharan presentation, composition, and organization of motifs seen in stone reliefs is obvious. The linear progression of the scenes and their separation into individual episodes with architectural dividers (here gaily painted borders replace the columns) reveal the influence of the Gandharan style. In addition to a general conformity in the lay out of the illustrations, frequently there is an exact agreement with Gandharan compositions and figural dispositions. Important correspondences were also found with the art of Amaravati and Nagarjunakonda.

The Qizil murals from the Peacock Cave demonstrate an early stage in the evolution of narrative. The stories are represented in a complete manner and occupy a primary area of decor. The temptation was told in two parts, the death a cycle of four events. But a few others, like the birth and seven steps, were conflated, and the four exits were merged into one, suggesting the imminent decline in narrative interest. Both the use of horizontal narration and the literalness of the depictions strongly suggest that these murals were based on an illustrated scripture, which called for a continuous narration of the complete biography. However, since no early illustrated scriptures of the biography have survived in India or Central Asia, their existence is hypothesized; though they are preserved in China and Japan.[76] Based on the apparent conformity of details in the murals in the Peacock cave, the *Lalitavistara* seems to have been the preeminent text.

Similarities in iconography were also noted. The flaming shoulders of the Buddha are a most unusual feature, and it is surprising to see them in Amaravati, Qizil and Gandhara. So too the rarely depicted four exits and miracle of pairs appear at all three sites. In these representations the figure of the Buddha is slightly larger than life size or human in scale, physically distinguished by his halo and ushnisha, as well as central placement in the narrative action. Later period illustrations show him much larger than the narrative characters of the setting. The eminence of the scenes of the temptation and first sermon, presented in large size and importantly placed in both the anteroom and main chamber, is very significant. Such subjects are of clear concern to members of the pre-Mahayanist sect, who practicing self-discipline and meditation, had to combat the distractions to a peaceful mind. Thus the temptation was a metaphor of the difficulties encountered during meditation which is in accord with primal Buddhism when the demonic members of Mara's army were less abstract and non-personified ills such as sleep, sloth, exhaustion, hunger, thirst, fear, craving, and anger.[77] The temptation is then an inspirational model of the heroic achievement of illumination through meditation. Similarly the first sermon has a special significance. The first preaching celebrates both the initial sermon given on that day when the world shared the benefits of Buddha's enlightenment and the creation of the *sangha* or monastic community. It was the *sangha* who were responsible for the dissemination of the doctrine beyond the life span of Shakyamuni. Therefore, the illustration of the first sermon celebrates the centuries old transmission of the beliefs through the vehicle of the monastic devotees.

Thus the murals from the Peacock Cave at Qizil present a clear statement of Sarvastivadin art. Narratives of the life of the Buddha dominate this pre-Mahayanist site. Many similarities with the arts of Kushana India and Andhra Pradesh, also Sarvastivadin in their affiliation, exist in the subject, iconography and presentation. This evidence helps establish a corpus of material that can be identified as Sarvastivadin art.

2. CAVE 110 (Stepped Cave, Treppenhöhle)[78]

Cave 110 preserves a more complete life cycle of the Buddha Shakyamuni. Attributed to the second style by the Germans, this cave has a vaulted fore hall (which was destroyed) and a square cella, but neither a central pier nor ambulatory. The walls taper at the top to form a simulated barrel vault. On the door and rear walls are lunettes that carry an image of large-scale seated Maitreya and the attack of Mara, respectively.

The painting style is extremely naturalistic especially in the rendering of the human figures, a legacy of the Hellenistic school's influence on the art of Gandhara. Most of the characters have a light skin tone. Warm flesh tones outline and shadow the anatomical forms. These hues suggest the three-dimensionality of the arms, shoulders, and legs, and accentuate the interior modeling of the fleshy forms like the chest and stomach. The delicate designs of the jewelry—earrings, arm bracelets, necklaces—and textile patterns are drawn with great finesse. The hair lies close to the head. The *ushnisa* of the Buddha is a small, discrete protrusion covered with wavy hair. For the Buddha's garments, a special style is appropriated—a double line defines the folds of cloth that closely cling to the body. This drapery pattern is reminiscent of a late style of Gandhara, identified by Hallade as deriving from Sassanian art.[79]

Approximately the same size as the narrative figures, the Buddha maintains his importance in the scene by his central placement or by the actions of the accessory figures that are always directed toward him. Brilliant blue and vivid aqua green are the main hues, with a white or teal blue background that is shared by contiguous panels. Separating the scenes are painted framing elements adorned with delicate floral designs of white petals on an ochre or a blue-green field.

Being the largest image in the room and placed in the most important location, in a lunette on the upper rear wall, the attack of Mara is as prominent here as in Peacock Cave (and Cave 8, Höhle der sechzehn Schwerttrager, ascribed by the Germans to the seventh century). (FIGURE 9) This is not the scene in which to observe the naturalistic technique of the Qizil artist, as the wild composite creatures that make up Mara's army dominate the composition surrounding the seated Buddha, who is unfortunately now totally effaced. The lunette, having been taken back to Berlin, is largely destroyed; only the lower right

corner survived. (FIGURE 9a) Mara, crowned and dressed from head
to toe in scaled leather armor, is shown twice: on the left trying his
smooth words, and on the right about to draw his sword.

Like the Peacock Cave, the side walls of the main chamber have
registers of stories from the life of the Buddha. These read like a scroll
continuously from right to left. As in the ritual triple circumambulation
of the stupa in India, the faithful walk around the cave three times for a
complete viewing of the life, reading each section in its entirety before
proceeding to the next. Each of the three horizontal divisions on the
side wall has seven square panels, the rear has only five; the lowest
register is completely destroyed. All surviving 57 scenes are uniform
in size. Beginning at the top right wall are the nativity scenes.

RIGHT WALL

1. In typical Gandharan fashion, the conception shows the
bodhisattva's mother Maya, lying on a bed on her right side, her head
resting on her right arm. (FIGURE 10 left) In the foreground of the
palatial setting are two female attendants: one figure, seen from the
rear, kneels; the second sits asleep in front of the bed. Two standing
female guards frame the composition. True to Indian prototypes, the
queen is buxom, scantily clad in diaphanous skirts, scarves, and rich
jewels. Above Maya, the subject of her dream, the bodhisattva,
descends into her womb. His figure, adorned with gold, suffered great
damage and is most difficult to make out, for vandals scratched the
gold off. For the first time the bodhisattva is depicted neither
metaphorically as a six-tusked elephant nor riding one.

2. The interpretation of the dream is also shown in a palatial setting
(FIGURE 10, top middle). At center is the bodhisattva's father,
Suddhodana, crowned and haloed, sitting on a low stool in the posture
of royal ease; next to him is Maya, seated in the cross-ankled position.
To the right the Brahmin sage Asita sits with his legs crossed at the
ankles. His right hand is extended forward in conversational gesture as
he delivers the prophecy:

> *He who will be born in your household will become either a*
> *supreme emperor who will possess the flying wheel (Chakravartin)*
> *or he will leave home to "seek the Way," attain Buddhahood, and*
> *bring release to the Ten Directions.*

3. The miraculous birth takes place in the next panel. Maya reaches for the limb of a flowering tree in the Lumbini Garden as she gives birth; her sister stands on the right. (FIGURE 10a)   To the left the god Brahma kneels to catch the baby as he emerges from Maya's left flank. Indra stands nearby.   Unlike the nativity cycle represented in Cave 76, the scene of the seven steps is not included.

Many miracles accompanied the bodhisattva's birth, among them the simultaneous birth of male creatures throughout the kingdom:

> *Eighty-four thousand elders all gave birth to male children and eighty-four thousand stable horses all bore colts. One of them was unique: his coat was all white, and his mane was like a precious pearl; because of this, they named him "Special soaring"(Kanthaka). In the stable, eighty-four thousand white elephants were born; the hair and tusks of one of the elephants were as white as pearls, his mouth had six tusks.80*

Similar to Kushan representations, the illustration of the miraculous simultaneous births shows Kanthaka, the prince's mount, being nursed by its mother. Here at top right the mare is not drawn in perfect profile, but like the Hellenistic ancient standards, turns her head back to watch the foal. Unlike the Gandharan composition is an added detail described in the scripture—an elephant nursing its young in the bottom right.

4. It is here that the seven steps appear in a panel with the first bath. Each event occupies half the allotted space. (FIGURE 11 top middle, 11a) On the left the naked child stands on a stool bathed by a corona of intertwined snakes that arch in the sky over his body and issue streams of "warm and cool water."   The corona of dragons derives from the GXYJ, which is the only version to describe two *nagaraja* brothers.81 The traditional way of showing the first bath in Gandhara is to render the *naga*s as anthropomorphic divinities.   It is only at Mathura that the shower is given by nagas represented as snakes—with human upper bodies and a corona of snake hoods over their heads. This unique example of the adoption of the Mathuran imagery is something of an anomaly that may have been transmitted by the Sarvastivadins, who were active at both sites.

The naked child takes his first steps on the right and raises his right hand in an unusual gesture—palm facing out, index and thumb forming a circle. The left hand hangs by his side. A divine deva with fluttering scarves hovers overhead. In accordance with the texts, lotus petals spring up as his foot touches the ground.

5. Much like the Indian versions, the return from the Lumbini Garden is in an elephant-drawn palanquin, but here Maya is conspicuously absent. (FIGURE 11, top right) Attendants lead the mount.

6. and 7. Destroyed.

REAR WALL
8. and 9. Destroyed.

10. The youthful years spent in the palace are the subject of the next series of depictions. The specific content of this scene is not apparent. (FIGURE 12, top left)

11. The prince is standing, a figure kneeling before him. (FIGURE 12, top mid) Next, turned to the right he walks, a servant following. At center is a tree. Perhaps this is the walk to school, a popular scene in Gandhara that is not found in the texts. The scriptures relate only the lesson in school.

12. The next series of scenes comprise the athletic competitions that demonstrated the physical superiority of the bodhisattva. First there was an elephant stuck in the city gates. (FIGURE 12 top right, 12a)

> *Devadatta was the first to go out. When he saw the elephant blocking the gates he tried to expel it with one blow, but when he grasped it, it became unconscious. Then Nanda found it and dragged it to the side of the road. Later the heir apparent . . . felt great compassion, slowly came in front it, placed his hand on the elephant, lifted it and pitched it outside the city walls, causing the elephant to be revived and revitalized.*[82]

The event of the throwing of the elephant is told in continuous action. The unconscious creature lies in the middle of the panel, and a princely figure on the left attempts to drag the carcass. Next, the bodhisattva stands over the beast. Last, at center, he holds the elephant in his right hand about to hurl it over the crenellated city walls in the right background.

LEFT WALL

13. The contests of strength and other events from the adolescent period continue on the left wall, beginning with the wrestling competition.[83] (FIGURE 13, top left) In the foreground is a dark-skinned contestant with his legs spread for balance; a light-skinned youth is seen from the rear. Both are dressed in short *dhotis* (skirts). To the right is a seated female spectator, maybe Yashodhara, for whose hand, the XXBJ scriptures explain, the contests were held.[84]

Next is the archery contest. Standing on the left the young prince, dressed in a short dhoti and fluttering scarves, holds the bow in his outstretched left hand and pulls the string with his right. (FIGURE13, top middle, 13a) Shown again to the right, the young prince holds an arrow in his left hand. In the distance is a bird's eye view of the stream that gushed forward when his arrow entered the earth, a detail not found in Gandharan sculptures, but described in all of the texts. Neither other competitors nor the archery targets are drawn. The story has been reduced to its climactic conclusion: *"The arrow shot (by the prince) pierced seven (target) drums and entered the ground causing a spring to gush forth."*[85]

14. Completing the displays of physical superiority is the sword competition. (FIGURE 13, top middle right) It is important to note that this event was not described in the extant scriptures and thus not common among the biographical depictions of Gandhara; it only was represented at Hadda.[86] Three contestants stand flat-footed in frontal position; they are separated by the painted motif of thin vertical piers. The first contestant, wearing a turban, dhoti and scarves, raises his sword in his left hand. The next, crowned, holds his weapon in his right hand in front of chest; his left rests on his hip. Last is the bodhisattva, naked but for a short dhoti and jewels. He has a halo and light skin. His sword is in his left hand; his right hand is in front of his hip. Delicate modeling of the torso, arms and face is done in a lighter hue.

15. The wedding is painted with the same economy of means. The prince stands on the left, his palms joined together, both index figures

and thumbs forming a circle, the palms facing out, fingers pointing up. (FIGURE 13, top right) His bride, ample-breasted Yashodhara, stands next to him; an attendant flanks each of them. In Gandhara it was usual to include a sacred flame between the figures, for circumambulating it three times was an important part of the wedding ritual. Its absence here suggests that this was not the local custom.

16. This scene is unidentified. The prince walks with an attendant. On the right he bathes in a river.

17-18. As in the Peacock Cave, the four encounters are combined. (FIGURE 14) Here two are presented in each panel. The bodhisattva enters the composition from the left, riding in a chariot drawn by Kanthaka. In the background is a single tree; seated in the foreground is the sick man, an emaciated character with a distended belly. (FIGURE 14a) Behind him is the old man. Supporting himself with his staff, he wears only a loincloth and is so thin his ribs protrude. The last two encounters are arranged in a similar manner. On the left is the vision of a monk with an alms bowl; in the upper right the dead man is shown wrapped in a shroud, borne on a stretcher, and attended by a single figure. (FIGURE 14b)

19. Destroyed.

RIGHT WALL SECOND REGISTER
20. The first meditation takes places out-of-doors. Asked to oversee the plowing of the fields by the king, the young prince, exhausted, seeks rest under a leafy tree. While seated there he is moved to compassion for the toiling farmer and oxen and the destruction of life caused by the tilling of the earth. Worms are exposed with the upturned clods of earth and birds swoop down to eat them. The youth begins to meditate. As he sits a miracle occurs, despite the movement of the sun, the shade of the tree is immobilized to protect him.

> *The sun's rays were strong and bright, and the tree (under which he sat) had a crooked branch that provided [constant] shade for his body (despite the movement of the sun).*[87]

At Qizil the prince sits in the pensive posture—ankle resting on the knee, the hand, upholding the head, is balanced on his knee—not the yogic cross-legged position of Gandhara.[88] (FIGURE 10, bottom left) Kneeling before him is a light-skinned attendant who performs the kowtow and a dark-skinned one looks up in adoration; both are responding to the miracle of shade.

The vision which stimulated the first meditation is to the right: the blue bull toils pulling a plough; Indra, a bejeweled and dark gray-skinned figure, hovers over the animal as mentioned in the GXYJ.[89] The flowering trees that flanked the composition are now lost.

21. The prince goes for a ride near the city gate on the right, in the middle is the city goddess of Kapilavastu wearing a crown. The light-skinned figure of the prince on horseback has been effaced; Chandaka stands nearby on the left. (FIGURE 10, bottom left)

22. Next the prince kneels, begging permission to leave home. The royal parents want to keep him at home and the request causes great concern. The queen extends her arm to comfort the king, who raises his right hand to his head. This gesture is described only in the GXYJ. A dark-skinned servant kneels near the prince on the right. (FIGURE 10, bottom right)

23. The setting for the prince's departure from home is the harem. Awoken one night he gazes about him and the women in the harem appear deformed by sleep. He has a vision of the women transformed into sacks of skin containing pus and blood. The gruesome aspect of this vision is not illustrated. Rather, in Indian fashion, the lascivious beauties are shown in postures of deep sleep. The Qizil version is nearly an exact replica of the Gandharan bas-reliefs.[90] (FIGURE 11, bottom center) Yashodhara reclines on the bed, her right arm draped over her head; at the foot of the bed, the prince, awakened, is seated. Sleeping maidens are in the foreground. One dark-skinned figure on the left, seen from the front, leans on a large drum; another, on the right, shown in profile, is similarly abandoned to sleep.   A rich architectural arcade and coffered ceiling convey the palatial setting. Remnants of the midnight blue background are still visible.

24. This is an illustration of the bodhisattva's great departure; rejecting his family and kingdom, he leaves the palace. (FIGURE 11, bottom right)

> He called Chandaka, gravely ordering him to saddle the horse with the equipment for the wilderness. Worrying about the sound caused by opening the gate, he walked to and fro in the palace. The god knew his thoughts and sent yakshas to carry Kanthaka by lifting the horses' hooves.[91]

In the Qizil painting the prince, in profile, rides his white horse. He is followed by the now familiar figure of Indra, and leading the party is the groom Chandaka holding an umbrella. Floating creatures, their legs gracefully extended in the air, bear the hooves of the horse. Standing nearby is a sensuous female. Is this the city goddess who in the texts tries to dissuade the prince from leaving home? There are still traces of the dark blue backdrop of night and small white flowers fill the sky. In the left background is the crenellated city gate. On the right, confronting the escaping prince, is Mara, dark-skinned, crowned, and clad in armor, who also tries to prevent the prince from leaving. His presence, marked in the TRBJ, also occurs in scenes of the great departure in Gandhara, for example at the site of Kunduz.[92]

25. and 26. Damaged.

REAR WALL

27, 28, and 29. These scenes did not survive but in all probability were related to the enlightenment cycle. The prince's farewell to his horse and groom and their return to the palace, his six years of austerities in the forest, and his meetings with the brahmin ascetics may have been among the lost subjects.

30. Highly stylized landscape elements and water plants identify the bath in the Nairanjana River, which marks the end of his six fruitless years of practicing austerities in the forest. A haloed bodhisattva dressed in loincloth, stands in the river; wavy lines and a blue color delineate the water. (FIGURE 12, bottom center) On the right, now dressed as a Buddha, wearing monastic apparel with the right shoulder exposed, he emerges from the river. This scene illustrates the important physical transformation of the bodhisattva into an ascetic.

He has discarded his princely jewels, exchanged his luxurious attire for the simple clothes of a hunter and cut off his hair.

31. After rejecting the austere life of ascetic existence, the bodhisattva begs a meal of the maiden Sugata. Both she, dark-skinned and kneeling, and a second figure standing beside her, offer up bowls of gruel to the Buddha standing on the left. (FIGURE 12, bottom right) On the right the Buddha is shown twice. Holding the bowl up with two hands he pronounces his thanks for the meal and confers blessings on the maidens. On the far right, he stands eating its contents. The scene is set against a blue background scattered with gold and white flowers. The women's garments, jewels, and sandals are done in an extremely fine style. The white beading of their adornments and the delicate floral patterns of their sheer silk garments are particularly well rendered.

LEFT WALL SECOND REGISTER
32. The pre-enlightenment cycle includes many encounters with well wishers. The first is the Naga Kallika and his wife. (FIGURE 13, bottom left) On the left the standing Buddha reaches his hand out to the kneeling Nagaraja who is identified by his attributes of crown and hood comprised of many cobra heads. On the right Buddha extends his hands in a gesture of greeting, accepting an offering from a kneeling figure. A luxuriantly blossoming tree in the background separates the two figures.[93] This may be the tree spirit wishing him good fortune as illustrated in Gandhara and narrated in the XXBJ:

> *In the midst was one tall tree that was especially beautiful; one branch after another had dense foliage. The colors of its flowers were so lush that they resembled heavenly adornments. At the summit was a celestial banner of good fortune. [Near it] was the king of the grove of trees.*[94]

33. Next a grass cutter proffers fresh cut grass for the bodhisattva to sit on. To the right is the grass cutter, at center is the bodhi tree, and on the left is the Buddha. (FIGURE 13, bottom middle)

34. Only the defeat of Mara is illustrated. The Buddha is seated on the grass seat; around him are worshiping figures, some of whom are clearly Mara's defeated forces. On the right, in a gesture of

supplication, stands Mara. (FIGURE 13, bottom right) The abbreviated telling of the event is no doubt due to the large-scale and detailed rendering of the temptation in the lunette.

35. After enlightenment, the merchants Trapusa and Bhallika offer the Buddha another meal. In typical Gandharan style, which closely follows the scriptural tradition, the merchant donors, dressed in tunic and trousers with swords at their waist, stand at either side of the centrally seated Buddha. In the upper part of the panel are the Four Guardian Kings, who, flanking the Buddha, offer a bowl for the Buddha to receive the food. (FIGURE 14, bottom left) These two scenes, which had been distinct in the northwest, are conflated at Qizil.

36. The homage of King Bimbisara of Magdha, the subject of the next panel, is told only in the GXYJ and *Lalitavistara*.[95] (FIGURE 14, bottom right) During the period of his wandering prior to enlightenment, the bodhisattva encountered King Bimbisara. So impressed was the king, he offered the bodhisattva his empire if he would only agree to stay with him. Explaining that he had renounced the world, the bodhisattva promised that after achieving enlightenment he would return to preach to the king. Here is the depiction of his return visit after enlightenment. On the left the Buddha is seated beneath a flowering tree; seated nearby, on a low stool, is the king. This scene is heavily damaged.

37. After enlightenment the Buddha is tempted to expire, having exhausted his karma. However, the gods entreat him to teach his doctrine. After much consideration of a worthy audience, the Buddha decides to preach to the five ascetics who lived with him in the forest. The first sermon takes place amidst flowering trees; the members of his first audience surround the Buddha. (FIGURE 14, bottom left)

38. This scene of a regal couple seated under a royal canopy approached by a figure, with his arm raised over his head, is unidentified. (FIGURE 14, bottom right)
    The remaining 17 scenes, now totally effaced, surely would have portrayed the conversions, perhaps displays of miraculous powers like the miracles at Shravasti. It would have been interesting to know if the descent at Samkassa were depicted, when the Buddha went to heaven

to preach to his mother who had died seven days after his birth. Afterwards, he descended to earth on a triple staircase at Samkassa. The scene is illustrated elsewhere at Qizil (Caves 4, 98, 178, 192, 224). The death cycle would also have been told including the farewell to Mallas, the Buddha's lay followers, farewell of his disciple Kashyapa, burning of the bier, and the division of the relics.

In summation, Cave 110, though undated, is characteristic of an early stage of narrative art at Qizil. With its reliance on western prototypes for narrative technique, composition and figure style, the influential role of Gandharan art is apparent. Similar to Gandharan art, the Qizil murals share completeness in the portrayal of the biographical cycles and a literal depiction of the events that suggests a reliance on illustrated sutras, or copybooks. However, there are times when details found in the scriptures, but not in the pictorial traditions of India, are illustrated. The inclusion of the elephant in the simultaneous births, King Suddhodana's hitting his head in grief in hearing of his son's decision to leave, and the Buddha's returning to preach to King Bimbisara, are but a few examples. It seems likely that an illustrated scripture, based on Gandharan pictorial narratives, was instrumental for the Qizil artists. This probably was the *Lalitavistara* since both sites belonged to the Sarvastivadin sect. Moreover, like the organization of the Gandharan bas-reliefs on the body of the stupa, the images are read in a left to right direction similar to the reading of a scroll. However, it should be noted that details absent from the scriptures and found in the pictorial art are also omitted, like the absence of the ritual flame in the marriage ceremony, which may be attributable to local custom.

In Cave 110 and the Peacock Cave narratives play a primary role in the decorative and iconographic scheme—as the main decor, they occupy a major area of the cave. This is indicative of an early stage of development. Within the biographical scenes, the storytelling is still expansive, and sometimes more than one panel is used to illustrate an event. Multiple narrative characters are present in each scene. Both the primary and secondary figures are drawn in full scale, with the handsome details of their garments, the intricate textile patterns, and elegant adornments meticulously rendered. Still important to the scenes are the settings which, whether palatial interiors or outdoor environment, are pictured with care and interest.

Also characteristic of the early phase is the consistent artistic dependence on western prototypes. A general concordance with

Gandharan art is evident in the disposition of figures, posture, or other details; sometimes there are exact reproductions of Gandharan compositions. At times there is a clear correspondence with the art of Afghanistan, particularly the similarity of the themes of the sword fight and the treatment of the four exits. Moreover, the paintings from Cave 110 exhibit a Hellenistically inspired naturalism in the delineation of the figures' proportion, features, treatment of the garments and in the artful application of the shadows and highlights. The heroic muscular body and idealized beauty of the figures closely partake of the classical tradition.

Despite the expanded and seemingly complete narration of the biography, the first stage of reduction in narrative detail is detectable. In some cases only the conclusion of a series of episodes is shown (archery). Several panels combine two scenes into one—bath and seven steps, four exits, gift of food by the merchants and offering of the bowls. But this is not the extreme abbreviation of scenes and joining of events characteristic of the later stage of narrative evolution. That stage, manifest in the later caves, is marked by a repetitious progression of seated or standing Buddha images differentiated only by the minuscule narrative personae that accompany them.

While the pictorial narratives are important in Cave 110, there are contemporary caves with a similar organization of the main chamber but a total absence of narratives. The scheme of dividing the side walls into two or three horizontal zones filled with multiple large rectangles enclosed in floral frames is familiar. Although the overall decorative scheme of the cave is the same, the contents of the squares differ. The compositions house an unvarying series of large, centrally placed images of a seated Buddha flanked by an audience. One example, Cave 80, is ascribed to the first stage of construction.[96] (FIGURE 28) Here two rows of large, framed images of seated Buddhas are painted in squares on the door and two side walls. Other aspects of the design and iconography of the caves are the same. The rear wall of the main room has a large niche that once held the central sculpted icon, and above it, in a lunette-shaped niche, is a painted image of a seated Buddha on a throne. There is also a scene of the death on the back wall of the rear chamber. An alternative plan for the side walls of the main chamber employs the excavation of rows of square niches (that were once filled with icons) such as in Cave 27 which has two rows or Cave

99 with three registers.[97]   In general caves with rows of painted rectangles dominate the decorative plan of many of the Qizil caves.

Thus, Cave 110 and the Peacock Cave are unique for the important role played by narrative scenes. In other caves at Qizil there are only segments of cycles, most commonly of the death.   No other extant complete treatment of the life of the historic Buddha seems to have been attempted. When biographical scenes appear, they are usually not in the main room or in a primary area of the decor.[98]

II. CAVES WITH SCENES OF THE LIFE OF THE BUDDHA AS SECONDARY DÉCOR

Scenes from the life of the Buddha appear in various locations in the Qizil caves; sometimes they are contained in lunettes over the door, flanking the central niche, on the side walls or on the rear chamber walls. Caves 99 and 175 have several scenes drawn from the early life (birth, seven steps, first bath, four exits, life in the palace, and descent of Mara) painted in lunette shapes on the side walls of the rear chamber. Several illustrations from the life occur in other caves: the first meditation in Cave 227; the gift of grass (Caves 80, 163, 171); the attack of Mara (Caves 69, 76, 98, 163, 171, 175); the first sermon (Caves 38, 69, 98, 189, 292, 193, 198, 205, 207); the visions during enlightenment (Caves 80, 189, 227); the taming of the flaming snake (Caves 110, 205, 224); the conversion of the Kashyapa brothers (Caves 8, 98, 175, 193, 196, 205, 207, 224); the descent at Samkassa; (Caves 4, 98, 178, 192, 224) as well as the parinirvana cycle. None of these caves has an entire cycle, only one or more scenes.

According to the dating established by Chinese scholars there are three periods of construction to which they assigned the following caves. Caves belonging to the first period (third to fourth century) include Caves 6, 38, 47, and 80. The second period (fourth to fifth century) comprises Caves 3, 7, 13, 17, 27, 35, 36, 58, 77, 98, 99, 100, 101, 104, 110, 118, 129, 171,175; and ascribed to the third period (sixth to eighth century) are Caves: 8, 70, 161, 189 190 and 234.[99] Not all caves were ascribed periods.   Looking at the appearance of narratives in the various periods of construction, it appears that it was during the second period that the scenes flourished, with a clear tapering off in the third period. Only the most noteworthy narrative examples will be discussed here.

Among the three groups of caves designated by the Germans as the Maya Caves, number 19 of the second plan, Cave 205 (Mayahöhlen), undated, has a most unusual depiction of events in the life of the historic Buddha.[100] Cave 205 has a fore hall, barrel-vaulted square main cella with central square pier, and ambulatory. On the ambulatory wall to the right of the niche is an extraordinary painting— a portrayal of a servant holding up a cloth on which the four principal events in the life of Shakyamuni are illustrated. The story represents breaking the news of the death of the Buddha to one of his royal followers, King Ajatasatru. At Qizil the story appears in eight caves.[101] The king's minister, fearful of the king's response to the news of the Buddha's death, devised a scheme of depicting the four great events and showing them in their logical progression so that the death would be presented as the natural consequence of the birth, enlightenment, and first sermon. (FIGURE 16,16a) Ajatasatru, dressed in brilliant blue dhoti and scarves, is seated on a dais, his ankles crossed; his wife and minister flank him. To the right a servant unfolds the cloth revealing it to the king. The cloth is rectangular. In the lowest left is the birth: Maya's position here is reversed, as she leans her right arm on her sister, to give birth from her left flank. Perhaps at Qizil the left side, as in China, was the side of honor and substituted for the right. Kneeling on the left is Indra; behind him is Brahma. In the upper right is the attack of Mara; the Buddha is seated in *bhumisparsa mudra* (right hand pointing to the earth, calling it to witness). The use of this gesture speaks of a later date, for it was only at the end of the Gandharan period that it was utilized; by the Guptan era (fifth century) it was almost universally employed.[102] The mudra is not seen in early Chinese art until the sixth century. On the right Mara, in true north Kushan style, is about to strike with his sword; his demonic army surrounds the Buddha. In the foreground is a fallen warrior, lying prone.

The lower right corner has the first sermon: the Buddha sits in teaching gesture (*dharmacakra mudra*—the fingers held high, imitate the turning of a wheel); the monks are on either side of him. In the parinirvana, the Buddha reclines on a bed resting his head on his right arm, the posture associated with his final address to his devotees when he imparted his last instructions and benedictions, as described in the *Mahaparinirvana sutra*. More commonly, he lies flat on his right side, dead. As in the early Gandharan examples, there are few mourners in attendance. Seated in the right corner is Subhadra, the last convert ordained during the Buddha's final moments; a young princely figure sits at the head of the bed, a monk and two more haloed princes stand behind it. This is close to the traditional Gandharan composition: the Mallas, aristocratic lay devotees, stand behind the bed, while monks attend at the head and foot of the couch, and Subhadra is seated in the foreground meditating with a corona of flames engulfing him.

These illustrations exemplify the later stage of narrative depiction when only the four main events are shown and these are treated in an extremely abbreviated fashion—only the essential figures are represented and the setting all but disappears. There are many ways in which an epitomized version of the life appears in India. The earliest formulation of an epitomized cycle of the life of the Buddha encapsulated the four most important events. Though important in the ancient Indian oral tradition, the four scenes do not appear in the art until considerably later. It is not until the later Gandharan era and the last phase of decor at the monument of Amaravati that the four-scene group functions as an architectural adornment on stupas, as well as on small architectural models of stupas that acted as reliquaries and traveling shrines.[103] In addition, judging by later scriptural decoration from India and Nepal, the set of four scenes may have been used as frontispiece design for scriptures.[104]

Although the events from the life seen in Cave 99 are also epitomized, they draw upon an entirely different artistic source. On the side walls of the rear chamber, behind the main niche, are lunettes with biographical scenes that are not formally separated from one another, but placed together. (FIGURE 17, 18) There is no consistent direction in which to read the scenes, as those in Cave 110, and the chronological sequence is skewered.[105] On the left wall the murals portray a few episodes from the nativity. Beginning on the left is an abbreviated scene of the *Dipamkara jataka*. This is the story of the last incarnation of the bodhisattva prior to his birth as Siddhartha. Dipamkara Buddha, one of the Buddhas of the past, stands to the right; before him, performing a kowtow, is the young brahmin Sumadhi, his flowers of homage scattered on ground, his hair spread out as a carpet for the Buddha to trod. For this act of reverence he is rewarded with the future birth as the Buddha Shakyamuni. Next are the nativity scenes: at the center of the panel are the seven steps. A standing naked figure of the child is shown frontally. To the far right is the birth: supported by her sister, Maya stands with her right arm raised, the baby issues from her right flank. On the left a kneeling divinity catches the child. In the opposite lunette are the four exits, now in poor condition. Buddha stands on the left; lying in the foreground is what appears to be the sick man; to the right is a stooped figure, perhaps the old man. The rest is difficult to discern.

In contrast to the complete and linear telling of the biography in the previous caves, these examples do not appear to be based on an illustrated scripture. Rather they resemble scenes from the life found on architectural models. Commonly, reliquaries are decorated with biographical scenes; though rare, a few are extant. Typically a small square-base model has a lunette on each of its four faces housing a scene from the life; some examples of traveling reliquaries have multiple scenes incorporated into the architectural decor in miniature scale.[106] The selection of scenes in such architectural models is different from those with a set of four; they are not part of an epitomized set. Sometimes a chronological grouping, like the early life, is chosen, as is evident in Cave 99.

A third type of reduced narrative format is seen in several scenes from the biography in Cave 118 (the cave with the Ring Bearing Doves, *Höhle mit den Ringtragenden Tauben*).[107] This cave has a fore hall, square cella, tent-like ceiling; the narratives placed over the door. This type of interior organization of the space and decor becomes important farther east, in Gansu. As one approaches the entry to the main cella, there is a giant standing Buddha and devotional group flanking either side of the doorway. Painted over the threshold are the offering of food by the merchants Trapusa and Bhallika combined with the gift of the four bowls by the Guardian Kings and the first sermon. In each case the centrally seated Buddha is flanked by smaller narrative figures creating a rhythmic decorative scheme. Occupying the right side wall is the *Dipamkara jataka*. At center is the Buddha, flanked by praying monks and deities. On the right the Brahmin ascetic Magdha approaches with his floral offering. The lower part of the picture is destroyed. However, Grunwedel in an earlier expedition noted a prostrate figure in that area. These paintings are indicative of the last manifestation of narrative evolution characterized by an extreme paring down of the elements of the story to small accompanying figures attending a larger icon. Soon even these small-scale remainders of the biography disappear.

III. SCENES OF THE BUDDHA AS A MINOR THEME

The following caves incorporate scenes of the life of the Buddha in the ceiling decor. All of the ceilings are painted with a lozenge-like pattern. Each diamond shape comprises a triangular arrangement of mountains; at the bottom of the lozenge is a seated Buddha. This treatment of the mountainous landscape as overlapping lumpish triangular forms has its origins in Sassanian art.[108] Similar mountain forms appear in the landscape settings of hunt scenes on such Sassanian vessels as the vase in the National Collection, Teheran.[109] At Qizil there is some variety in the definition of the mountains, whether treated as abstract or more naturalistic forms, in the size of the Buddha figure, in the size and number of attendants, and the degree to which the narrative content of the unit is recognizable. Ma Shichang has identified three types of ceiling design based on the shape and number of peaks that form the setting for the seated figure.[110] Three additional trends are discernible. In earlier caves atrophied narratives may alternate with the seated Buddhas in the lozenge designs. Secondly, there is a growing diminution in the number of the figures attending the centrally seated Buddha. Lastly is the conformity of the arrangement of figures in each of the lozenges.

It is important to note that there is no apparent iconographical organization among these images, no chronology is suggested in the placement of the various scenes, and no single event is given prominence over another. Precedents may be found in the painted decor in Indian cave-chapel ceilings where small figures are interspersed among the designs, perhaps best preserved at Ajanta. In Cave 1 for example squares within squares or circles within circles alternate with or incorporate figures from the everyday world—animals and foreigners as well as flying deities. Another type of ceiling decor exists at Bamiyan in Afghanistan, but these geometrical designs are highly organized iconographical mandalas housing images of bodhisattvas. At Qizil, the narrow central ridge of the ceiling has celestial images painted—sun, moon, flying Buddhas, the wind god, and a double-headed bird. These in combination with the flanking mountains housing Buddhas on the slopes of the ceiling similarly refer to the vault of heaven. Distinctly different are the repetition of the landscape elements and the lack of a hierarchical arrangement, which appear to be unique to the area of Xinjiang.

Caves with the ceiling lozenge pattern composed of a seated Buddha and narrative figures in a mountainous setting include Cave 7 (Höhle mit dem Freskoboden); Cave 27; Cave 38; Cave 171; Cave 69; Cave 77 (Höhle der Statuen); Cave 80 (HolletopfHöhle); Cave 85 (Shatzhöhle A); Cave 101; Cave 104; Cave 110; Cave 114 (Höhle mit dem Gebetmuhle); Cave 118 (Hippokampenhöhle); Cave 171; Cave 172; Cave 175; Cave 178; Cave 179; Cave 186 (Mittlere Höhle); Cave 188 (Höhle von vorm 12 Buddhahöhle); Cave 192; Cave 193; Cave 196; Cave 199; Cave 205 (Höhle mit der Maya 2 anl.); Cave 224 (Höhle mit der Maya 3 anl.).

There are 50 lozenges painted on the ceiling of Cave 38 from the early period; the rows are alternately filled with seated Buddhas or seated bodhisattvas.[111] (FIGURE 20)   For the somewhat large-size Buddhas there is usually one figure in attendance.   In contrast, the diamonds containing a seated bodhisattva have a narrative content that is conveyed by the actions of the attendant figures and other small details that identify the story. Despite the rigid geometry of the overall design, the interior pattern of the lozenges with narratives varies widely—each has a unique composition.   These have a white background, while the Buddha-filled designs are painted on a green field. Two narratives may be scenes from the life of the Buddha. In one a bodhisattva rides a white elephant, which may be a reference to the conception.   In the other a bodhisattva practicing austerities is flanked by two threatening blue-skinned demons.   Abbreviated illustrations of jatakas like the *Hungry Tiger* also appear.[112]   The mountains that fill the diamond pattern on the ceiling are extremely stylized conical forms painted in brilliant opaque colors. Scattered among the mountain backdrop of the seated icons are depictions of animals—rams, paired peacocks, or deer. The ceiling of Cave 17 (Höhle mit dem Bodhisattvagewolbe) ascribed to the fifth century has 48 simplified narratives in the lozenge pattern on the ceiling with up to three small figures in each diamond shape.[113] (FIGURE 21) Each unit has jatakas or scenes from the life told with minimal narrative detail against a backdrop of alternating colors of green, white, blue, or black. Among the identifiable jatakas is the local favorite, the *Hungry Tiger*, related in a truly jubilant style. Drawn in a lively and life-like manner, animals—antelopes, deer, bluebirds, doves, snakes, and monkeys—are scattered throughout the composition.[114]

In some caves the figures around the seated Buddha suggest narrative scenes. Though reduced to a single attendant figure, the composition can still recall an event from the biography. For example, two scenes from the enlightenment cycle are identifiable by the relatively large figure accompanying the Buddha in Cave 80 also from the early period. (FIGURE 22) In one lozenge the centrally seated Buddha is tortured by a demon during the attack, and in another Naga Muchalinda, a cobra deity, wraps himself around the seated Buddha to protect him during his prolonged meditation following enlightenment, a rarely depicted event in Central Asia or farther east. (FIGURE 21)

In later caves the narrative content is dropped altogether. The single figures that accompany the Buddha in the ceiling designs of Caves 34, 32, and 171, ascribed to the sixth century, are undistinguished. Most of them are monks, ascetics, or kings who make an offering to the Buddha. In these later caves the arrangement of attendant figures surrounding the central image of the Buddha of each lozenge is standardized; sometimes they comprise a triad formation, like the unvarying ceiling design of Cave 175.[115]

IV. SCENES OF THE PARINIRVANA

Without question the most important event of the life of the Buddha painted at Qizil is the scene of the death—nearly all the caves have versions of it. Typically, death scenes appear in a separate architectural unit—a rear chamber behind the square central niche on the rear wall. Two side aisles approach the rear chamber, allowing for ritual circumambulation. The deathbed farewell is placed on the back wall and often the division of the relics is on the opposite wall.

In India, the scene of the death of the Buddha evolved under different circumstances from the rest of the narrative cycle. As portrayals of human suffering were eschewed, the architectural monument, the stupa, was the first representation of the death. Ubiquitous in India, the stupa was the primary focus of devotion for five hundred years. As a container of the Buddha's relics, the stupa indicated both his physical presence and his passing away. It was only during the Kushan era that the heroic death scene based on Hellenistic images of dying was created. On Gandharan monuments the image of the expiring Buddha is usually the conclusion of the narrative cycle. Most often shown in human scale, the Buddha is reclining on a funeral bed at the center of the composition, his disciples surrounding him. Moreover, following the text of the *Mahaparinirvana sutra,* the subsequent events in the death cycle were illustrated—acts leading up to and including the cremation, putting out the fire, the battle for the relics, and division of the relics.

Scenes of the parinirvana continued to be represented in the Guptan era (fourth to seventh centuries). With the creation of an epitomized set of the eight great events in the life of the Buddha and the adoption of the format of a freestanding stele carved with the set of eight, the image of the death remained important. As the crowning element, the reclining Buddha with a few mourners around the bed was placed at the top of the stele, often in conjunction with a small stupa, the ancient symbol of the death, carved above. It was probably during the Guptan era that the colossal image of the reclining Buddha was created. One such over-size sculpture done by the Guptan Mathuran artist Dina is found in the literary records.[116] An extant example of a huge reclining Buddha from this period is present at Ajanta in Cave 26. Both the icon of the dying Buddha and narrative details of the event are sculpted.

Among caves at Qizil there is a pretty strict conformity with Gandharan compositions, narrative characters and details of the death cycle. But the scale of the Buddha is clearly oversize in relation to the monks and mourners. As in the Gandharan representations, the disciples are prominent individuals who can readily be recognized. Ananda, the youngest, who stands by the head, was the personal companion of the Buddha and is associated with deep personal commitment. As a result of his importance in the *Mahaparinirvana sutra,* he is given the primary position. The eldest of the disciples, Kashyapa, singled out because of his extraordinary intellect and wisdom, is associated with the more philosophical nature of the doctrine. He is usually placed at the feet, for the story is told of how he was traveling when the Buddha died. Arriving belatedly he bid his farewell by touching the feet of the Buddha. Third in importance is Subhadra, the last disciple to be personally admitted by the Buddha. He was greatly advanced on the path to enlightenment, and after but one sermon, attained supreme understanding moments before the Buddha's demise. Subhadra is often seen seated in front of the funeral couch surrounded by a blazing fire that symbolically represents his enlightenment. Traditionally the disciples did not attend to the death preparations, which were left to the lay disciples. It was the Malla chieftains who undertook all responsibility for the funeral activities; thus, they are shown standing as princely figures behind the bed of the reclining Buddha. Sometimes a bearded, half-naked deity attends the funeral. This is Vajrapani, bearer of the thunderbolt, who appears in other Gandharan bas-reliefs of the life of the Buddha, but whose presence is rather mysterious, as he is not described in the texts.[117] Framing the composition are twin flowering trees.

Precedents for the general composition, the portrayal of the emotional states of the mourners, their figural disposition and their individual characterizations are found in northwestern Indian reliefs of the late Kushan era (third-fourth century). In general these depictions of the death are not marked by great displays of emotion. The three primary disciples, Ananda, Kashyapa and Subhadra, are almost never shown expressing grief. In general the other monks are not in attitudes of bereavement, but stand solemnly, though secondary figures may demonstrably mourn. The emotional tone of the scene is one of heroic strength in the face of personal loss, a mark of the achievement of non-attachment. Towards the end of the Kushan period, an increase in the emotional reaction of the mourners is clearly discernible and the size of the reclining Buddha increases dramatically in proportion to the mourners.

Following the Gandharan illustrations of the death cycle, the Buddha is placed at the center of the composition, and the activities are conducted around the still figure. Attendants flank the wrapped bier, attend the cremation fires and put out the flames with long-handled water pots. For the battle of the relics, the eight contending tribal chiefs are symmetrically placed outside the city gates, seated on their mounts—elephants and horses. For the happy resolution of the conflict—the equitable distribution of the relics—the sage Drona is seated at center with eight reliquaries; the contending parties flank him.[118] Outside of the primary importance placed on the deathbed farewell, all scenes related to the death cycle, including the cremation and division of the relics, are afforded the same importance.

Cave 80 (Hollentopfhöle), identified by the Chinese scholar Su Bai as an early cave belonging to the first stage, has several scenes from the death cycle. As an early example Cave 80's version of the parinirvana scenes is relatively simple. The death has ten disciples mourning the Buddha and in the division of the relics Drona is at center flanked by six Malla kings. A more elaborate example also belonging to the first stage is Cave 38 (Höhle mit dem Musikerchor), ascribed to the fourth century.[119] The rear wall scene of the parinirvana is in good condition except for the effaced areas where vandals rubbed off the gold. Covered in a dark monastic robe, Buddha relines on his right side, resting his head on his right hand, with his feet lined up one atop the other. (FIGURE 22, a) Three monks are at the feet; the kneeling one is probably Kashyapa. Subhadra sits at head of the bed, shown from the rear. Small white flowers blossom on the dark green leaves of the sala trees placed at the head and foot of the bed. Assembled behind the bed are six crowned and jeweled Malla princes, some dark, some light-skinned. A row of stupas, each housing a seated Buddha, occupies the walls of the flanking aisles.

Scenes from the death cycle appear in all phases of construction at Qizil. Rather typical is the representation of the death cycle in Cave 8 (Höhle der Sechzehn Schwerttrager) ascribed to the seventh century.[120] The rear wall of the back chamber had a large-scale painting of the death scene, now in ruinous condition, which relied on lines of darker pigments drawn along the contours of the parts of the body, giving a naturalistic effect. Celestial figures in attendance, like *mithuna* (loving couple), reflect the Indian ideal; they are elegant, fleshy and sensuous. On the opposing wall was the battle and division of the relics. In the foreground eight kings on horse and elephant mounts battle each other. Above at center Drona is seated holding his portion of the relics. Six kings, haloed and crowned, flank him, holding their reliquaries in their hands; behind them is a second row of six haloed and crowned figures, two of whom are kings holding reliquaries.[121]

The parinirvana of Cave 48 is noteworthy for its depiction of grieving mourners.[122] Though mostly destroyed, the murals retain the painted figures, which are drawn around the bed as well as on the side walls. (FIGURE 23) Only details of these remain—a weeping figure naked to the waist is at the foot of a tree, a strong wind blows his scarf and his hair. At the foot of the bed is the kneeling Kashyapa; he is so emaciated that his skeletal structure protrudes beneath his skin. He wears a patched cloth garment that exposes his right shoulder. Another monk with his hands clasped together bows his head in grief. Numerous devas hover overhead on the ceiling of the rear chamber.

The depictions in Cave 205 are remarkable for their conflation of scenes of the death cycle and the directness and frankness with which the cremation is told. The mural has been reconstructed from large fragments and is now housed in Berlin.[123] (FIGURE 24, a) The centrally placed ornate coffin is slightly open to reveal the Buddha, lying on his right side, his head supported by his hand. A funeral shroud of braided variegated ribbons encases the body. The lid of the coffin is ablaze. Kashyapa kneels at the foot, his palms clasped together. Behind him are two monks and a deva. On the left, by the head, a mourning figure, haloed and crowned, reaches out in grief. Nearby, Ananda lifts the lid, behind him are two haloed and crowned figures. The battle and division of the relics are preserved in the upper area. Outside the battlements of the city of Kushinagara, the warring tribes ride horses and an elephant. (FIGURE 25,a) Above the city gates is the division by Drona, who is at center. Seated around him are the pacified combatants, each holding a reliquary with their portion.

There is a remarkable intensification in the portrayal of the grieving mourners in the rendering of the cremation in the Cave 224, designated as A by Grunwedel.[124] The compositions of the rear chamber, well described and published by Le Coq, are now reconstructed from over two dozen fragments.[125] (FIGURE 26, a) As in Cave 205, the body of the Buddha is wrapped in a variegated ribbon shroud; the coffin is almost closed, and flames engulf the lid. On the right and left of the upper area are the Malla nobles, kneeling with urns in their hands to douse the flames. An unusual feature is the exaggerated postures of lamentation the mourners assume. In front of the coffin are two mournful monks: one, a dark-skinned figure is seated on the ground, his head bent forward; the other, light-skinned, reels forward, his arms swaying above his head. At the foot of the bed are two haloed princely characters; one holds a flywhisk, the other an urn mounted on a long pole. One curious addition is the balcony painted above the cremation scene. Three figures, dressed like Indian royalty, are at the center; the one on the right leans forward, his two arms extended before him in a gesture of woe. On the far left and right are figures, dressed in wide-lapeled tunics, wearing neither crowns nor jewels, who perform acts of self-mutilation—cutting their foreheads with knives, an ancient practice among the people of the steppes.[126] (FIGURE 26,a) Above them are devas descending with garlands.

Cave 201 should be mentioned for its extremely simple rendering of the death. Only Kashyapa, who, wearing a patched cloth robe that reveals his emaciated body, kneels touching the foot of the Buddha. This fresco also is in Berlin.[127]

A second format used in representations of the parinirvana consists of a large-scale sculpture of the reclining Buddha with painted narrative figures on the wall behind. This type of mixed media format was used in a cave designated by Le Coq as the second cave-chapel east of the second small gorge of the stream of the Settlement *(Zweiten Tempel Ostlich von der Zweiten Kleinen Bachschluct der Siedlung)*.[128] Although the head has been destroyed, the ornately carved bed with decorative rugs and the body of the Buddha wrapped in a shroud and emitting flames are all well preserved. Rows of flying geese are painted on the wall near the ceiling. Caves 1 (FIGURE 27) Caves 197 and 198 also have large-scale sculptures of the reclining Buddha on the rear wall with narrative details painted on the wall behind.

Scenes of the death on the rear wall also occur in the following caves: Cave 7 (Höhle mit dem Freskoboden); Cave 9; Cave 14; Cave 17; Cave 18; Cave 43; Cave 47, ascribed to fourth century, is no longer extant; Cave 58 (Höhle der Behelmeten) has the division of relics on the wall opposite. Cave 63; Cave 69; Cave 92; Cave 100; Cave 101; Cave 107; Cave 114 (Höhle mit dem Gebetmuhle) has the extinguishing of the flames of the bier; Cave 118, Cave 123; Cave 171; Cave 178 (Cave 3 Schucht Höhle); Cave 161, Cave 188; Cave 201; Cave 206; Cave 207 has the division of the relics; and Cave 254. Several scenes from the death cycle are painted in room A of the cave with a Chimney *(Kamenhöhle)*, which has the burning of the coffin on the opposite wall. Above the flaming corpse are eight small stupas. The division of the relics is painted on another wall of the cave.[129] Two others caves identified by the Germans also have examples of a reclining Buddha that are less well preserved.[130]

In summation, the death scene at Qizil is of paramount importance. At no other site is the event given such prominence. In India, where the representation of human suffering was eschewed, it is relatively infrequent. It is only in northern Gandhara that the image appears with any frequency. The passing away of the Buddha, testimony to the frailty of the human condition, is of doctrinal importance. The model of the stoic monks in the earlier representations is consistent with the doctrine of non-attachment. However, when the narratives of the life of the Buddha gave way to large-scale icons, and believers sought to worship the icons rather than emulate the heroic life, his passing took on another connotation. Thus, the emotional representations of the grieving followers around an increasingly large image of the reclining Buddha reflect the growing practice of *bhakti* (devotion).

CONCLUSIONS

The importance of these caves cannot be overstated since they preserve the earliest painted examples of a complete cycle. Moreover the site yielded many examples of biographical narratives for which a number of formats were employed. These different narrative techniques each reveal the varying ancient Indian prototypes.

The continuous narrative style is clearly based on the Gandharan linear telling of the story. Independent scenes are strung out horizontally and read during ritual circumambulation. Such caves as the Peacock and Stepped Cave that utilize this technique relate nearly a complete story of the life, which when read in this manner preserves the ancient didactic function of the biography. Concordances among the illustrations at Qizil, Gandharan and Amaravati art may be the result of the role of the Sarvastivadins who were active in these locations. Such agreement between the visual material and the literary accounts suggests that it may have been the *Lalitavistara,* a text important to the Sarvastivadins, which was the common basis for the illustrations.

The epitomized format showing the four most important scenes on a single surface is also employed. This technique, characteristic of a later phase of narrative development in India, was first seen during the mature period of Gandhara and Amaravati. It was later brought to a climax under the Sarnath sculptors of the Guptan era and appears in Cave 19 of the Maya Cave in the illustration of the story of King Ajatasatru. This story within a story is the earliest painted example of the four great events in the life of the Buddha in this region. This format remains important in later Buddhist art. The use of a reduced number of scenes, not limited to the four events, on Gandharan traveling shrines and perhaps lost portable paintings were the basis for the biographical representations used as a secondary theme in the interior decor of caves like 99. In the last phase of narrative illustration isolated scenes, not representing an epitomized biography but seemingly randomly chosen, are found in unimportant places and in small scale.

Qizil artists created many modifications in the format, presentation and details of the narratives. Qizil artists appear to have created new themes and compositional formulas. For the first time the following themes were presented—pensive prince posture, the arched frame of demons in the attack, the use of intertwined dragons for the first bath and the placement of the temptation on the north wall. Another modification was the adoption of the ceiling and the area over the doorways for narrative scenes. In addition there was a unique emphasis and development of the pictorial cycle of the death events. The death image appears in most of the caves, its primacy being evident in its prominent placement and its large size. Innovative architectural organization of the interior ritual space accommodates the placement of the important image of the dying Buddha in the rear chamber with flanking aisles that allow for circumambulation. These are noteworthy contributions to the evolution of the pictorial biography that had a direct impact on Chinese Buddhist art.

The decline in narrative interest may be traced not only in the decreasing number of illustrations of the biographical scenes but also in all forms of narrative illustration. The depiction of jataka scenes once shown in large scale with a concentrated effort in rendering the details and the sequence of the story—a particularly fine example is Cave 80, though little else of that cave survives—also gradually disappear. (FIGURE 28) The trend towards simplification of narrative details is also observable in the preaching scenes where the number of attendants in the audience decreases in size and number. For example, Cave 7 of the earlier period has a single register of compositions that fill the side walls of the main cella. Each composition has a preaching Buddha surrounded by a varied and relatively large-scale audience.[131] By the time of Cave 100, the interior scenes of the rectangular compositions filling the walls of the main room have only four figures flanking the centrally seated Buddha.[132] In later caves such as 129 the interior scenes show an oversize Buddha with only two flanking figures. (FIGURE 29)

2. TATARU

Not much remains of the wall painting at the caves at Tataru.[133] Close in style to the first period at Qizil, remnants of figures are drawn in blue, green, and brown hues. The ceiling barrel vault designs of Cave

13, now blackened, resemble those of Qizil Cave 34—the five partite mountain forms that rise behind the seated Buddha painted in alternating colors. A small detail of what may have been the temptation is in the rear chamber of Cave 17. The partial depiction comprises a seated meditating bodhisattva with a crowned Mara-like figure on the right holding a sword. Fragments of the ceiling painting include a meditating Buddha in small open stupa-like form, meditating bodhisattvas, and an attendant angel in a mountainous setting inhabited by animals.

3. QUMTURA

The site of Qumtura, 20 kilometers southeast of Qizil, at the lower flow of the Muzart River, has dozens of caves with painted embellishment of similar style and development to those at Qizil. Chinese scholars ascribe some caves to the fourth century, but these have little of the original decor; only the architectural layout suggests the close relationship between the two sites. Some of the caves have representations of the Attack of Mara. In one example in upper ranges of the thousand cave group (Grunwedel's Ming-oï) displays elements seen in later Indian art. Mara, crowned and dressed from head to toe in scale armor, aims an arrow at the Buddha on the right. Perhaps this is a metaphorical representation of his physical seduction, which was represented earlier by his daughters. Mara has multiple arms and grotesque features. Some of his demonic warriors also have multiple heads and eyes, like the three-headed creature on the right, in addition to the more usual horrific features—pointed ears, fangs, claws and animal heads. Figures with multiple appendages are late to appear in Buddhist art, and may be identified with the later post-Guptan (seventh century) Vajrayana movement in eastern India.

Here too the main cella may have a barrel vault, like Caves 10 and 11. The Qumtura-style ceiling lozenge design filled with Buddhas seated among stylized mountains and flanked by small-size attendants is seen in Cave 24, Cave 43, 46, and 63 in particular.[134] Some of the later caves ceiling paintings, for example Cave 13, preserve the lozenge pattern decoration. This cave shares the typical Qizil plan with two aisles carved on either side of the central square pier and a rear chamber. In many of their themes the Qumtura caves correspond in style to the later phase of Qizil art. The organization of decorative motifs of Cave 34, for example, is heavily dependent on caves like Cave 110—panels fill three registers of the side walls of the central chamber, but here each panel contains a seated or standing Buddha and the narrative context is lost. Now the narrative figures have become a pair of considerably smaller flanking attendants. As a result of the limited number of figures and abbreviated settings and props, identification of the episodes is most difficult.

Death scenes are similarly placed on the rear wall of the back chamber of the cave temple. Cave 14 is distinguished by its parinirvana depictions, which have bodhisattvas behind the funeral couch, in addition to the more usual mourners. Cave 16 has a representation of the death of the Buddha painted in the Chinese mature Tang style with an emphasis on stylized naturalism. The drapery of the figure clings to the body, revealing the swelling forms beneath. Standing behind the bed are six Chinese courtly figures (two with halos) who alternate with six fiercely crying monks; above them the leaves of the sala tree are drawn. The area in front of the bed has not survived. There does not appear to have been any angels descending from the sky painted in the upper area.[135]

4. BEZEKLIK

The site of Bezeklik, on the northern trade route located 600 miles northeast of Khotan and north of the Taklamakan Desert also has cave shrines excavated from the living rock with painted interiors. This site is considerably later in date, being ascribed to the eighth to ninth centuries. The murals of these cave chapels exhibit both Persian and Chinese Tang style characteristics. By this late period few scenes of the Buddha are illustrated. There are remnants of what once was the first sermon, now only the base of the image remains with four very naturalistically rendered deer flanking an ornate Wheel of the Law. Two divinities on cloud swirls rush down to flank the wheel.[136] Another has a heterogeneous audience listening to the Buddha's sermon.[137] The parinirvana is also represented at Bezeklik, though the extant examples at the site in Cave 18 and 33 are ascribed to the tenth century and later.

The unique longevity of the parinirvana scene, in contrast to the other biographical events, is witnessed here. Its popularity is due to the Mahayanists, who revered their version of the text that promised future life in heaven. This made the demise of the Buddha a portrayal not so much of the end of his terrestrial career as of the rich rewards promised by the Mahayanist doctrine. The parinirvana, then, represented salvation. Like the meditating figure, importantly symbolizing the means to achieve enlightenment for the pre-Mahayanist school—the dying Buddha, when placed at the top of the Guptan stele or on the rear wall of the cave—in Mahayanist terms suggests universal transcendence of human limitations. The universal concern of the doctrine is conveyed through the ever-expanding number of mourners and their heterogeneous characters. One example of the parinirvana has a crowd of foreign dignitaries including Persians and Arabs.[138]

ENDNOTES

1. Hambras, "Central Asia," *Encyclopedia of World Art* 1959: 826.

2. Excavations in Soviet Central Asia, the region to the north east, have been reported in G. Frumkin, *Archaeology in Soviet Central Asia* (Leiden, 1970). Evidence of contact with the Kushans is provided by coins found at the sites of Kobadiyan (now Mikoyanabad) in the Kafirnigan Valley, see p. 66; Talkhar, see p. 68; Tadzhikistan, see p. 76; the palatial complex at Toptak-kala in Khorezem, see p. 97. Ancient Kharosti documents were discovered in a Buddhist monastery at Karatepe, northwest of Termez, see p. 11.

3. M. Bussagli, *The Painting of Central Asia* (Geneva, 1963): 13.

4. Among which is the *Taizu ruying benji jing,* in Nanjio, *Daizokyo*, vol. III, no. 184.

5. Fa Xian, *Foguoji*, translated by Samuel Beal, *Buddhist Records of the Western World* (London: Kegan Paul, et. al. 1875, Rpt NY, 1968): xxvii-xxvix.

6. *The Travels of Sung Yun,* in Beal, *Buddhist Records*: lxxxvii.

7. *Siyuki,* Beal, *Records*: 18.

8. *Datang siyuki*, translated by Beal, *Buddhist Records*: 18.

9. Charles Eliot, *Hinduism and Buddhism* (London: Unwin and Allen, 1921) 3 vols., vol. I: 303. For a discussion of Sarvastivadin beliefs see Andre Bareau, *Les Sects du Petit Vehicle* (Saigon, 1955): 131 ff. Two of the special philosophical views that distinguished the Sarvastivadins were that an *Arhat* can fall from *Arhatship* and that continuity of thought constitutes meditation. See also Salomon 1990: 7 and following for a discussion of the importance of this sect in Xinjiang and China.

10. E. Foucaux, *Lalita Vistara* (Paris, 1880) translated the Tibetan version into French, Samuel Beal, *The Romantic Legend of Sakya Buddha* (London: 1875, rpt Delhi: Motilal Banarsidass, 1985) translated into English a Chinese version the *Fobenjing (Abhinishkramana sutra)* rendered into Chinese by Djnanakuta, ca. sixth century. An inscription at the end of this scripture names the Sarvastivadins.

11. See C. Sivaramamurti, *Amaravati Sculptures in the Madras Museum* (Madras, 1956).

12. See Akira Hirakawa, "The Rise of Mahayana and its Relation to Stupas, " *Memoirs of the Toyo Bunko Research Society* vol. 22 (1963): 57-106 and Elizabeth Stone, *The Buddhist Art of Nagarjunakonda* (Delhi: Motilal Banarsidass, 1994): 13ff, discuss the relationship between Mahayanism, the

Sarvastivadins and the worship of the stupa noting the importance of cult images for these proto-Mahayanists.

13. *Along the Silk Routes: Central Asian Art from West Berlin State Museums* (Berlin, 1982): 24-49 gives a most informative summary of the various European explorations of Chinese Central Asia.

14. Hartel 1982: 22.

15. A. Stein, *Serindia* (Oxford, 1921) vol. IV: 163, found near Domoko.

16. A. von Le Coq, *Die Buddhistische Spantantike Mittelasiens* (Berlin: Verlag Deitrich Reimer Ernst Vohsen, 1928) vol. VII: 27.

17. K. Sha, *Buddhist Literature in Central Asia* (Calcutta, 1970): 34, stated that Luders found a copy of the *Buddhacarita* in the Turfan region, see p. 98.

18. Hartel 1982: 22. Khocho, the old Uighur capital, yielded several Manichean texts; the eighth century ruler Bugug Khan (759-780) was converted to that faith.

19. Scholars like J. Rosenfield, *Dynastic Art of the Kushans* (L.A: Univ. of California Press, 1967) have questioned to what extent and when the Sassanians came to take control of Gandhara, see p. 116 ff. The evidence of coins and an inscription of Shapur I at Naqshi-i-Rustam that records the accomplishments of the ruler are cited.

20. A. Godard, *The Art of Iran,* trans. by M. Heron, M. Rogers, ed. (London: G. Allen and Unwin Ltd. 1962): 142.

21. A. Soper "Aspects of Light Symbolism in Gandharan Sculpture," *Artibus Asiae,* vol. XII (1949): 252-283.

22. *Chugoku sekkutsu kiziru sekkutsu,* 3 vols. (Tokyo: Heibonsha publ., 1983) vol. I: 15 ff. Japanese scholars, who worked in tandem with the Qizil Research Institute and Chinese archaeologists like Su Bai, have come to the conclusion that there were three periods of construction. The first, comprising Cave 38, is ascribed to the period 310+/- 380, which is considerably earlier than the western dating of the caves. See 163 ff. For Cave 69, see vol. II: pl. 3.

23. Hartel 1982: 82, pl. 19; Le Coq found this 1922, 026 IV: 25; it is from the "largest cave," inv. MK III 8419.

24. P. Harper, *The Royal Hunter: Art of the Sasanian Empire* (NY: Asia Society, 1978): cat. no. 3, a fourth century silver gilt plate with figure hunting lions, has this kind of treatment of the mountains under the feet of the lion; it is in the Iran Bastan in Teheran (ht. 6 cm., di. 28.5 cm.). The vase, see cat. no. 22, is from ca. the seventh century, and now is in the National Collection, Teheran (ht. 17.5 cm.). For Qizil see *Chugoku sekkutsu, Kiziru,* vol. I: pl. 20ff.

25. Rosenfield 1967: 235.

26. A. Godard and J. Hackin, *Les Antiquities bouddhique de Bamiyan* (Memoires de la Delegation archeologique Francaise en Afghanistan, Paris: Les Editions G. van Oest, 1928): 68ff, fig 25, 26.A.

27. *Chugoku sekkutsu, Kiziru* vol. I: pl. 83ff from the early period Cave 38.

28. Also A. von Le Coq, *Buried Treasures of Chinese Turkistan* (reprint, Hong Kong: Oxford Univ. Press, 1985): pl. 8. Nestorian Christian remains were also found.

29. Le Coq 1985: 58, pl. 9, sees this as a representation of Manes.

30. Hartel 1982: 175, pl. 112; pp. 176-181, pls. 114-119. See also Le Coq, 1985: 30 ff.

31. A. Farrer and R. Whitfield, *Caves of the Thousand Buddhas: Chinese Art from the Silk Route* (NY: G. Braziller, Inc., 1990): 144.

32. F. Tissot, *Les Arts Anciens Du Pakistan et de l'Afghanistan,* (Paris, 1987): 120-121.

33. Rowland 1984: 165 ff; for painting, see p. 187ff.

34. Tissot 1987: 122, pl. 15.

35. Miran for example is one of the more important archaeological finds in the region with its *Visvantara jataka* painting of shrine MV. The painting has an inscription identifying the subject: "This is Isidata, the son of Bughani"; the site is ascribed to the third-fourth century. See A. Stein, *Innermost Asia* (Oxford, 1926): 171; see also *Serindia*, vol. IV: 398.

36. B. Degens, *Monuments preIslamique d'Afghanistan* (Paris: Memoires de la Delegation archeologique Francaise en Afghanistan, 1964): Pl. II no. 11, from area MK 32.

37. Hambis and M. Hallade, *Toumchouq* (Paris: Memoires de la Delegation archeologique Francaise en Afghanistan, 1964): 119, 141.

38. Stein, *Ancient Khotan*, vol. 1: fig. 61 ff.

39. *The Art in the Caves of Xinjiang,* Sun Da Wei, ed. (Xinjiang, 1989): 4.

40. A. Howard has provided these two Chinese sources in her article on the dating of Qizil, "In Support of a New Chronology for the Kizil Mural Paintings," *Archives of Asian Art,* vol. XLVI (1991): 68-83, she cites the *Bhiksunipratimoksa* from the *Chusanzangjiji*, in Taisho vol. 55, no. 2145: 79c-89a.

41. *Siyuki*, Beal: 19-21.

42. Initially Le Coq accepted this but later in life placed both styles a century later.

43. Waldschmidt, on the basis of literary evidence found in the Red Dome cave as well as scriptures and inscriptions, proposed a sixth and seventh century date. E. Waldschmidt, "Beschreibender Text," in Le Coq, vol. VII: 24 and 27.

44. Hartel 1982: 47-49.

45. Rowland makes the two styles contemporaneous in the fifth to sixth century; B. Rowland, "Review Articles: Art Among the Silk Roads, A Reappraisal of Central Asian Art," *Harvard Journal of Asian Studies* vol. XXV

(1964): 257-60; also his *Art and Architecture of India* (Great Britain: Penguin Books, reprint 1984): 185. Soper has ventured to move the evolution of the second style up to the mid-fifth century, A. Soper, "Northern Liang and Northern Wei in Kansu," *Artibus Asiae,* vol. XXI, no. 2 (1948): 146.

46. The most important of these is the joint encyclopedic study of the Qizil caves *Chugoku sekkutsu, Kiziru sekkutsu.* More recently are the Chinese studies, *Zhongguo meishu quanji,* vol. 16: *Xinjiang shiku bihua,* Su Bai, ed. (Beijing : Wenwu, 1989); *Xinjiang shiku bihua* (Beijing, 1989); and *Guizi shiku,* Han Xiang, ed. (Xinjiang, 1990).

47. *Guizi Shiku* 1990: 323.

48. Su Bai, "Kiziru sekkutsu no keishiki kuwa to so no niendai," *Chugoku sekkutsu, Kiziru,* vol. I: 162ff.

49. Le Coq 1928, vol. VII: 132, described finding the cave under rubble and sand, the brilliance of the murals' pigments and the metallic hue they gave off. Because of Grunwedel's objections to removing the whole cave, only two murals were brought back to Berlin on this trip. At a later time Le Coq returned and took the whole cave back.

50. Su Bai "Kiziru sekkutsu," 1983: 163. For dating of styles see p. 174; the second style more generally is ascribed to the period 395+/-65 to 465+/-65.

51. Grunwedel 1912: 91 for floor plan, discussion on p. 87 ff; photos of the narratives figures 199 and 200; Le Coq, 1928, vol. VII: 16, 69, further identified and described the scenes.

52. P. Karetzky, "The Act of Pilgrimage and Guptan Steles with Scenes from the Life of the Buddha," *Oriental Art,* vol. XXX, no. 3 (1987): 268-275.

53. In fact the baby, it is explained, was kept in a protective enclosure. During the time that the bodhisattva was in her womb he was pure and unsullied by (human) filth. TRBJ, p.473 b26.

54. XXBJ: 463 c9. Although this text stipulates ten months, the pregnancy was of normal duration, for this is the Chinese way of counting age. *Abhinishkramana Sutra,* Beal p. 42, explains that the Lumbini Grove was located in Maya's father's house.

55. See *Zhongguo meishu quanji,* vol. 16: 55-56, and 42-45.

56. M. Eliade, *The Sacred and Profane,* trans. W. Trask, (NY, 1958): 30, in this way mythic heroes take symbolic possession of the earth.

57. Beal 1985: 44, similarly in other Chinese translations, the earliest is the XXBJ: 463 c13.

58. XXBJ: 463 c13.

59. For a nativity scene from Amaravati in the British Museum, see Robert Knox, *Amaravati* (London: British Museum Press, 1992): 13ff and

Sivaramamurti 1956: fig. 41, p. 100-101. These scenes show no image of the Buddha; his presence is only suggested. Similarities also exit with the bas-reliefs from Nagarjunakonda, which were heavily influenced by the art of Amaravati. See Stone 1994, for example fig. 210.

60. GXYJ: 630b20.

61. XXBJ: 467a

62. Ibid.

63. J. Dye, "Two Fragmentary Gandharan Narrative Reliefs in the Peshawar Museum," *Artibus Asiae*, vol. XXXVIII (1976): 219-245, compared the Qizil and Gandharan examples, finding a great deal in common, including the conflation of scenes, garments, chariot, attendants, and vision; see p. 240.

64. Beal 1985: 118, the prince rides a chariot in this text.

65. Rosen 1994: fig. 227 which was reproduced but not discussed by Rosen; also fig. 224, p. 75 a dome slab from site 2 which identified by Rosen as one of the four exits actually is only a representation of a corpse, no encounter is portrayed as in fig 227.

66. Beal 1985: 187.

67. XXBJ: 469 b19.

68. B. Degens, *Monuments pre-Islamique d'Afghanistan*, Memoires de la Delegation archeologique Francaise en Afghanistan (Paris: Les Editions G. van Oest:, 1964): Pl. XVI, fig. 52, no. 128, site P, and respectively Pl. XIX, fig. 63, no. 155, site K. Musee Guimet, Paris, inv. no. MG20995; also has a very small fragment of this type. Two large icons of the starving Buddha may also be cited: one in the Peshawar Museum, inv. no 799 from Takht-I-Bahai 1908, another is in the Lahore Museum inv. no. 2099; see H. Ingholt and I. Lyons, *Gandharan Art in Pakistan* (Connecticut, 1957): fig. 52.

69. Rosen 1994: fig. 228 bottom; see also figs. 165, 193 and 221. For Amaravati see Sivaramamurti 1956 pl. LXIII.

70. Alexander Soper, "Aspects of Light Symbolism in Gandharan Sculpture," *Artibus Asiae*, in three parts: vol. XII (1949): 252-283, 314-330, and vol. XXII (1950): 63-82. Esp.

71. Rosen 1994: 218

72. Beal 1985: p. 304. The ability to perform miracles was won when he achieved enlightenment, see The TRBJ: 478 a7. The GXYJ: 649 b28, says it was performed to convert the Kashyapas.

73. In contrast to these discrete images are the extremely large size steles that show superhuman size icons which are also identified as the Miracle of Shravasti, these appear to be Mahayanist; see Karetzky, "The Post-Enlightenment Miracles of the Buddha; Texts and Illustrations," *Orientations* (Hong Kong) Jan. 1990: 71-77.

74. There is one relief found in northwestern Pakistan at the site of Swat; it is now in the local museum; see, D. Faccenna, *Reports on the Campaigns of 1956-8 at Swat* (Rome, 1962) 3 vols., vol. I: 39, pl. CXXXXXIII, inv. no. 431. See also S. Czuma *Kushan Sculpture* (Cleveland, 1950): 194, pl. 104. Francois Tissot, *Les Arts Anciens Du Pakistan et de L'Afghanistan* (Paris, 1987): 108, fig. 115; several of these were found in Afghanistan; one is in the Musee Guimet. The image also appears at Paitava Shotorak in Afghanistan, but there an oversize Buddha dominates a large size stele and Shotorak has been identified as a Mahayanist site. See also J. Meunie, *Shotorak* Delegation francaise en Afghanistan (Paris, 1942

75. Sivaramamurti 1956: pl. XLVII-1 and pl. XXXVIII-2. Sivaramamurti identifies this as the Shravasti miracle and quotes the *Dhammapad-atthakatha* (III: 38).

76. The earliest extant illustrated scripture of the life of the Buddha is preserved in Japan and ascribed to the eighth century, it is presumed to be based on a somewhat earlier Chinese scroll, see T. Kameda, *E Inga Kyo: Nihon Emakimono Zenshu*, vol. XVI (Tokyo: Kadokawa Publ. Co.,1969). See also Chapter IV.

77. P. Karetzky, "Mara Buddhist Deity of Death and Desire," *East-West*, vol. XXXII (1982): 75. XXXVIII-2. Sivaramamurti 1956 identifies this as the Shravasti miracle and quotes the *Dhammapad-atthakatha* (III: 38).

78. So named by the Germans for the formidable steps in front of the cave that are still problematic to climb. See Grunwedel 1912: 117-119; Le Coq has photo illustrations of most of the paintings: vol. III: 33-8, pl. 6-10; vol. VII: 38, pl. 7. For more recent illustrations see *Chugoku sekkutsu, Kiziru*, vol. II, pl. 107 ff. The Germans took the lunette with the attack of Mara back to Berlin, where the only part that remains, the lower right corner, is housed; see Hartel. 1982: 92, cat. no. 28.

79. Ingholt 1957: 36.

80. XXBJ: 465 a18.

81. GXYJ: 625 c28.

82. XXBJ: 465.

83. The wrestling competition is not mentioned in the GXYJ, in the TRBJ: 474c the crown prince wins easily, and in the XXBJ: 465c, Nanda, having beat Devadatta, concedes the crown prince's superiority.

84. XXBJ: 465, see introduction.

85. XXBJ: 465c; this event is not described in the TRBJ; but is treated in an exactly similar manner as the GXYJ account; see, p. 628c.

86. Degens 1964: pl. II, no. 6.

87. XXBJ: 467c.

88. The first meditation is unique in that it is variously placed in the different scriptures; the only one to have it after the four exits is the XXBJ.

89. GXYJ: 628a. For this scripture see *Daizokyo*, vol. III, no. 189: 632 and no. 186: 505 respectively.

90. *Chugoku sekkutsu, Kiziru*, vol. II: pl. 110.

91. TRBJ: 475 b19. It is at this point in the biography that the first meditation takes place. Here also, the deity Mara attempts to forestall the prince's illumination.

92. TRBJ: 475 c-20.

93. Though the Chinese identified the figure as the Naga Queen, this identification is not possible as both human figures are clearly nude to the waist and male. Compare these to the preceding depiction of the milkmaid Sugata.

94. XXBJ: 470 b29.

95. GXYJ: 650b ff.

96 *Chugoku sekkutsu, Kiziru* vol. II: pls. 43-66; for dating see p.172.

97. For Cave 27, see *Chugoku sekkutsu, Kiziru* vol. I: pl. 73; for Cave 99 see vol. II: pl. 87.

98. Waldschmidt, vol. VII: 37, points out that these appear rarely on the cella walls, and mainly in the barrel vaults. One example is the Kashyapa Cave of the common type (fore hall, square cella, pier and ambulatory); on the barrel vault of the main room are scenes from the animal and human incarnations of the Buddha. One representation has the Buddha seated under a tree, protected from the adversities of weather by the Naga Muchilinda, during his first night of enlightenment. See Grunwedel 1912: 119.

99. Ding Mingyi, Ma Shichang, "Qiziru shiku de fufu bihua (Kiziru sekuttsu no butsuten hekiga)," *Chugoku sekkutsu, Kiziru,* vol. III: 170-227; especially see p. 207 ff.

100. Here too the Germans removed murals to transport home; this is housed in Berlin inv. no. MIK III8437. Grunwedel 1912: 162ff ascribed the cave to the middle seventh century, but believed the drawing on cloth to be in a much earlier style. See also, Le Coq, 1928, vol. VII: 21. For extant fragment, see Hartel 1982: 86, cat. entry 24; who identified the royal couple, and the earthquake (in the lower right) that took place when the Buddha died.

101. *Chugoku sekkutsu, Kiziru* vol. II: 220, it is painted in Caves 4, 98, 101, 178, 193, 205, 219, 224.

102. S. Weiner, *Ajanta: Its Place in Buddhist Art* (Berkeley: Univ. of California Press 1980): 60.

103. For a discussion of the formulation of a set of four see Karetzky 1987: 268-274. One example of a miniature Gandharan stupa base with the four scenes from a private collection is found in P. Pal, *Light of Asia* (LA: LA County Museum of Art, 1984): 53; entry 1. Another traveling shrine, a

damaged diptych from Pakistan in the S. Eilenberg Collection in the Metropolitan Museum of Art, NY, has two scenes, the birth and death preserved. See Pal 1984: 55ff. Several fragmentary examples of small traveling shrines are in the British Museum.

104. A polychrome book cover from Bihar in the Los Angeles County Museum, ascribed to the eleventh century and one from Nepal dated 1054 have eight scenes from the biography; see, Pal 1984: 59.

105. *Chugoku sekkutsu, Kiziru* vol. III: pls. 35-36.

106. F.R. Alchin, "A Cruciform Reliquary from Shaikan Dheri," in *Aspects of Indian Art*, P. Pal, ed. (Leiden, 1972): 15. There is one dramatic exception to this, a traveling shrine found in Gansu of uncertain place or time of manufacture with dozens of scenes carved on its interior, see A. Soper, "A Buddhist Traveling Shrine in an International Style," *East and West* vol. 15 (1955): 222ff. See also See D. Rowan, "A Reconsideration of an Unusual Ivory Diptych," *Artibus Asiae,* vol. XLVI.4 (1985).

107. Grunwedel 1912: 119; Le Coq 1928, vol. VII: 74.

108. Hartel 1982: 82, pl. 19; Le Coq found this 1922, 026 IV: 25; it is from the "largest cave," inv. MK III 8419.

109. Harper 1978: cat. no. 3, cat. no. 22, as previously mentioned. For Qizil see *Chugoku sekkutsu, Kiziru*, vol. I: pl. 20ff.

110. Ma Shichang, "Qizilshiku zhongxinshude zhushikudingde houshide bihua" (Kiziru sekkutsu chushin chukutsu no shushitsu kutsu cho no koshitsu no hekiga), *Chugoku sekkutsu, Kiziru*, vol. II: 170-236; see p. 173 ff.

111. *Chugoku sekkutsu, Kiziru* Cave 38, vol. II: pls. 82-145.

112 . This story tells the previous life of the bodhisattva when he sacrifices his life to feed a starving tigress and her cubs.

113. *Chugoku sekkutsu, Kiziru* Cave 17: vol. II: pl. 55-72 (a common type—a barrel vaulted room with square pier, a niche on its front face which bore the now missing major icon and two aisles that led to a rear room).

114. These paintings in Cave 8 are illustrated in *Chugoku sekkutsu, Kiziru* vol. I: pl. 13-14. Traces of a mural of the cremation of the Buddha are still visible on the back wall of the rear chamber— Kashyapa stands at the foot of the bier. On the opposite side was a row of stupas. Cave 32, ascribed to the sixth c., see pl. 76; Cave 34, ascribed to the sixth c., see pl. 78-81.

115. Ibid., vol. III: pls. 5- 6 and pls. 15-20 respectively.

116. S. Subrahmanyam, "Dina, The Mathuran Gupta Artist," *The Golden Age*, Karl Khandalavala ed. (Bombay: Marg, 1991): 125ff.

117. For example, the cave in the north gorge, left of the gorge (3) with the Inscription, *Höhle in der Nordlichen Schluct L. Von Der Schluct (3) Mit Der Inschrift* has the burning of the coffin is on the back wall of the rear room and the division of relics opposite. Vajrapani appears at the foot of the coffin, throwing his *vajra (*thunderbolt) away in anguish.

118. For example, the usual placement of the death, with the burning of the coffin on the facing wall, is found in the so-called Maya Caves of the third plan (see Grunwedel 1928: 24). The Preta or Third Cave has an Iranian style lantern roof with a *garuda* bird at its center and five pictures of a teaching Buddha on each wall of the main room.

119. This cave has a painting in a lunette over the door of a preaching Maitreya, seated with crossed ankles, surrounded by a celestial audience of ten figures. On the side walls, above the three large paintings of a Buddha preaching to an audience, is a balustrade with crowned couples, eating, drinking, or playing music—flute, string instruments—from which the cave derives its name.

120. The sidewalls of the main chamber of this cave, in contrast, have a single register of three large rectangular panels each with a Buddha preaching to a group of monks and divinities. Holes remain on the upper walls that may have once supported a wooden balustrade. On the walls of the aisle are large sized standing images of the Buddha with a smaller figure in attendance; one has the Buddha holding a begging bowl, the donor kneels to the right in small scale.

121. A large central pier similarly dominates the Cave in the North Gorge, left of the gorge (3) with the Inscription, *Höhle in der Nordlichen Schluct L. Von Der Schluct (3) Mit Der Inschrift.* It also has several large compositions of a preaching Buddha with an audience on the side walls of the main chamber. The burning of the coffin is on the back wall of the rear room and the division of relics is opposite. The burning of the coffin differs in minor details: behind the now closed coffin and flaming pyre are three small painted stupas with tall spires; Vajrapani appears at the foot of the coffin. The division of relics does not differ from the common prototypes of Qizil.

122. *Chugoku sekkutsu, Kiziru* vol. I: pls. 154-156.

123. Grunwedel 1928: 24; there is no illustration of this scene only the author's description of it. The Berlin Museum acc. numbers are MIK 8438, respectively. See *Zhonguo meishu quanji*, vol. 16: 78-81, fig. 100-101. There is another example of this scene in one of the Maya Caves of the second plan illustrated in Le Coq 1928, vol. IV: 9, pl. 6; inv. no. IB 8438.

124. Grunwedel 1912: 169; Le Coq 1928, vol. IV: 73.

125. Le Coq 1928, vol. VI: pl. XV, inv. no. IB 8861; also Grunwedel 1912: 46, fig. 91. See also *Zhongguo meishu quanji*, vol. 16: 91, fig. 115.

126. Le Coq 1928, vol. VII: 81, mentions Herodotus' history of the Scythians who practiced self-mutilation during mourning.

127. *Zhonguo meishu,quanji* vol. 16: 93, fig. 118, inv. no. MIK III 8891.

128. Le Coq 1928, vol. VI: 73, pl. 11, inv. no. IB 8891, 445 X 463 cm.

129. Grunwedel 1912: 47 discussed but did not reproduce a photo of these paintings.

130. One example is on the upper niche of the Temple in the Gorge; all that remains of the colossal statue is the podium (80 cm high) which rests against the rear wall. Two mourning monks are painted on the left; Le Coq 1928, vol. V, pl. 1556, inv. no. IB B8487; 73 X 29 cm. The second example has nothing left of the Buddha figure only the painted music-making devas on the ceiling remain. See Le Coq 1928, vol. VI, pl. 2a, p. 65, inv. no. 8841B; measuring 178 x 59 m.

131. *Chugoku sekkutsu, Kiziru* vol. I: pls. 14-26.

132. *Chugoku sekkutsu, Kiziru* vol. II: pls. 87-91. The side walls of the central room of Cave 100 have three registers filled with rectangular compositions of preaching Buddhas, the rear wall has a niched icon flanked by two smaller, now empty, niches. The rear chamber has a representation of the death.

133. *Chugoku sekkutsu, Kiziru* vol. I: 179 ff.

134. *Zhonguo meishu quanji*, Cave 24: fig. 160, p. 124; Cave 43: 166-167, p. 130-131; Cave 46: fig. 173-4, p. 139-40; Cave 63: fig. 176-180, p. 141-145.

135. *Zhonguo meishu quanji* vol. 16: 123, fig. 159. Berlin Museum inv. no. MIK III 8912.

136. *Zhonguo meishu quanji* vol. 16: 196, fig. 226.

137. F. Andrews, "Central Asian Wall Paintings," *Indian Arts and Letters* vol. VII. 4 (1934): 14, pl. VII.

138. Andrews 1948: 75, Pl. XXIV and Pl. XX. The shrine is designated XXXXI A-C and the painting found on the end wall measures 5 feet in width.

CHAPTER II

PICTORIAL BIOGRAPHY OF THE BUDDHA IN CHINA

INTRODUCTION

Stories of how Buddhism was transmitted to China are often told: monks and missionaries made their way east preaching and performing attention-getting feats to demonstrate the superiority of their beliefs. One of the best-known legends associated with the introduction of Buddhism concerns Han Emperor Ming (58-75) who dreamed of a golden deity flying over his palace. When it was explained to the Emperor that this was the Buddha, he dispatched men like Zai Yin to search out more information.[1] Scholars have questioned the myths surrounding the introduction of Buddhism into China. One source of confirmation of the date of its entry is the record of foreign monks who came to proselytize. The Indian Kashyapa Matanga, or Ku Sho, for example, supposedly came to China with Zai Yin in 67 C.E. A more reliable but casual reference is the mention of Buddhist monks in the city of Luoyang in a poem by Zhang Heng 78-130.[2] Early documentation is also found in Xiang Kai 's famous memorial to the throne dated 166, which gave an account of the life of the Buddha. In the text he quoted events in the biography as a moral standard for the errant emperor, too preoccupied with his court beauties:

> *The Buddha did not pass three successive nights under the mulberry tree, he did not wish to remain long for this would give*

rise to an attachment to and a liking (for the place). That was
extreme refinement. The gods sent beautiful maidens to tempt him
but he said these are nothing but sacks of skin containing blood
and he paid no further attention to them. His concentration was
like this so he attained illumination.[3]

In the *Wei Lue,* compiled by Yu Huan ca. 239-265, a similar
description of the Buddha's origins and early life are recounted.[4]

The first place where Buddhism was practiced in China was in Peng-
cheng in modern Henan, but it was nearby Luoyang, the capital, which
became the famous center of activity in the Han. The Baimasi (White
Horse Temple) was probably the first to be established. Although the
temple is still extant, visiting the site reveals that nothing from that
time has survived.[5] Certain artifacts also point to the introduction of
Buddhism into Sichuan in this early phase.[6]

Owing to the extreme reverence for the written word in China,
translation of the sutras took place almost as soon as Buddhism
entered. The activities of several Indians are recorded in the temple in
Luoyang in the first century: notably Kashyapa Matanga and
Dharmaraksha, also known as Gu Falan. Of the foreign monks
involved in such activities in Luoyang, An Shigao was the most
eminent. A royal Parthian, An arrived in the mid-second century and
lived there for twenty years. He and two assistants—An Xuan and Yen
Foutiao, a Chinese convert—are credited with over 55 scriptural
translations. Zhi Chan arrived in 167, as did Kang Mengxiang; Kang
Zhu from Sogdia was also there. At the end of the second century Ki
Yao, Ku Fosoh, an Indian, and several monks of Tibetan origin were in
residence in Luoyang. It is said that not many Chinese were Buddhist
at this time, and that the temples were for the foreigners.

Gradually, support for Buddhism grew, but it had to overcome
several obstacles in order to be acceptable to the Chinese. First and
foremost the Indian prince, who discovered the religion of renunciation
nearly a thousand years earlier, must have seemed particularly remote
to the Chinese. Added to this was the nearly inexplicable fact that he
rejected all worldly fame, riches, and family. This was in direct
conflict with traditional Chinese mores. On a very basic level, the
Chinese were not attracted to an asceticism that espoused vows of
chastity and poverty, for they had a rich appreciation for the material
world. However, the China had some recognition of poor ascetics
being closer to spiritual truth. Certainly, the hermetic existence

of a meditative life in the forest was highly regarded in China, but these recluses were secular paragons of virtue who rejected worldly ties; they were not described as mendicants.   Often their reclusion was a retirement from court responsibilities.

Among the Buddhist practices that were difficult to accept was the necessary rejection of personal identity and the family.   For the Chinese, filial piety and ancestor worship were the highest responsibilities entrusted to future generations. By choosing the life of a religious, monks rejected not only their parents but also four generations of ancestors; ignoring their needs was considered criminal. Shaving the head and other observances were also considered to be a breech of filial piety, for the body was considered a gift of one's parents—to defile or abuse it was gross ingratitude.

Chinese Buddhist literati addressed these issues in the choice of the scriptures they translated and in their commentaries. Buddhism was in large part made acceptable because of the efforts of apologists and exegetes who explained the doctrine in native terms, using Taoist vocabulary or less frequently Confucian values.   Three scriptures translated by An Shigao, for example, directly address the question of filial relations in their titles.[7] In the late Han, translation activities accelerated, both the earlier pre-Mahayana and Mahayanist scriptures were rendered into Chinese. In the major centers of central China like Luoyang and Chang-an as well as places along the Yangtze valley in Shandong and Anhui, the number of monks and monasteries multiplied.

At the end of the Han dynasty, in an atmosphere of social upheaval and uncertainty, Buddhism became more popular. Political chaos ensued when noble families and eunuchs, seeking only personal wealth and power, came to dominate the government. Their behavior caused a gradual dissolution of faith in the government; their lack of concern for the welfare of the people was alarmingly apparent. Coincident with the natural disasters at the end of the Han, peasant uprisings eroded central authority and confidence in the system of government.[8]   Disorder spread. This was a defeat of Confucianism as well, for many turned away from the social responsibilities associated with the failing ideology to find comfort in the doctrines of individualism. The appeal of Taoism and its goal of harmony with the laws of nature and an untrammeled lifestyle lived in seclusion was great, as was the appeal of the so called "Dark" practices that sought to extend one's life to immortality through proper breathing, diet, and other disciplines. The personal salvation offered by Buddhism was yet another attractive alternative. Mahayanist scriptures put forth the concrete rewards of faith with their descriptions of hell and a paradise ruled by the Buddha of infinite life, Amitofu (Amitabha). Buddhist deities dedicated to universal salvation acted as an individual worshiper's personal aide. These deities could transfer the merits of their good works to the pious. Such tenets were adapted to the demands of filial piety: the rewards of meritorious practices and prayers were directed to the benefit of parents and past generations.

In the post Han century China was subject to a series of short-lived and poorly unified regimes known as the Three Kingdoms period.[9] The inability to resurrect a powerful central government left authority and national defense weakened. With the power now decentralized, China was prey to foreign encroachments. In 317 the north was invaded by barbarians, forcing a large segment of the population to flee south. From this point onward the north was ruled by a succession of barbarian regimes and the south suffered a continuous series of native rulers. Political uncertainty plagued the populace. In these chaotic times the doctrine of self-fulfillment and the quest for spiritual peace were ever more attractive.

The character of Buddhism in the south was quite different from that in the north. In the south, many of the gentry and literati, having escaped the barbarian invasion, were dedicated to preserving Han traditions. But in addition to this conservative aristocracy were the southerners drawn to the philosophical aspects of the new religion. Literati pursued translation activities and wrote commentaries on the scriptures. Among the important figures was Hui Yuan (334-416), a classical scholar who converted to Buddhism. Hui Yuan was one of the early proponents of the paradisiacal cult of the Buddha of Infinite Life. Another literatus, Zhi Dun (314-366) was instrumental in translating Buddhist ideas and terminology by using Taoist analogies and borrowing Taoist terms. Zhu Daoqian (365-434) was also important in the transmission of Buddhism, reconciling many of the disparities perceived in the numerous scriptures of Mahayana and pre-Mahayana sects. One important Mahayanist scripture, the *Vimalakirti Nirdesa*, relates the story of how a highly regarded intellectual, Vimalakirti, fell ill, and the Buddha requested one of the divinities to go down and visit him. As the scripture relates, the bodhisattvas were reluctant to go because they would become involved in a debate with him, so the bodhisattva of wisdom was told to visit him. The scripture takes the form of the great debate between the secular figure, representing native wisdom, and the Buddhist god. Of course in the end the god wins the debate, but only after the native tradition is given its due regard.

By the sixth century Buddhism found state support in the south. It was in the monarch Wu of the Liang (r. 502-549) that the ideal Buddhist king found expression. Wu's patronage of the Buddhist community was lavish. He sought to collect revenues by having himself held ransom by the temples; he proclaimed vegetarian days; and sponsored the ordination of monks and the building of temples. But unlike Ashoka who was universally tolerant, he initiated repressive measures against the Taoists, forcing them back into the laity. Prince Gang of Jinan (the future Qian Wendi) of the Liang dynasty was also a great patron of Buddhism who sponsored many extravagant projects. He had an artificial bodhi tree erected that had representations of the life of the Buddha on it. This description of it is from the *Guang hong ming ji* (XV):

> Then, thinking on the beginning of all of our salvation, he has erected a tree of Bodhi. The four seas have given up their rarities (to it) and the hundred crafts have spent their cunning. With chased gold, carved jade, mirrors strung together, festoons of pearls it is fashioned in the likeness of the Snow Mountains and its shape is that of a flying canopy. . . . Majestic is the wondrous form (of the Buddha?) shading those curving branches; as resplendent as a gold mountain, as venerable as linked moons. (One sees) the pious maiden at the time when (the Buddha began again) to eat; the figures of the gods offering their four bowls; the strewn propitious grass (that was used for the Buddha's seat), and the linked fluttering of bluebirds (overhead); the quelling of the thunder-spitting Mara, and the rout of his mountain-bearing devils; strange shapes in ornamental materials beyond the power of words (to describe). Here truly (has been revealed) a wondrous karma for the creation of good; here is the profound felicity of (spiritual progress. . . .). [10]

Although the large literary corpus of southern Buddhist translations, exegeses, and commentaries are preserved, little of the art has survived. Of the few icons preserved at places like the Wanfosi temple in

Sichuan, narratives are exceedingly rare.[11] Most of the steles present a large icon of the Buddha flanked by the members of his entourage—bodhisattvas, monks, guardian kings, and angels—in reduced scale.

By contrast, Buddhism in the north won the sponsorship of the barbarian kings early on. Finding sympathy with the non-Han religion, these rulers were enthralled by the display of supernatural powers possessed by proselytizers who could make it rain or who promised to enhance the ruler's power against their enemies. Northern rulers supported the building of temples and endorsed the ordination of thousands of monks. As a result, Buddhism was better endowed and far more widespread in the north. But under the Northern Wei regime Buddhism suffered its first proscription in 445. Influenced by a powerful Taoist monk, the emperor repudiated the monastic community for its abusive practices and dereliction of civic responsibilities. Monks took vows of poverty yet they appeared to be indolent and non-productive, living off the efforts of the laity. More importantly the temples grew rich on tax-exempt income from industries run on temple lands. With the discovery of a cache of arms and stash of liquor in a monastery, a violent, but short-lived persecution ensued. This event led to the laicization of monks, confiscation of temples, and destruction of artistic monuments. In the wake of this devastation, however, was a restoration that created new, lasting monuments that are still preserved. With the restitution of Northern Wei imperial support, the religion flourished, its adherents multiplied, and its institutions proliferated.

By this time the life of the Buddha was a well-known story. The *Wei Shu* in the chapter on Buddhism and Taoism written by Wei Shou (506-72) has an abstract of the biography.[12] The description is detailed and complete in its coverage.

> *He who is spoken of as Buddha was originally called Shi-jia-wen which being interpreted means "Capable of Benevolence." That is to say, his virtue being fulfilled and his way complete, he is able to save myriad beings. . . . Shakya was the son of the King of Jia-wei in Tianju (India). Tianju is a general appellation, while Jia-wei is a specific name. Now Shakya in the fourth month on the eighth day at night was born out of his mother's right side. At birth his extraordinary features were thirty-two in number and heaven rained down auspicious portents in response thereto also thirty-two in number. The scriptures of the Buddha's origin explain this*

in full.   Shakya achieved Buddhahood at the age of thirty.   He converted the manifold for forty-nine years.

As in India, religious images were worshiped by washing, adorning, and parading them through the streets. This type of celebration was particularly undertaken on the day commemorating the birth of the Buddha. The first mention of this practice occurs in the Song dynasty of the period of division in the south. Celebrations, pageants, and processions were led through the streets of the city; both masked figures and entertainers are said to have taken part in the galas.[13] A later reference, from the *Luoyang qielan ji*, records the representation of the conception—Shakyamuni riding a white six-tusked elephant in the air—on a three-story pagoda inside the Si-yang gate of the city.[14] There, for the commonly observed holiday celebrations of the Buddha's birthday, an image of the conception was taken out and paraded through the streets accompanied by flower throwing, banner flying and incense burning:

> *The decorations and ritual paraphernalia were all of gold or jade; the originality of the workmanship would be difficult to describe. On the fourth day of the fourth month the image was always brought out, preceded by pi xie monsters and lions. Sword swallowers and fire spitters would prance everywhere; the pennants and streamers tied overhead were exceptionally ingenious. For strange arts and odd costumes there was nothing else comparable in the whole city. When the image would stop the onlookers would block the way, trampling each other until somebody was killed.*

A number of such celebrations of the birthday are recorded elsewhere. Images of the newborn Buddha, naked and standing in a basin used for ritual washing, have survived in Japan from the Nara period (eighth century) and in Korea,[15] which suggests that there probably were similar icons in contemporary China. Another event in the life of the Buddha annually celebrated and Japan is the day of the great decease or passing away of the Buddha, the parinirvana. In this case paintings of the event were exhibited on the day so designated, February 15.[16]

ARTISTIC EVIDENCE

One of the major problems in dealing with the early narratives in China is the vast amount of lost material. Due to the tumultuous history of the continent with its civil wars, natural disasters, foreign invasions, and the targeted destruction of Buddhist monuments during the anti-Buddhist proscriptions, little is left. The major extant source of material are the cave temples of north China, which being in remote locations and sometimes sheltered by their natural surroundings, escaped the wholesale destruction of temples in the capitals and large metropolitan areas. In Gansu province, there are several sites, each with many dozens or even hundreds of caves: Binglingsi, Maijishan, and Dunhuang are among the most prominent. At Datong in Shanxi there are the Yungang caves, and in Henan the Longmen and Gongxian caves. Sichuan also has several sites with multiple rock-cut caves. Most early caves have a single chamber; later ones become more complex. In China these highly decorated caves are for worship rather than monastic use.

With the exception of the cave material, artistic sources of the narrative scenes of the life of Shakyamuni are extremely limited. However, there are some impressive extant sculptures. First are the large steles carved with Buddhist decorations and inscriptions. Second are several small objects such as traveling shrines and reliquaries. Later, in the Sui period, the biographical cycles are appropriated for pagoda decor. Lastly is the literary evidence recording the titles of works of art, sometimes with descriptions of their appearance, which were lost to history in their pictorial form.

Looking over the Buddhist material in China, there is an apparent dearth of pictorial biographies. Certainly, much has been lost to the vagaries of history. But among the extant material, the number of icons far exceeds that of pictorial narratives. This proportion is maintained in all media—cave murals, freestanding stone sculpture, and even literary sources. Biographical narratives were surely instrumental in the introduction of the doctrine into China, the Buddha's life being a paradigm for instruction. Easy to tell and often amusing, the stories of the four exits, the temptation of Mara, and even the death were particularly well suited to explaining the main tenets. Yet, interest in the pictorial biography seems to have suffered decline soon after its introduction. But for a brief period in the early stage of Buddhist art in

China, the large-scale icons came to be the focus of worship. Remarkably, there are at least two extant pictorial biographical cycles, each at a major site—Dunhuang and Yungang. These two examples are quite different from each other. Those at Yungang are much earlier, carved in stone and clearly dependent on Gandharan prototypes in style, composition and narrative technique. Those at Dunhuang were made later, occasionally utilize the scroll format, and seem more dependent on the illustrated narratives from Xinjiang.

As Chinese Buddhism underwent its dramatic accommodations to native style and culture, so did its art. After the brief introductory phase characterized by a nearly slavish imitation of Western icons, the process of sinification took place. By the end of the fifth century the muscular heroic Gandharan Buddha with broad shoulders, fleshy belly, and thick thighs becomes slender and narrow-bodied. The previously exposed areas of the torso and shoulders are swathed in layers of heavy material draped to resemble a long, silk gown. The facial features are Chinese. In sum, the sculptural values of the west are gradually replaced by the linear aesthetic of Chinese art—three-dimensional modeling, through highlighting and shading forms, is lost among graceful and rhythmic linear designs.

In this period of accommodation, the focus of worship shifted from the singular life of the noble ascetic to a paradisiacal view of the cosmos inhabited by the innumerable Buddhas and bodhisattvas to whom individual appeal could be made. These new deities were more contemporary and accessible in a way the historic Buddha ceased to be. Scenes of the life of the Buddha present the historic person, portraying him in normal scale; the details of his biography, inextricably tied to his life in India, were no doubt strange and at times difficult to understand. In contrast the members of the Mahayanist pantheon offered a new capacity to aid humanity in the search for salvation and, as E. Zurcher has shown, an eschatological movement began in China as early as the fourth century and reached a' peak in the sixth. Scriptures predicted the decline of the faith in a degenerate age and an apocalyptic renewal when new deities could help the faithful in a way that Shakyamuni no longer could.[17]

In the later period, beginning in 550 and continuing through the Tang, increased mercantile traffic on the silk route results in a more frequent interchange of ideas and images. There were more monks coming from the West and Chinese going to India. Interest in foreign cultures expanded, reaching a climax in the great internationalism of the Tang era. As early as the Northern Qi to Sui periods, the Buddha image underwent another transformation—now the fussy linear patterns of the drapery became more simplified and the bodily forms regained their three-dimensionality, appearing as geometric shapes. Increasingly, elements of naturalism were introduced until the Buddhas of the Tang resembled their Indian counterpart's yogic fleshy body, exposed to view, with detailed anatomical articulation that included the navel and nipples. The body's forms pressed behind the diaphanous drapery. Almond-eyed and curvaceous-lipped sensuous Indian faces appeared among the entourage of the Buddha, and the central deity himself was cast as a dark-skinned Indian.

At this time narrative forms were reintroduced to China and sparked a new style of painting. Buddhist narrative scenes reappeared at Dunhuang and other cave sites. Extant in Japan is an illustrated scroll that is believed to preserve closely the ancient Chinese Tang original. Moreover, Chinese art historians of the Tang recorded a number of lost paintings by famous artists of scenes of the biography.

NARRATIVE STYLE

The three stages of evolution of narrative—expansive, abbreviated and epitomized—are observable at many of the sites in China. Most often the detailed presentations, the more ancient in India, chronologically precede the other two in China as well. The prototypes on which these narrative styles are based are varied, and in analyzing the contrasting styles, different kinds of artistic sources can be distinguished. Two Indian narrative formats of the extensive style were transmitted to China: the rectangular form with the most important event at center and secondary details drawn on the periphery and the horizontal format of continuous narration. Here too the Indian chronological evolution of these two formats is observable in China: the rectangular precedes the horizontal. Furthermore, this is the beginning of pictorial narrative art in China, for prior to the introduction of Buddhism there is no evidence of continuous narrative illustration. Though Chinese art has many instances of illustrations of historical and literary themes, these commonly comprise individual scenes that present a single isolated episode or event. Han dynasty tombs have murals and sculpted or painted tiles that show images of the deceased, chariots, banquets, and other entertainment, even the acts of hunting and salt mining, but these activities are not told in multiple scenes nor in continuous action.[18] As for extant evidence of scroll painting in China, the most ancient Chinese scrolls, attributed to the fourth century master Gu Kaizhi, are universally acknowledged to be copies dating from many centuries later. It is important to note that Gu was a celebrated painter of Confucian themes and Taoist scenery who also won fame depicting Buddhist subjects such as the *Vimalakirti Nirdesa*.[19] Soon after the narrative technique and the scroll format were introduced into China with Buddhism, they flourished, reaching the first stage of development during the so-called Period of Division or Six Dynasties and achieving the height of expression and popularity in the ensuing dynasties—notably the Tang and Song.

PICTORIAL BIOGRAPHY OF THE BUDDHA IN GANSU PROVINCE, CHINA

Gansu, traditionally the most northwestern province of China, was the terminus of the silk route. It was both the starting point for merchant caravans and military expeditions journeying west, and the entry point for western traders, emissaries, and Buddhist missionaries. According to the annals of the *Han Shu*, Dunhuang was made into a commandery in 111 C.E.[20] During the barbarian regimes, the northern corridor was under the control of a succession of minor dynasties. Though traditionally not considered part of China, Gansu's relation with China proper intensified when these Hu peoples invaded the north. By the late fifth century the Hu peoples were sinicized and the art of Gansu exhibited the influence of Chinese artistic traditions. By the Tang era, the art produced in the cave-chapels exuded a very cosmopolitan air, closely resembling the murals produced in the capitals of Chang-an and Luoyang.

As a result of high-level commercial and military activity in Gansu, Buddhist patronage thrived. Cave-temples were excavated under the direction of monks and their sometime military or merchant patrons. The earliest evidence for these caves dates to the opening decades of the fifth century. At that time several sites were under Northern Liang control in the Gansu area. Chinese archaeologists have recently studied Wugemiao, Yumen changma, Wenshushan (Mazhongsi, Jintasi and Qianfodong), Dunhuang, Maijishan, and Binglingsi.[21] The Northern

Liang King Mengxun, of the early fifth century, is remembered for his Buddhist activities of commissioning caves to be constructed, images made, and scriptures translated. The conquerors of the Northern Liang, the Northern Wei, who were active until the first third of the sixth century, continued to support work at most of the sites excavated under their predecessors. Under succeeding dynasties—Northern Zhou, Sui, and Tang—patronage of the caves continued. Later dynasties maintained the sites, repairing and remodeling older caves. The considerable body of artistic evidence at the cave-chapels of Gansu allows for a number of kinds of studies in the evolution of religious painting, sculpture, architecture, religious practices, and iconography.

As in Xinjiang, the caves in Gansu province are excavated from mountains conveniently located near to or by the banks of rivers that provide both a conduit for travel and a source of water. Usually carved high in the rocky bluffs, they are fairly inaccessible now, unless the government has reinforced the necessary structural supports and constructed access routes to the caves.[22] The caves of Gansu are stylistically similar to one another. For example, those ascribed to the Northern Liang are small squarish rooms whose walls are filled with painted images and in some cases stucco sculptures. Caves commissioned during the Northern Wei era have a consistent style that reflects Xinjiang prototypes: a larger space (often decorated to resemble a fore hall and main chamber) dominated by a central square pillar. Later caves tend to be large square rooms, often with a niche at the rear.

Among the earlier caves excavated under the Northern Liang, biographical narratives are infrequent. So far, a cave at Binglingsi with its inscription of the year 420 is the earliest dated cave in Gansu and narratives are not a part of its iconographical program.[23] At the slightly later site of Maijishan, narratives function as a minor motif, being extremely few in number. The grottoes at Dunhuang are however, exceptional, for they have a considerable amount of Buddhist pictorial narratives, many of which are illustrations of jataka tales.[24] Though the painted stories from the life of the Buddha are not nearly as numerous as other Buddhist themes, still the murals from Dunhuang are a rich source of information.   This pictorial evidence allows for a consideration of which scriptures were illustrated and how the biographical scenes fit into the decorative program in terms of physical placement, thematic relevance, and iconographic content.

1. MOGAO CAVES AT DUNHUANG

Although the opening of the caves at Dunhuang is traditionally ascribed to the middle of the fourth century, the earliest ones are attributed to the period of the Northern Liang occupation of the first two decades of the fifth century.[25] Excavation and decoration continue until the fourteenth century. Similar to Qizil, the caves at Dunhuang can be divided into three phases according to the placement, size, and frequency of the narratives. In the earliest phase narratives are a major theme and figure prominently in the decorative scheme. In the second phase events in the life of the Buddha are rare and cast in secondary areas. Caves of the third phase relegate narratives, now severely reduced in scale, to insignificant areas, with the exception of the parinirvana scenes, which enjoy a brief renaissance.

I. CAVES WITH NARRATIVES AS THE MAIN THEME

Cave 275

The earliest group of caves, comprising Northern Liang Caves 275 and 272 are heavily dependent upon western prototypes. In general, there is a characteristic reliance on the art of Xinjiang. The murals share a similar color scheme—red background with primarily red, black, and tan articulation of the figures. The anatomy is drawn naturalistically: line and shade define the musculature and fleshy parts of the body. Analysts of the Dunhuang Institute believe that oxidation of the iron content in the pigment resulted in the blackening of the lines. Now many darkened contour lines over-emphasize the drawing rendering the three-dimensional forms of the body. Convincing modeling in dark tones and highlighting of forms suggests the remote ancestry of Indian art, as does the fleshy exposed body, which resembles the Guptan ideal of beauty—broad shoulders, narrow waist and protruding belly. Skirts and scarves that drape the figures are defined with care, suggesting the quality of cloth as it wraps about the body and falls into swags. The facial features are clearly non-Han. In sum, they have a non-Chinese appearance. Other Northern Liang dynasty caves at sites in Gansu also share these characteristics presenting a fairly consistent style of painting.[26]

Cave 275 is a small cave with no central pillar.[27] The upper areas of the sidewalls have niches with sculptures of the Buddha or a bodhisattva and below are painted narratives. Following the interior organization of Indian ritual spaces, the major icon occupies the rear wall. But the decor of the Liang dynasty caves of the mid-fifth century at Dunhuang is already affected by the new soil in which the art was transplanted—the tops of the niches have architectural frames shaped like a pagoda or Han-style tiled roof and bracketing.

The earliest biographical narrative at Dunhuang is the depiction of the four exits painted on the lower section of the south wall of Cave 275. When during a later period the cave was extensively redecorated, a wall was erected that covered the murals; however, the Dunhuang Research Institute has restored some of the original Liang dynasty murals. Set against a red background, white-skinned figures are shown with a bare minimum of setting. Only two of the sorties—the meetings with the ascetic and with the old man—are still completely visible, for one large chunk of the original wall has fallen away. The story is told in a processional manner. On the far left in the mid-ground the prince, mounted on an impossibly small horse, is passing out of the city gate. (FIGURE 30) Drawing the gate on a diagonal accomplishes a feeling of spatial recession. The white two-story structure has a blue tiled roof and red paint articulates its Chinese-style bracketing system. To the right the groom, Chandaka, explains the plight of old age to the young prince. The old man on the far right has white hair, mustache, and beard; his thin, naked body is covered with only a loincloth. Two devas fly overhead. To the left is the second encounter: the prince stands beside the bald-headed ascetic, who wears dhoti skirt and scarf draped over one shoulder. In the upper area are flying angels. To the far left all that remains of the third encounter is the city gate setting; the rest of the wall has toppled. On the lowest zone of the sidewalls are a row of angels and a register of alternating red and white triangles.[28]

Cave 254

In Cave 254 the main representations of biographical scenes appear in the antechamber. Similar to Cave 275, scenes from the jatakas and the biography occupy the main section of the lower wall.[29] But this cave, ascribed to the early Northern Wei period (439-534), has a more complex plan.[30] Although it is a single large room, the illusion of two rooms is accomplished through the treatment of the ceiling and wall decor. A simulated gable with painted rafters creates the impression of a fore hall; the main room, dominated by a central rectangular shaft, has a flat ceiling. Carved into the four sides of the square pier are large-scale niches containing icons of seated Buddhas. As in Xinjiang, the central pillar symbolically alludes to Mount Sumeru. These icons on the pier are the main devotional focus and can, in accord with ancient Buddhist ritual practice, be circumambulated. Articulation of the sidewalls is typical of phase one: painted at the top is a row of celestial musicians, next is a series of stucco seated Buddha images housed in fanciful frames. Below is a zone of narratives. The thousand Buddha theme fills the interstitial spaces (the mid wall area between the fore-hall and main room and on lower sidewalls of the main room). The colors of this cave are quite extraordinary— predominantly blue-green and green, unlike the earth colors—ochre and red—of the other early caves. A similar color scheme is also found at Qizil.[31]

The Temptation of Mara occupies the lower middle part of the south wall of the antechamber. (FIGURE 31) A large scale, dark-skinned, semi-nude bodhisattva is seated in lotus position. His garment covers the left shoulder; the other is bare. His right hand is in the gesture of "calling the earth to witness" (*bhumisparsa mudra* pointing to the ground); the other hand holds the ends of his garment. Painted above his head is the flowering bodhi tree. To the right is the figure of Mara, who is much smaller in size than the Buddha and yet considerably larger than the other narrative figures. Dressed as an Indian prince with flowing scarves and a large halo, Mara holds both hands clasped in front of his chest. As at Qizil, Mara's daughters in their seductive poses are on the left, on the right they are transformed into old hags— crouching and stooped, they hobble away. Soldiers stand on either side glaring at the Buddha—five on the left, two on the right. They are dressed in military armor, broadly painted in alternating stripes of blue and black. Lying before the Buddha, two defeated warriors humbly kowtow. Ranged in the upper area the demonic members of the army are drawn in a breath-taking variety of deformities and horrific combinations: ram-headed, snaked-headed, elephant-headed, gastro-encephalitic, multi-headed, and snake spitting. Grimacing and twisting, they threaten with weapons, knives, bows and arrows; muscular bodies whirl and turn; one is about to hurl a mountain. In all, this is a perfect replication of the compositions found in the Qizil murals and Gandharan bas-reliefs.

Painted on the opposite wall of the antechamber is a rarely portrayed scene—the conversion of Nanda, the Buddha's younger cousin. The Buddha, a large iconic figure, is centrally placed; flanking him are a monk and a haloed prince drawn in rather large-scale. Above are a row of bodhisattvas, two standing disciples, and six monks seated in meditation in their caves. At the very bottom of the composition are mountain-like forms; the reluctant Nanda is on the left being persuaded to join the order. In the foreground are two couples reflecting the happy conjugal life Nanda was so reluctant to reject, an event prominent in the *Lalitavistara* and the art of Amaravati and Nagarjunakonda.

Caves 263, 260, 428-- Depictions of the Attack of Mara

The attack of Mara in the antechamber of Cave 263, also from the Northern Wei Period, is similarly drawn but not as spectacular in its garish details.[32] Sections of the cave have been repainted, but a large part of the south part of the fore hall has been uncovered to reveal the Northern Wei period murals. The centrally seated Buddha is light-skinned, with bright blue hair, a convention also seen in Qizil. This change derives from a literal interpretation of the texts, all of which describe the newborn's blue-black hair, one of 32 marks of beauty, or *lakshana*.[33] In all other details, the compositional arrangement is comparable. The triple attack is depicted simultaneously, with the action synoptically shown. On the left are the lascivious daughters; on the right they are transformed into hags. Some of the demons stand as isolated naked figures, their fleshy Guptan-style bodies rendered in various skin tones. The rest of the demon army fills the upper areas. Another Northern Wei cave, 260, has a related painting of the attack in the antechamber,[34] and the temptation still figures importantly in Cave 428, despite its late date of execution—during the Northern Zhou dynasty (557-581). In painting style, the latter scene differs only slightly from previous examples. Here, in north Gandharan fashion, Mara draws his sword, while his son tries to restrain him. Both the seduction and rejection of his daughters and the demonic army are comparably represented.

Cave 428

To the far left of the depiction of the attack in Cave 428 is a large-scale rendering of a stupa whose prominence is a reflection of the continued sanctity afforded the western object. Like the ancient prototypes, the painted stupa has a scene of the nativity as part of its decor (FIGURE 32). Housed in an arched frame, Maya grasps the branch of a dimly drawn tree with her right hand. The child issues forth from her right side. Presumably this is based on an actual reliquary that bore scenes from the life on all four sides, probably drawn from the other important events of the biography—the great departure, attack of Mara, and first sermon. Motifs like the garuda bird and earth spirits or *yakshas* suggest a Gandharan prototype, but no single extant stupa can be cited.[35]   Soper notes structural similarities with the Ashokan reliquary once housed in a temple in Zhekiang named after the famous relic, "Ayuwangxi."[36]   On the basis of affinities in appearance and decorative themes, he proposes a northwestern place of manufacture and fourth-century date for the model of the Dunhuang stupa.   The rendering in Cave 428 establishes the presence of architectural models decorated with biographical scenes in China.

The murals of Cave 428 are indicative of a transitional stage. The size and placement of the biographical scenes on the lower area of the wall of the main room are characteristic of phase one, but a new style of narrative presentation is heralded in the jataka paintings. (FIGURE 33) As in Qizil, the walls flanking the entrance door of Cave 428 are appropriated for narrative themes. But here the *Mahasattva* and *Visvantara jatakas* are rendered in the long scroll format. The repetitive nature of both the settings and the telling of the events reflect the influence of illustrated scriptures. Such effects, the result of the one to one relationship between the text and illustrations drawn above, are observable in the Japanese hand scrolls of the life of the Buddha, *E-Ingakyo*, the earliest extant illustrated sutra. At Dunhuang the continuous horizontal scroll format, too long to fit on the wall, is divided up and transposed into three registers. The direction of the composition alternates with each register: right to left, left to right, and right to left. This awkward adaptation of the scroll to the wall surface is evidence of the artist's lack of familiarity with the new format. It seems likely that the origin of the scroll, like that of the stupa, was western. As one of the earliest pieces of evidence of scroll painting in China, these murals are extremely important. Moreover, the painting style reflects the sinicization process in which Chinese aesthetic values are adopted: the figures are clothed, slight of build, and have Chinese features. There is no attempt to define the anatomy or render the three-dimensional forms of the body. No longer on a red background, the narrative unfolds against a white ground, the kind used for calligraphy. Figures are drawn with lines in red and blue with accents in red, blue, green, and orange. The characters are considerably smaller but, for the most part, naturalistically related to their environment, with the occasional landscape motif out of scale. (FIGURE 33)

In its iconographical program Cave 428 is also transitional. The biographical scenes are still important, but Mahayanist themes appear. The rear wall has the Twin Buddha Miracle of the *Lotus sutra* and the upper parts of the sidewalls display the thousand Buddha theme that declares the universal character of the doctrine. There is also an image of a colossal Buddha wearing a robe upon which a cosmological diagram of hell, earth, and heaven are painted.[37] Placed at the center of the back wall, recalling the cave temples of Qizil, is a large parinirvana scene.[38] Although the rear wall icon is still important, it is secondary to the pier as the focus of worship.

As for the iconographical context, the biographical scenes in phase one occupy a place in a vertical hierarchy of motifs arranged on the walls of the caves. At the top are flying angels; next are seated Buddhas, bodhisattvas, and the thousand Buddha theme on the upper wall. At the middle level of the walls are the biographical scenes and donors; near the bottom are earth creatures. In other caves with central square pillars this organization of spiritual themes is even clearer. On the square central pillar which represents the cosmic axis, creatures of greater spirituality are at the top, others are placed below in order of their rank. In this scheme, the life of the historic Buddha is treated as a supernatural event on earth.[39] (FIGURE 33a) Thus the historic Buddha is but one stage in the spiritual evolution that culminates in a multitude of Buddhas. But at this point the historical Buddha is still familiar and important to the viewer.

In summation phase one illustrations of the biography are relatively large scale and placed on the main area of the walls, either in the false anteroom or in the main chamber. The themes are an integral part of the decor. At first the rectangular format is used for the narrative (Caves 254, 275); later the horizontal layout is adopted for continuous narration (Cave 428). In the early caves the themes and painting technique rely on western models in the color scheme, appearance of the figures, and the manner of rendering their bodies and draperies.

Later Chinese equivalents replace the foreign style and narrative details.

II. NARRATIVE SCENES AS SECONDARY DECOR

In the second phase accommodations to Chinese art and thought are evident. Figures are no longer western in appearance nor are their bodies exposed, characteristics that are far more obvious in the painted narratives than in the more conservatively treated sculptural icons. Thick clothing obscures the figures' anatomy. Now a white background replaces the western red ground. Instead of the bold outlines of the earlier style there is a fluid linearity in the drawing style that recalls Han carvings and calligraphy. Delicate lines render the contours and interior drawing of the figures, architecture, landscape, and details of the story.

The scenes that tell the story of the life of the Buddha undergo a dramatic transformation in their placement, size and frequency of depiction in the decorative scheme. It is actually possible to catalogue the decline in interest in the life of the historic Buddha not only by the growing scarcity of the depictions, but by their decreasing size as well as their relegation to inferior areas. [40] Ascendant Mahayanist themes, such as the twin Buddhas and the thousand Buddha motif, cover the walls with straightforward statements of the growing pantheon of supernumerary Buddhas ranged throughout the cosmos. Prominent among the works of the second phase is Cave 290 of the Northern Zhou Period.[41]

Cave 290

Cave 290 with its complete cycle of the life of Siddhartha, from his birth to enlightenment, is unique at Dunhuang. The theme however is painted in very small size on the lower section of the ceiling. The dated inscription from the reign of Zhen Guang (520-4) has been repudiated, and the cave is ascribed to the Northern Zhou era.[42] In plan, the cave, like that of 428, has a simulated fore-chamber with false gable and a main room dominated by a central square pillar. The sidewalls of the cave are divided up into three areas: the lowest has donor processions, next is the thousand Buddha theme, and at the very top is a row of music-making devas.

Of the five texts that narrate the life of the Buddha translated into Chinese before the sixth century, the *Guoqu xianzai yinguo jing*, seems to be the one upon which the paintings are based.[43] For this text, which obviously accommodates Chinese cultural preferences, provides the most parallels with the details of the compositions of Cave 290. In addition, the date of its translation is close to the mid-sixth century period when the cave was decorated. However, there is no illustration of the opening passages of the GXYJ beginning with the *Dipamkara jataka* or the portion of text that describes the excellent character of both the Buddha's mother Maya and father Suddhodana. At Dunhuang the story begins on the east wall with the conception and ends long before the scripture does. There are omissions of other scenes recounted in the sutra as well. Despite these divergences, there is a general adherence to the unfolding of the story as told in this text.

In its pictorial treatment, Cave 290 is similar to Cave 428. The continuous narration of the horizontal scroll format is transcribed to the wall surface by being divided into three registers. The compositional direction of each register changes: left right, right left, left right. Though the scenes are to be read in continuous fashion, each scene is independently composed and has its own setting. There are no formal architectural dividers between them like the Gandharan examples; rather the disposition of narrative elements clearly distinguishes the individual scenes. Cartouches are drawn which might have identified the content of the individual scenes, but these were never inscribed.

A: EAST WALL TOP REGISTER

A1. The scene of the conception recalls Gandharan style: Maya lies in bed, her body obscured by bedding. Beside her is a maid. (FIGURE 34 top right) The women's quarters are distinctly rendered: a single-story structure with gabled tiled roof and lateral halls. There are three structures on the right and five on the left arranged in a zigzag manner to suggest recession into depth. In each end hall is a servant. Maya, as stated in the texts, dreams that a white six-tusked elephant has entered her side, but this very important detail is omitted.

A2. Queen Maya reports her curious dream to her husband. Both are seated together in the palace. Most of the main characters are dressed in Chinese long-sleeved, floor-length court robes; the servants wear the more traditional "barbarian" garb—round-necked, long-sleeved tunic and trousers.   Two servants flank the palace.   The artist has not illustrated the interpretation of the dream.

A3. Aware of her pregnant state, Maya withdraws from the women's quarters to enjoy the solitude of the Lumbini Garden. (FIGURE 34 top left) A few leafless trees in the background, a lotus flower, and a low bush on the left indicate the setting. Maya is dressed in a long, white, long-sleeved, belted robe. There are three handmaidens in attendance.

A4. The king is alone in the women's quarters. (FIGURE 34 top right)

A5. The birth is rendered as described in the text. Standing among a few lumpish hills on the left on which a quadruped walks, Maya raises her right arm and the child issues forth from her sleeve. (FIGURE 35 top mid)   There are several concessions to the Chinese sensibility. Because the sight of a baby issuing from her flank was objectionable, the artist has done his best to obscure the fact by making it seem as if the child is coming out of her sleeve.   Also a heavy Chinese robe shrouds Maya's curvaceous body; she now has a halo.   The Wusung tree, a Chinese poetic image, is identified in the text as the name of the tree that she grasps for support; this "tree without sorrow" is here summarily drawn and faintly visible. As in the western prototypes, like the "Steppenhohlen" at Qizil, Maya's sister is shown on the left supporting the queen; but in Cave 290, Brahma and Indra have lost their divine identity. Unlike the Qizil representation, the simultaneous births are not portrayed.

A6. Lotus blossoms mark out the path of the seven steps that the newborn prince walked just after birth. (FIGURE 35, top mid) Only six are indicated, two beneath his feet and four others, perhaps the seventh is too faint to see. Indra and Brahma, shown as princely deities, are on the right of the child, accompanied by a third figure; on the left are two worshiping devas. The young prince raises his right hand; as in the texts, he makes his first proclamation.
    As at Qizil, the newborn is as tall as the adults and naked but for a loincloth. His halo is leaf-shaped, unlike the flanking figures Indra and Brahma whose halos are round. Two delicately drawn trees are placed in the background behind music-making devas.

A7. The celestial bath is given in the west by *nagas*, snake gods joined together to form an oval body mandorla, but at Dunhuang and Qizil these are interpreted as dragons.[44] (FIGURE 36 top) Intertwining in alternating colors, all of the dragons are drawn in profile but for the central one which is frontally shown. In India nagas are tutelary deities, but such is not the Chinese tradition and the substitution of dragons is apt, for they, like nagas, are aquatic and beneficent creatures. Dragons are also a valid choice in mythological terms: a familiar symbol of the eternal duality in Han dynasty art,[45] they represent creation—the mystical union of yin and yang. This policy of substitution of the familiar for the unfamiliar or for the objectionable has been identified as a characteristic of the Chinese translation technique of Buddhist scriptures; here we see it at work in the illustrations. Other narrative details have also been transformed into Chinese equivalents such as the object upon which the baby stands: a low Chinese dais with cusped decor replaces the western tri-legged stool. Also the artist at Dunhuang has added a landscape setting of rocks and hills in the foreground.

A8. The entry into Kapilavastu is rendered with all the pomp and splendor that is described in the texts: Maya, embracing the crown prince, rides in a chariot drawn by yoked dragons with flying streamers and musicians. Maya with her son in her lap sits in the back of a chariot; an attendant in front holds the reins of the dragon steeds. The entourage is accompanied by devas. (FIGURE 36 top right) Once again there is a telling exchange: a team of dragons draw the palanquin, instead of the naga, lion, or elephant of the western renditions. Here too Chinese prototypes replace foreign images, in this case it is the dragon chariot from the *Songs of the South*, which transport shamans through the ethereal realm.[46] In the pictorial arts the illustration of the *Luoshen Fu* attributed to Gu Kaizhi has the closest parallel: the goddess of the Luo River is in a chariot drawn by dragons, and the chariot has similarly shaped sides and a round canopy over head strung with streamers.[47]

A9. Approaching the chariot from the left is Suddhodana and his retinue. Informed that his wife has given birth to a son, he joyfully rides out on horseback to meet them. A servant holds a royal canopy over his head, he is in the company of three outriders. (FIGURE 37 top mid)

A10. The last scene is difficult to see in its entirety. There is a tiled roof pavilion beyond which is an elephant on whose back is a flaming jewel. (FIGURE 37 top left) Perhaps these are the seven possessions of the Chakravartin given to the prince at birth, but the general, minister, horse, wife, and flaming wheel are missing.

B: EAST WALL: SECOND REGISTER

B11. The first scene of the second register may be the naming of the child. The baby is shown as large as an adult, haloed, and wearing only a loincloth. (FIGURE 37, second register, middle right) His father and a servant accompany him. Brahmin elders are assembled on the left; their leader kneels reverently with his hands piously clasped.

B12. The following group of scenes relates the taking of the child into the ancestral temple to be blessed:

> *As they approached the city, but had not yet reached the gates, the Brahmin sages all said: "It is fitting that the crown prince pay his respects to the images of the gods." They carried him into the temple, and then the various statues all fell forward. The brahmins said among themselves: "The crown prince is truly a god, truly excellent. He caused the gods to reverence him." Though they named him crown prince, they called him god of gods.*

The chief brahmin carries the child, who has been drawn in natural scale; they are at the temple's entrance. Two attendants follow. The temple is a single-story main hall with lateral chambers drawn in a zigzag manner—two on the left, three on the right. On the right the elders with the baby proceed to the chapel. In the background are a group of leafy trees.

B13. In the next scene a view inside the chapel reveals the chief brahmin holding the baby with two attendants nearby. (FIGURE 37, second register, mid)

B14-18. are illustrations of the Thirty-two miracles that accompanied the birth of the Buddha. All of the texts agree that there are the Thirty-two signs, differing only in their sequential arrangement and in some minor details. The miracles begin with:

> *A brightness scattered all about, up to the twenty-eighth heaven and down to the eighteenth hell. Everywhere was illuminated. The reflected light was so great that it made day of night. And heaven sent down thirty-two marvelous responses:*

and

> *The earth shook mightily (while tomb mounds remained undisturbed). Roads and byways cleaned themselves, and the noisome places became sweet smelling. The withered old trees within the borders of the kingdom all burst forth with flowers. Gardens spontaneously produced rare sweet fruits. The earth bore lotus flowers as big as cartwheels.*

The artist attempts to portray the miraculous happenings literally. In the limited narrative technique of the sixth century, the results are sometimes comical. For example the first miracle's *"Roads and byways of themselves were cleansed, the noxious places became sweet smelling."* the artist has made use of human agents sweeping the ground with a broom to show the divine happening which defies pictorial representation. (FIGURE 36 middle register, center) Strewn on the ground are huge lotus buds and in the background are lightly drawn fruit trees. For *"The deaf, blind, and those suffering from all manner of diseases were completely healed"* the artist has painted a small figure enclosed in a box-like shelter who is apparently defecating. (FIGURE 36 middle register, right) The artist has rendered the discomforts of the disease, not being able to picture the cure. At Dunhuang several miracles may be rendered in the same scene.

B15. It may be that for the miracle *"Within the realm all the pregnant women gave birth to sons,"* two of the figures are drawn sitting in a pavilion and before them a messenger reports the miraculous simultaneous births, which elsewhere represent all thirty-two miracles.

B16. A single-story pavilion houses an attendant. Before him is a rack with neatly folded clothes that depict: *"Garments and bedding were hung on racks."* Illustrating the lines: *"Winds cleared away the clouds and the sky was brilliant. Heaven sent down a fine rain that spread fragrant moisture everywhere,"* is a composition of a space cell comprised of trees; at center is a divine being and to the right a sky demon stands. (FIGURE 35 middle register, left) This is a typical post-Han depiction of a sky creature like those found in the third century Yinan tomb in Shandong, with its chicken legs, flowing hair, animated wings, and open mouth.[48] In the upper right a stream of water with lotus buds may be an attempt to depict the fine fragrant rain.

B17. Placed in a small pavilion is a flaming jewel that resembles a leaf-shaped mandorla; in an adjacent pavilion is a servant with another jewel-like object and an attendant. The mandorla represents here, as on statues of the Buddha and other divinities, the emanation of brilliant light. (FIGURE 35 middle register, center) These pictures illustrate:

> *Treasures hidden in the earth all came forth of themselves. Jewels stored away unveiled their brilliance. Supernatural pearls, bright as the moon, were suspended in the palace halls. There were (like) lamps lit in the sky that were never used again.*

B18. Next is a quite literally rendering of: *"The sun, moon, and constellations all halted. Shooting stars came down to attend the crown prince's birth. The jeweled canopy of the god Brahma arched over the whole palace."* To the upper right are the sun and moon, and a small but ornate pavilion with four columns is Brahma's canopy. There is a ram drawn in the sky, a reference to a constellation sighted at the time. On earth a youth is seated in a tiled-roof single-story building. (FIGURE 35 middle register, center)

B19. In the foreground are two large jars on bases, above them are two basins filled with mounds of food. Illustrating *"A myriad of precious jars hung filled with sweet dew. A hundred heavenly tasty dishes were spontaneously spread out in front."* (FIGURE 35 middle register, center)

B20. On the right is the chariot made of the seven precious materials and drawn by celestial spirits to render the miracle of *"Heavenly spirits yoked to a sweet dew chariot came pulling a treasure."* A horse pulls the chariot (which exactly resembles the one in the first register). Two devas fly along side it, one leads. Next, the king sits in his palace; in front of him is a winged lion in a setting typical of Dunhuang—conical mountains and a few wispy trees. (FIGURE 34, middle register, left) Above him are two courtly looking figures and on the right three servants flank a pavilion. Perhaps this is an illustration of: *"Five hundred white lions' male cubs coming forward from the Snow Mountains (the Himalayas) stationed themselves at the city gate."*

B21-24. Suddhodana is seated in his palace. On its roof are two divine females. In the upper right two heavenly, haloed beings with fluttering scarves descend. (FIGURE 34 middle register, right) Two additional celestial maidens hold small bowls in their hands. These pairs of divine females only suggest the richness of the scriptural account.

> *All the houris of heaven appeared above the (royal) handmaiden's shoulders. The daughters of the dragon kings circled around the palace before taking their places. The myriad jade maidens of heaven holding peacocks' whisks appeared in the palace halls. The houris of heaven, holding golden vases filled with fragrant essences, ranged themselves in attendance in the air.*

B25. At center an aerial view of a lake is treated rather abstractly as a rectangular shape, trees surround it. (FIGURE 34 middle register, right) The accompanying text is: *"All rivers with their myriad currents halted, (their waters) clean and pure."* Within the rectangle are two naked figures, who may be, as in the westernized art of Gandhara and the Silk Road, anthropomorphic representations of water spirits. This conception is familiar in China, where rivers like the Xiang and Luo were personified as divine females. The register ends with a hilly landscape, a leafy tree, and a small quadruped running off to the left, which may allude to: *"Poisonous vipers hid themselves, while auspicious birds flew about singing."*

C: THIRD REGISTER EAST WALL
C26. Here a hunter with a bow and arrows rides on horseback in chase after a group of deer running to the left through a range of small stylized mountains illustrating: *"Those who fished, hunted, or harbored feelings of anger and evil, simultaneously became benevolent and merciful."* (FIGURE 34 third register, bottom right)

C27. This illustration of a figure being pulled by two others from a flaming pit may be a representation of hell, for one of the miracles was *"All the torments in the prisons of the earth (the hells) were halted."*

C28. Next is a pavilion, beside it a haloed figure kneels reverently, which perhaps illustrates: *"Tree spirits appeared in human (form), bowed their heads in worship. And at the same time in the sixteen great kingdoms there was naught that was not elegant and rare beyond (measure)."*

C29. The narrative resumes with the following scenes. The rishi Asita who lived in seclusion on Fragrant Mountain, Gandhamadana, is in deep meditation when he becomes aware of the miraculous events. By these supernatural signs, he knows the Buddha is born. Here he is shown seated in his mountain home in a meditative pose: Asita supports his chin on his right hand; his left leg is bent beneath him. (FIGURE 34, bottom register, left)

C30. This is a totally abstract rendering of a very large, extraordinary flower. Perhaps it is the *udumbara* of the text, which fell to earth spontaneously producing Lion Kings and alerted Asita of the birth of the bodhisattva. [49]

C31. Asita, dressed as an ascetic in dhoti and scarf, his hair drawn up in a topknot, sets out for Kapilavastu to see the newborn. (FIGURE 36, bottom register right) Transported by magical power, he flies through the air. On the left a messenger reports his arrival to the king who is seated in his palace. Behind the palace, servants are instructed to prepare the crown prince.

C32. Asita reads the special signs, or *lakshana*. (FIGURE 36, bottom register, right) Haloed and seated on the left, the sage holds the baby in his arms; his right arm is bent, the right foot rests on his left knee, just as in Gandharan representations. The king is seated on a low dais. Asita predicts the child's twin destiny—world ruler or world savior. On the right are servants. An interesting genre detail is the king's slippers placed beneath his seat.

C33. Harem women attempt to entertain the prince lodged in his palace. This must be one of the seasonal residences that Suddhodana had constructed, decorated with precious objects, and filled with innumerable beautiful and talented women. He hoped that these pleasures would distract the prince from his religious calling.

C34. Because these attempts to amuse the prince fail, the king summons his advisers to devise other stratagems. (FIGURE 36, bottom register left) In the GXYJ they suggest education. Suddhodana is in his hall. Seen from the rear are his three advisers seated in front of him, three others stand in the background. A servant waits outside the chamber.

C35. Suddhodana has arranged for a teacher, Visvamitra, to educate his son. The king stands in his palace awaiting his arrival. On the left is a servant. A minister of the court kneels before the chosen tutor, and the prince approaches on horseback. (FIGURE 37, bottom register, center) Two men attend the brahmin scholar, one of whom holds a parasol over his head.

C36. The young prince is in a two-story palace with two attendants. Visvamitra approaches on horseback with his two servants. Although all the texts agree as to the outcome of the lesson, the GXYJ describes the interchange in great detail—the crown prince had knowledge of 64 languages and provided a moral maxim for each of the letters of the Sanskrit alphabet. Cave 290 does not include the familiar Gandharan scenes of the ride to school in an ox cart, a detail that was described in only one of the texts,[50] or the lesson at school. In Chinese style the tutor visits the home of the pupil.

D: WEST WALL TOP REGISTER
D37. On the west ceiling are the events in the adolescence of the crown prince. These illustrations begin with Suddhodana again consulting his advisers who this time suggest the prince engage in the study of the martial arts. (FIGURE 38, top register right)

D38. This is the first of a reoccurring image—the dejected prince in his palace.

D39. A figure is seated in a pavilion accompanied by two servants. In the background is another building housing two figures; there is no specific event to associate with this scene. (FIGURE 38, top register left)

D40. Siddhartha leaves the palace gates; on the right, within the gate, are Suddhodana and a servant; a second attendant stands near by; and a third sweeps his path.

D41. Painted here is the elephant that got stuck in the city gate and blocked traffic. In one text the king wants to test his son's strength and has the elephant placed in the city gates; in another a jealous cousin, Devadatta, stuns the elephant with a blow dealt with his fist. A younger cousin, a more benevolent soul, tries unsuccessfully to dislodge it from the city gates. (FIGURE 39 top register right)

D42. The young prince approaches, picks up the elephant carcass with one hand, and hurls it over the city walls. The Qizil prototype, much indebted to western artistic traditions, is altered here. In the Stepped Cave the elephant is shown twice—the bodhisattva, naked but for dhoti and jewels, stands astride the animal, and then holds it in his right hand about to hurl it; his left hand rests on his thigh. In contrast the Dunhuang painter has the fully dressed prince holding the elephant over his head in his right hand; his left rests at his side. Did the artists have no idea as to the size and weight of such a creature? The narration describes not only the magnificent strength of the crown prince but also the miraculous recovery of the elephant.

On the left side of this scene is the wrestling competition. Here, as at Qizil, the crown prince watches his two cousins engage in a test of strength, but at Dunhuang the two episodes are conflated into one scene—the winner of the match is Nanda who concedes superior strength to the crown prince, as described in the text of the XXBJ.[51](FIGURE 39, top register middle)

D43. In the archery contest the three cousins stand in a line inside a pavilion, holding their bows and arrows ready. On the left the targets are arranged horizontally; there are seven iron drums, as stipulated in the text. At the bottom of the panel are conical hills. (FIGURE 39-41 top register right) The Qizil convention of using a rectangular shape for an aerial view of the body of water that sprang up when the prince's arrow entered the earth is employed here but the rectilinear shape has been replaced with an undulating oval placed between the third and fourth targets.   The long narrative that relates the retrieving of the prince's grandfather's bow is not included, nor is the sword contest which, though not described in the sutras, was sometimes illustrated in Afghanistan and Qizil.

D44. The victorious prince rides a white horse; a servant holds a parasol over his head.   On the left is the city gate--a two-storied building with lateral wings.   By the doorway are two servants. Welcoming the crown prince on the road are five figures on the left, four on the right.

D45. The following scenes relate the nuptial events.   To the right Suddhodana and Mahaprajapati, the prince's stepmother (Maya had died a week following childbirth) come out of the palace to greet the crown prince's father-in-law, who kneels before them. Behind him is a servant. On the left is the palace, treated in a unique way. Behind the main chamber are two rooms, both parallel to the first; each has two servants, on the left are four more attendants. (FIGURE 41, top register)

E: WEST WALL SECOND REGISTER
E46. Suddhodana is seated in his palace instructing his two servants in the marriage preparations.

E47. A horse-drawn chariot leads the bridal cortege, which is similar to the one portrayed on the east wall with streamers flying from a circular canopy. (FIGURE 41 middle register left) Four people watch the procession pass on the road, four devas or angels in the sky play music. The marriage ceremony is not illustrated.

E48. Life in the harem has the prince and Yashodhara, his wife, in the main chamber; in the wings are attendants, some of whom play musical instruments.   To the right one of the crown prince's servants kneels before the king to report the prince's discontent.

E49. Very upset by the servant's report, Suddhodana calls his advisers to suggest the means by which they can prevent the crown prince from leaving the secular world. The king is in his palace with two servants; on the right, housed in an adjacent building, are four of his advisers.

E50. In the depictions of the four exits, the artist has tried to enliven the monotonous sequence of events by alternating the color of the mount and attire of the crown prince. (FIGURE 41-39 middle register) Each episode is similarly rendered. He exits the city portal on horseback; the gate is on the left, the groom on the right, and the subject of the encounter is on the far right. This is followed by a portrayal of the brooding prince at home, as he grows ever more sorrowful. (FIGURE 40 middle register) Here he is leaving the east gate when he encounters an old man, stooped over, and fully dressed (unlike Cave 254).

E51. The prince meditates on the nature of old age. Then he makes a second foray, this time exiting the south gate, and meets a sick man. In contrast to this early version of the scripture, the GXYJ incorporates much of Chinese contemporary thinking about illness.[52] This time the prince, riding a black horse, emerges from the city gate. (FIGURE 39 middle register left) There he sees the sick man sitting with his legs out-stretched, supporting himself on his elbows. Behind him on the left are additional figures.

F52. Once more the prince pensively broods in his palace.

F53. Now riding a white horse, his garments in a contrasting dark color, the prince encounters a funeral cortege. (FIGURE 39 middle register right) The hearse is a gabled chariot, typical of Han funerary monuments. On the surface of the gabled top are intertwining dragons ridden by a *xian*, an anthropomorphic symbolic representation of the immortal soul. This theme is common among mortuary articles, like those from Eastern Han tombs from Luoyang.[53] The lower part of the chariot has three panels; the two vertical ones now lack decoration. Two oxen haul the carriage; they are drawn quite naturalistically: the one in the foreground, in profile, lifts its head and whisks its tail; the second lowers its head. Leading the procession is a figure carrying a tray of the funeral offerings. The GXYJ text description of the image of the funeral chariot and banners concurs with the artist's rendering, unlike the Qizil representations:

> *Thus the crown prince went out for a ride in his chariot leaving from the west gate. The god again (miraculously) made a dead man in a funeral chariot with flying banners that was followed by a woman and boys crying as they escorted it. The crown prince asked what kind of man is this?* [54]

F54. The prince has returned to his home in an increasingly depressed mood.

F55. Riding his white horse out of the city for another excursion, the prince, in dark attire, has his fourth encounter, this time with a brahmin ascetic. (FIGURE 38 middle register center) The artist has painted the mendicant as Asita, in an untailored garment wrapped around the waist with the end thrown over the left shoulder, leaving his right shoulder bare. Chandaka, on the left, explains the religious convictions of the man who left home to wander the world in quest of the truth.

F56. The prince in the posture of royal ease is in his palace, more dejected than ever. In the side hall is Chandaka.

F57. This is the scene of the first meditation, an event that has been placed at the various stages in the texts.[55] In order to distract his son from a religious vocation, Suddhodana asks him to oversee the plowing of the fields. The young prince sits down in the shade of a tree and enters into deep meditation. The tree under which he is seated miraculously bends its branches to protect him.[56] Underneath one of the two trees painted on the right is the seated pensive prince (FIGURE 38 middle register right). The farmer and his ox are in the foreground. The second half of the story is told in the next register.

F58. Suddhodana rides his horse out of the city gate on his way to check up on his son. Next, moved by the miracle of the shade, he kneels before Siddhartha sitting under the tree. Chandaka stands on the left, and servant is to the right. The artist rendered the tree very large as if to draw attention to it and bring to mind the miracle that defied depiction.

F: WEST WALL THIRD REGISTER

F59. The prince is in his palace with Yashodhara and a servant. As he sits in meditation a deva flies down to tell him that it is time to fulfill his vow to leave home. He goes to the lateral chamber and instructs Chandaka to prepare Kanthaka. In the adjacent room Chandaka gets the horse ready. (FIGURE 38 bottom register right)

F60. The gods beg the prince to depart. Flying in the air, they hover with their hands pressed together.

F61. On the right is the city gate, on the left the prince rides Kanthaka, whose hooves are upheld by celestials to prevent any noise from awakening the palace inhabitants. (FIGURE 38 bottom register left) A principal event in the sutra has been omitted, the sleep of the harem women which so delighted western artists.

F62. Having ridden about 40 li outside of Kapilavastu, the prince dismounts Kanthaka, gives his royal jewels to his groom, and bids farewell to both of them. (FIGURE 39, bottom register right) In the sutras this is a very touching scene, the climax of which is the horse's grief; he kneels to lick his master's feet and tears roll down his eyes; this is just how it was painted. On the left is Chandaka to whom the bodhisattva has given his princely jewels.

F63. The return of Chandaka and Kanthaka to Kapilavastu is next; the groom holds the jewels in his right hand, the reins of the rider-less horse in his left.

F64. News of the great departure is a cause of immense sorrow in the palace. Suddhodana and Mahaprajapati come out to greet the groom, servants stand behind them. On the left, Yashodhara, overwhelmed by grief, embraces the horse's neck; exact compositional parallels may be seen on reliefs from Swat, Gandhara and Amaravati.[57]

F65. Suddhodana charges five men with the job of finding the prince and bringing him back. They stand in a line in front of the pavilion, receiving their instructions from the seated king. (FIGURE 40 bottom register right)

F66. The five men on horseback, in file, set off for the search. Small conical hills and a large leafy tree in the background suggest mountain scenery.

F67. Failure of the search party to bring the prince home and the prince's emaciated state are reported to the king who is in his pavilion with several attendants. (FIGURE 41 bottom register right)

F68. Chandaka reports his intention to the king. He will mount a second search party, and bring food and supplies to the prince.

F69. Chandaka finds the bodhisattva practicing austerities with the five men of the search party, who afraid to return home without him, joined him in his spiritual quest. (FIGURE 41, bottom register left)

F70. Having achieved enlightenment, and now a Buddha, he preaches the first sermon. Buddha is seated on a high, double-lotus pedestal, he has a large leaf mandorla and his hands are in the gesture of teaching. He is shown with four followers. The composition ends with mountain scenery.

Beginning with the decision to depart, many scenes were omitted, like the sleep of the women and cutting off the long princely hair (having discarded his identity as crown prince, the bodhisattva took off his sword and lopped off his hair). Did the Gansu artist intentionally neglect this because they were considered an impiety, for it was the Confucian belief that the body and hair were gifts from one's parents and to disfigure one's self was an act of ingratitude? In a similar cultural distillation did the artists reject the harem scenes and cover Maya's semi-naked, voluptuous body with heavy robes? Such promiscuous portrayals were perhaps offensive to the Chinese sensibility. Since human suffering was never considered a subject for artistic expression in China, the omission of the emaciated figure of the prince during his years of self-mortification is easy to understand. However the wedding ceremony, encounter with the hunter, and exchange of clothes, the first meal, gift of grass, and temptation of Mara, to mention some of the more important scenes, are all missing. These omissions are quite unaccountable in terms of iconography. The temptation in particular was of such significance that at times it alone was portrayed in large scale in caves of the earlier phase. In addition there is the curious inconsistency that the Buddha preached to four not the traditional five at the first sermon.[58] There is no satisfactory explanation. Such omissions are not the result of an incomplete text. Conversely, the artist has rendered many relatively insignificant scenes of the early life in scrupulous detail, following the text exactly, like the visit to the temple, the sage Asita going to the palace, or the selection of the schoolmaster. Such scenes are evidence of the style of scriptural illustration in which no selection of scenes is possible, because of the one to one relationship between the depictions and the text written below. As for the hasty ending to the illustrations of Cave 290, one may speculate that the patron who had commissioned these narratives had a special interest in them and aided the artists in their rendering by providing an illustrated sutra and explaining the narrative details. This patron may have lost interest in the project or grown sick, or perhaps the artist had misjudged his space and was forced to abruptly finish.

Other Western Wei and post Wei caves have many instances of narrative depictions of jatakas—like the Mahasattva and Syama--which remain popular despite the growing lack of interest in both scenes of the life of the Buddha and other pre-Mahayanist themes. For example the story of filial piety of the *Syama jataka* is painted on a narrow strip of ceiling of Cave 296 of the Northern Zhou. On the lower section of the main wall the *Sumati jataka* appears. In a similar fashion other jatakas appear on the ceiling of Cave 196 of the same period.[59] Caves 301 of the Northern Zhou and 302, 303, 417, 423, and 419 of the Sui also have stories of jatakas painted on the gabled ceiling of the forehall.

III. SCENES OF THE LIFE OF THE BUDDHA AS A MINOR THEME

In the third phase, depictions of biographical narratives appear in the most abbreviated manner. One familiar theme is the two small symmetrically placed figures of the bodhisattva on a mount in the two corners of the ceiling or on the rear wall flanking the main niche. Usually the birth, represented by the bodhisattva riding a white elephant is on the right; the great departure, with the bodhisattva riding his mount Kanthaka, whose hooves are upheld by four celestials, is on the left. Found relatively late at Dunhuang in Sui and Tang caves, this iconographical theme is also frequently seen both on stone stele and at other rock-cut caves.[60]

Cave 280, ascribed to the Sui dynasty, is unique for it pairs an abbreviated representation of the conception with the first sermon. (FIGURE 42, a) Painted against a white background, the bodhisattva descends on a white elephant. Light red, blue, and black pigments render fine linear patterns of Han, or Chinese style cloud swirls and lotus buds. Two Han celestials descend in addition to the four tiny attendants. For the first sermon the Buddha appears to be reading a scroll, five monks are in attendance and two celestials descend on cloud swirls. In Cave 278, also from the Sui dynasty, the more usual set is found. Here against a red background, the bodhisattva rides a black elephant, accompanied by four celestials. Kanthaka is portrayed as white and the escaping prince is attended by at least one celestial. The depiction in Cave 397 is similar, only the divine attendants are far more numerous (seven for the conception) and are drawn larger in scale.[61] This theme continues into the early Tang, for example in Cave 375.[62]

IV. SCENES OF THE DEATH: PARINIRVANA

Representations of the death are treated as a separate development in this study for they do not belong to the traditional narrative biographical cycle. They were not a part of the life as it appeared at Dunhuang and emerged much later than the other biographical scenes—the earliest example is attributed to the Northern Zhou period (550-570). The image of the death scene at Dunhuang is something of a paradox. In general, scenes of dying are extraordinarily rare in China. Representations of human suffering were never considered an appropriate subject for artistic expression.[63] This bias is reflected in the fact that in relation to the other narrative biographical scenes, not only does the death scene appear rather late at Dunhuang and at Maijishan,[64] it is depicted for only a short period of time—around two hundred years. Another anomaly characteristic of representations of the death here, as at Qizil, is that various formats are employed—narrative cycle, iconic mural, and/or sculpture.

Illustrations of the death may be divided into two categories: representations of the death cycle—the final farewell, preparation of the corpse, cremation, putting out the flames, and division of the relics—and large iconic images of the dying Buddha. As at Qizil, the death is portrayed on the rear wall of the chamber as a mural or a combination of a large-scale sculpture of the Buddha with painted narrative figures or complete sculptural representation of the event. According to the dating established by the Dunhuang Institute, the peak of these illustrations occurs during the Sui period, and they continue to be represented into the Tang. The death occurs fairly frequently in eight caves at Dunhuang over several periods: the Northern Zhou— Cave 428; Sui Caves 294 (Pelliot 126), 420, 295, 280; and Tang 158 (Pelliot 19), 440 (Pelliot 12), and 255 (Pelliot 58).

Not told in the early biographical sutras, the great decease is related in the *Mahaparinirvana sutra*, one of the popular texts found at Dunhuang.[65] Dharmaraksha, royal adviser to the Northern Liang ruler Mengxun translated this text into Chinese as early as the fifth century.[66] Despite the fact that Mengxun was a noted Buddhist patron, none of the caves from that era have an illustration of the death. The *Mahaparinirvana sutra* is unique in Buddhist literature because there are so many scriptural versions—some distinctly Mahayanist, others pre-Mahayana. Similarly, among representations of the death, some clearly relate to the earlier tradition, others are associated with Mahayanism. The clues to the interpretation of the scenes are in the details of the portrayal as well as in the iconographic-artistic context in which they are placed.

In contrast to the earliest representations, later portrayals of the parinirvana include not only members of different nations and various races but also divine beings among whom are bodhisattvas, guardian kings, and Buddhas. In the company of the thousand Buddha theme and the twin Buddha miracle, these later visions of the death take on the connotation of a heavenly assumption rather than just passing away. The death scene becomes a universally celebrated triumphal entry to the afterlife. Thus the later Dunhuang death scenes may be seen within the religious context of Mahayanism. Their appearance is altered and as a result so is their meaning. Although all Buddha's reincarnations throughout the eons followed the same earthly career, this scene is uniformly identified with Shakyamuni.

A. NARRATIVES OF THE DEATH CYCLE
Cave 294 and 420

Caves 294 and 420 illustrate the series of events according to the scriptures—the farewell, Kashyapa's late arrival, wrapping of the coffin, burning of the coffin, and battle of the relics. Prototypes for these kinds of scenes are present among the Gandhara bas-reliefs and the caves of Qizil but are so far absent among the Guptan-era artistic monuments. Though the compositions reflect the western prototypes, the style of expression is Chinese. Cave 294, attributed to the Sui dynasty, has six scenes from the parinirvana cycle told on the left sidewall.[67] The small size scenes are not separated by architectural units but by figural disposition. Beginning on the left, the Buddha is lying on a funeral couch, bidding farewell to his disciples. (FIGURE 43, a) The couch is placed on a diagonal and in reverse perspective, two space-creating devices common in Chinese painting. Monks in front of the couch are arranged in a semicircular group, further suggesting spatial recession. Haloed Malla princes stand behind the couch, as is traditional. A few hills to the right provide the only setting. In the second scene the Buddha, reclining on the bed with his followers crowded around it, is dying. In the background, two leafy trees drawn in a feathery brush style represent the sala grove. The group surrounding the Buddha has become more heterogeneous. In addition to the usual monks and royal Mallas are devas and bodhisattvas. The elder disciple Kashyapa stands in his traditional place at the feet of the master. The two female figures in the foreground are a new addition. Their identity is difficult to ascertain; this may be Maya, the Buddha's mother, as later she appears in the illustrations. In the third scene, which is substantially the same as the second, the coffin is ablaze, but the flames are not easy to discern. Devas descend on clouds to witness the proceedings. The fourth scene shares the same general distribution of compositional elements, but the coffin, no longer placed in three-quarter profile, is shown frontally with the figures assembled around it. In the fifth scene, which is higher up on the wall, all of the same elements are again present in the depiction of extinguishing of the flaming coffin. The battle for the relics is the sixth depiction: the cavalry, dispatched by the contending kingdoms, sets forth with charging lances. Below the brahmin sage Drona who stands among the battlements of the city divides the relics. This composition is close to the Qizil prototypes. The other characters are distributed in the two wings of the city wall that project into space. In China battle scenes are extremely infrequent; this battle of the relics being one of the rare exceptions.[68]

These scenes from the death cycle from Cave 294 are extraordinarily complete. Gandharan prototypes are apparent in the exact appropriation of compositions as well as in the literalness of the depictions. It seems clear that the paintings were based on an illustrated sutra in which western style figural compositions were preserved, though the technique of painting has been sinified. Fine outlines and an overall linearity replace the three-dimensional illusionism of western anatomical depictions. The dramatic use of space-creating devices in the rendering of the architecture, furniture, and figures reveals the growing confidence of artists in the Sui period. There is also a new awareness of landscape settings absent in the western prototypes.

Cave 420

Painted on one of the quadrants of the ceiling of Cave 420 are small-scale scenes from the death; the other three sections have illustrations of the *Lotus sutra*. The colors are extraordinary for Dunhuang—predominantly blue, green, and black with gold for the Buddha's skin.[69] At center of the north quadrant of the ceiling is a reclining Buddha that appears huge in size compared to the other figures. Bidding farewell to his followers, he rests his head on his right hand. Crowded behind the bed is a throng of nearly 70 figures including the more conventional mourners distributed at the head, foot, and in front of the bed. Two gorgeously blooming sala trees frame the upper area. Above the mourners bright lights and a rain of flowers signify the accompanying celestial events. Occupying the remaining upper section of this quadrant is a series of large-size, golden-skinned preaching Buddhas with an audience. To the left are several more episodes of the death cycle. In the upper left is the farewell of Kashyapa: the coffin is open, enclosed by mourning figures. In the lower right the coffin bursts into flames. In the right foreground is a landscape of piled-up blue and green hills. (FIGURE 43a)

Representations found among the cave-chapels at Maijishan should also be mentioned. Among the dozens of caves are two rare examples. These small murals conform to the size and placement of the narrative scenes at Dunhuang. But presented here is only the climatic farewell. These paintings, it is interesting to note, are ascribed to the Northern Wei period, somewhat earlier than the Dunhuang representations.[70]

B. ICONIC REPRESENTATIONS OF THE DEATH

Iconic representations of the death basically conform to the western standard that was conceived in India by the late Gandharan period (third-fourth century) and transmitted east through Xinjiang. The early

Chinese depictions, beginning in the Northern Zhou, are murals that stylistically belong to the first phase of narratives at Dunhuang. But there is not much interest in the narrative details or in the emotional content of the scene. Like the early Gandharan representations of the pre-Mahayanist ideology, these images present the doctrine of impermanence and non-attachment: the disciples of the Buddha, both monks and Malla princes, watch the proceedings according to their level of spiritual achievement. Those who had reached a higher level of understanding show no emotion. In this early phase, the parinirvana is shown in conjunction with the stupa, a combination commonly seen in the caves of Qizil. Such is the representation of Cave 428 at Dunhuang, the earliest at the site: the Buddha reclines on his right side, rigid and impassive, hands at his side. Prominent among the mourners is a kneeling elder monk, Kashyapa, biding farewell by holding the Buddha's feet, as described in the texts.[71] (FIGURE 44) Four sala trees painted behind the monks recreate the setting of the grove in Kushinagara. But the rest of the mourning monks and princely Mallas are lined up in two rows behind the funeral couch. This painting is singular in its abbreviated treatment of the mourning figures and lack of narrative characters placed before the couch. Against a red background, a thick and unvarying line broadly renders a sketchy portrait of the participants. Few of the monks are distinguished, only a tilt of the head or wringing of the hands suggests their emotion. The Malla princes standing in a row behind the bed are also undifferentiated. It may be that this brevity of detail is indicative of an early date of execution, before the complete iconography of the scene was determined in China. It is also likely that these narrative figures were simplified because they were incidental in comparison to the importance of the oversize Buddha. Here the interest is not placed on the narration of the events, so much as on the divine nature of the Buddha, exemplified through contrasting-scale relationships.

Later representations have more narrative details, the mourners are identifiable, and many more characters are included. The scene becomes increasingly emotional; the bereaved take on more dramatic postures of lament. Among the new characters is Maya, the mother of the Buddha. The role of Maya was described in the *Maha Maya Sutra* translated in the last quarter of the fifth century; this text describes her descent from the heaven of the Thirty-three gods to earth to bid farewell to her son.[72] In Cave 295's ceiling mural above the niche on the rear wall she sits near the body; in later depictions she is shown on a cloud descending from heaven.[73] (FIGURE 45) Trees of the sala grove frame the composition, which are simply rendered. In addition to the two angels in the trees, other individuals are discernible: the semi-nude, aged ascetic supported by a lotus blossom on the right is probably the tardy Kashyapa, bidding his long-awaited farewell. Kneeling at the feet are two other monks. Maya, seated on a lotus blossom, her feet resting on a lotus flower, bows her head in grief. Behind her is Ananda, the youthful personal attendant of the Buddha. Subhadra, the last convert, sits before the funeral couch, encircled by the flames of meditation. Behind the bed four monks and members of the Mahayanist pantheon are also present. Two bodhisattvas stand behind the bed demonstrably mourning. Next are several grieving Mallas—one pulls his hair in anguish, another leans over the dead body, the third throws his head back. Present also is a Buddha, wiping a tear from his eye. This portrayal seems truly ironic for the ancient concept of the nature of the Buddha is one who has transcended all attachment. All of the figures are dark-skinned, which may be due to the oxidation of unstable pigments. Cave 280's rendition of the parinirvana, also attributed to the Sui dynasty, is very close in style to Cave 295 but the pigments are predominantly red and blue with touches of black on a white background, and all of the figures are light-skinned. In the foreground, by the feet of the Buddha, a stupa takes the place of the meditating Subhadra.[74] Maya is alone, a more sympathetic figure at the head of the bed, dressed a long gown and a tall crown. Again a Buddha is present among the figures behind the bed. Extraordinary is the grief which leads one Malla to fall over the body of the Buddha and an angel in front of the bed to reel in anguish on his back, his leg extended, his divine scarves aflutter.

C. TANG DYNASTY PARINIRVANA SCENES

Representations of the death continue into the Tang. It is during this period that the colossal sculpture of the dying Buddha appears, as at Maijishan. In mural representations of the death, the absorption of native stylistic elements is most apparent. In accord with the new narrative interest in secular Tang art that is heralded in the Tang art histories, emphasis is on the drama of events, story-telling techniques, and a new awareness of setting. In this regard Cave 332 should be mentioned for the artful rendering in Tang style of the Buddha addressing Kashyapa from the coffin painted on the upper section of the southern wall.[75] The scene is set in an early Tang landscape painted in aqua, blue, and brown. The whole is executed with colors on the brush; outlines have been entirely eliminated.

A combination of sculpture and painting media is utilized in Cave 158 (Pelliot 19B) of the middle Tang, during the period of the Tibetan occupation of Dunhuang (781-848).[76] The colossal reclining stucco Buddha takes up most of the wall surface of the enormous cave. Behind it hundreds of mourners, members of many different nations and races, are painted. (FIGURE 46) Each is clearly differentiated and shown in attitudes of extreme grief. The exotic interest in foreigners is manifested during the Tang since the eighth-century paintings of Yan Liben, or the royal tombs excavated in Xian, like that of Prince Chang Huai dated 711.[77] An international gathering of mourners is also present at Bezeklik. Similar to Qizil's later caves, Cave 158 has representations of mourners performing native funeral rituals of self-mutilation. One of the bereft holds a knife to his chest, another lifts the blade to his ear; both are about to slash their flesh; a third impales himself on a sword. (FIGURE 46a) The figures are drawn in a style that emphasizes their irregular features in an exaggerated way, like caricatures. Furthermore the cave is shaped like a coffin with the coffered ceiling as a lid; one has the impression of being inside a casket. This type of architectural design was also present at Qizil. (FIGURE 46)

Cave 440 is unusual because the whole parinirvana is a sculpture housed in a large niche. The cave is ascribed to the late Tang.[78] At center is the reclining colossal Buddha; behind him stand much smaller stucco figures of mourners. Among the Mallas, monks, and others is a Buddha. In front of the bed is Subhadra in meditation; at the feet is a female, perhaps Maya. Painted on the walls flanking the niche are colossal standing bodhisattvas; the remainder of the wall surface is decorated with the thousand Buddha theme. This sculptural presentation of the death is reminiscent of the unique, three-dimensional clay tableau of the parinirvana in Horyuji pagoda in Japan. There it is one of the four scenes oriented to the cardinal directions that occupy the central platform of the main floor; the others are the division of the relics, the Vimalarkirti and Manjusri Debate, and Maitreya in Tushita Heaven. The compositions are dated 711 according to the inventory that recorded completion of the pagoda.[79]

The sculptural treatment of the parinirvana in Cave 255 (Pelliot 58) is similar in most respects to that of Cave 240.[80] Although the cave is ascribed to the Tang period, the hand of an ignorant restorer has rendered the faces of the mourners with smiles and expressions of wonderment.

CONCLUSIONS

This analysis of the pictorial biography of Shakyamuni at Dunhuang revealed a pattern of development in Chinese Buddhist art that is applicable at other sites.   Large-scale narrative paintings of the biography of the Buddha were given a primary place only in caves of the first phase, dating to Northern Liang and Northern Wei Dynasties, specifically Caves 275 and 254, as well as Cave 428 from the Northern Zhou. In this early period the importance of Shakyamuni is paramount as the creator of the doctrine; he was the first Buddha to be introduced and the only one that had a historical basis. This first phase at Dunhuang is heavily dependent on western style compositions, figural style and narrative techniques. In particular the rectangular format with continuous narration is employed. Although most of Cave 428 is consistent with Phase I, the representations found on the walls flanking the door anticipate the second phase.

The paintings of the second phase reject the western figural prototypes of Gandhara and Qizil. Gansu artists assimilate the foreign themes and styles by framing them in native pictorial conventions. The exploration with narrative techniques and the new format of the horizontal scroll were challenging aesthetic concerns; the Dunhuang material is among the earliest evidence of the initial phases of experimentation with the scroll format. The apparent lack of familiarly with narrative techniques may have contributed to the limited number of examples of the pictorial biography of the Buddha. The artists' awkwardness in employing the horizontal scroll is evident in Cave 428 and 290. It must have been daunting to employ the new method of continuous narration.

In the second phase biographical depictions (and jatakas) are relegated to a small area of ceiling. Cave 290 with its complete pictorial biography is the single example of a continuous narration of the life of the Buddha; a remarkable fact considering the late date of execution attributed to it by the Dunhuang Institute. A close parallel is found at Yungang's Cave VI in Datong, which is significantly earlier in date.   It is indeed puzzling that there is no contemporary and comparable example of a complete pictorial of the life of the Buddha at Dunhuang; no satisfactory explanation is readily at hand. The role of the biographical narratives follows the same general trend of decreasing importance in India, Central Asia, and China. But analysis of Dunhuang narrative technique revealed that though an early dependence on western examples of expansive narrative gradually became conflated and abbreviated, it later gave way in the sixth century to narrative experimentation with the scroll format.

The sinicized depictions not only bore a resemblance to Chinese art in their compositional motifs, garments, and architecture, but also its linear organization of human experience and meticulousness in illustrating the written word. Although these representations of the life of the Buddha lack accompanying sections of scriptural texts, the importance of the written word is evident in the sequential horizontal organization of the scenes, which read from line to line like writing. The exactitude in telling the story and its details also suggests a dependence on a literary source. This relationship is observable in a comparative analysis with the written versions of the religious texts which shows the painstaking and sometimes boring repetition of pictorial details that at times manifests a total disregard of aesthetic considerations.   There is a slavish devotion to the execution of the letter. Adherence to the details in the scriptures is often favored over the pictorial prototype. Is this due to the desire for religious merit accrued by the commission or execution of the sutras, or is it for these paintings, like incantations of a magic charm, exactitude is most important? The caves that show a very close correspondence between the scriptures and illustrations are those that employ the horizontal format, Cave 290 for example. Thus with the illustration of the first sermon, the artist follows the textual version, rather than the more common image of the first sermon with five adherents in the audience. In the parinirvana narrative cycles as well, there is a closer accord between the narrative details of the scriptures than the iconic traditions that preserve the Gandharan composition.

Although there is a lack of ancient western prototypes, it seems likely that illustrated scriptures were in circulation.   In Gandhara a reconstruction of a narrative cycle is made possible by considering the hundreds of fragmentary bas-relief scenes.   There the classically inspired, complete, chronologically arranged, biographical illustrations of the life of the Buddha suggest what was lost in transportable and more perishable media. There is also testimony to the existence of portable paintings of scenes of the life of the Buddha in the Maya Cave at Qizil. Painted on a cloth being shown to King Ajatasatru is a depiction of the four great events; but this example represents only four events and these are not told in continuous narrative style. When one considers the prevalence of later illustrations of the life of the Buddha throughout Southeast Asia, the presence of such formats seems even more probable. There also is the compelling evidence of a Japanese scroll illustrating the life of the Buddha (thought to be closely based on a Chinese original) ascribed to the eighth century, the *E-Inga Kyo*. (see Chapter IV)

Finally, artists became interested in the new horizontal scroll format so that they not only represented the story of the life of the Buddha and the jatakas in the long scroll form but during the Sui and Tang period they used it to render events from the *Lotus sutra*.[81] For the most part the other texts like the *Vimalakirti Nirdesa* and most of the images from the *Lotus sutra* were rarely shown in narrative style. The Vimalakirti debate, for example, usually took the form of two compositions that framed a door wall or the rear niche—on either side was one of the contestants encircled by his retinue. But in the Tang further experimentation led the artists to use the narrative format to portray other subjects. The perils from which Guanyin can save the believer in Cave 45 of the high Tang, or the travels to the ideal city from the *Lotus sutra* of Cave 217 of the early Tang, and other themes unfold on the cave walls. These efforts must parallel the developments in narrative secular art at court.

In phase three the narratives are reduced to a single compressed image that is shown as a symmetrical pair on the rear wall or ceiling of the caves. Most commonly these are the conception and great departure. It was also during the third phase that the large-size icons of the dying Buddha are presented on the rear wall of the caves. These death scenes are part of a narrative cycle or an independent scene. This last flourish of interest in Shakyamuni that begins in the Northern Qi-Sui period is extraordinary and due to a second wave of Buddhist art and iconography—now from Guptan India to Xinjiang. The death scene is not as common in either India or China as it was in Xinjiang. In neither place is the event given the kind of prominence that such heroic deaths merit in the west. This belated interest, late in the evolution of Buddhist iconography, may also be attributable to the prominence of Mahayanist versions of the *Mahaparinirvana sutra.* Thus the importance of the death scene is not so much the telling of the demise of Shakyamuni as the presentation of a set of new ideas.

V. SILK BANNERS EXCAVATED AT DUNHUANG

Among the later depictions of the life of Shakyamuni is a group of silk votive banner paintings found at Dunhuang. Although undated, they are generally ascribed to the Tang, and sometimes more specifically to the eighth century. The problem of dating is complicated by the Tibetan conquest of Dunhuang in 781 that ended in 848. Much of the extant material was the result of M. A. Stein's coup at the "library of Dunhuang" and was distributed by him between the National Museum in Delhi and British Museum in London.[82] Unlike the imperial commissions to excavate, sculpt, and paint a cave, these banners were relatively inexpensive works to sponsor. In painting style and iconography the banner paintings do not correspond to the art in the caves for they mark a later stage of popular Buddhism that has no counterpart in the cave-chapels. This manifestation of popular Buddhism attests to the fact that a cult centered on Shakyamuni was still vital among the lower strata of society.

The vertical format employed for the depiction of the narratives may be a result of their function. It seems certain that these banners were used in festivals, hung from cords at the top as described in the histories. Hanging painted decorations was an essential part of the festivities. Given the prevalence of the images of the nativity on the banners, surely some of these were hung in celebrations commemorating the Buddha's birthday.

The compositions comprise individual scenes arranged in a vertical hierarchy. The narrative organization now follows the visual pattern of Chinese script with earlier scenes placed at the top, the later at the bottom. Often plain black borders separate one composition from another. The selection of portrayed events suggests the epitomized cycles found on Guptan stele. Sometimes the scenes are thematically related, and occasionally the epitomized events recount a cycle; other times they appear to be randomly selected. Two examples have narrative details that are so confused that the scenes remain indecipherable. The cartouches accompanying the paintings that allowed for explanatory text may be erroneously inscribed;[83] more frequently they are left blank, like their counterparts on the walls of the cave-chapels.

The banner paintings seem to be related to contemporary artistic efforts outside of Dunhuang. The Tang art historian Zhu Jingxuan records the production of banners in the capital by the artist Zhen Hong of Zhekiang who was summoned to court by Ming Huang. Chen made twelve banners illustrating the *Sutra of the Buddha's Life*, which Zhu claimed were still extant in the ninth century.[84] In general the banners share stylistic affinities with courtly Tang objects, like those housed in the Shosoin, such as the famed biwa guard, the lady and tree screen, ceramic sculptures of court beauties, in addition to extant copies of court paintings.[85] The banner artists have appropriated many of the secular details of Tang art.

Most popular among the subjects is the nativity, perhaps reflecting the childbearing concerns of the patrons. The organization of events of the nativity portrayed on several banners corresponds to the chronology in the texts.[86] At the top of one banner are the symbols of worldly power, the Chakravartin's seven treasures, representing one of the twin destinies of the bodhisattva—the all conquering wheel, the wise minister, capable general, faithful wife, horse, elephant and rich treasures. (FIGURE 47) These are rendered in Chinese style: the wife is a Tang court beauty; the horse resembles the steeds of Han Gan 's Tang paintings;[87] the Chinese official and general are similarly transformed. Next is the celestial first bath—a fabulous cloud comprised of nine dragons forms a canopy that rains over the head of the child who stands on a lotus base supported by a rock. Plump court beauties stand together encircling the child. At the bottom of the banner are the first steps: standing on lotus blossoms, the child raises his left hand to proclaim, "This is my last birth!" Around him are another group of Tang style mid-eighth-century ladies-in-waiting—plump with high-piled hairdos and voluminous robes, they resemble the images on the Ladies Screen in the Shosoin.[88]

At the top of another banner the nativity scenes begin with three figures supported by a cloud outside Maya's quarters at the top.[89] This may be the conception. Below she is being escorted in a palanquin carried by six men, a composition strongly reminiscent of a scene from Gu Kaizhi 's *Admonitions Scroll*.[90] This scene, which represents her withdrawal from court and seclusion during pregnancy, was not previously illustrated. The third scene is the birth: set in a landscape of rocky mountains, the child issues forth from Maya's right sleeve. Two handmaidens support her; a third kneels to receive the child. Secular figures now replace the ancient deities of India. In the bottom zone the child takes his first steps and makes his proclamation.

Not all banners are concerned with the nativity; two examples illustrate scenes from the great departure. One has the traditional setting: on the left is the city gate, a heavy door studded with iron bosses that surely reflects contemporary structures.[91] Kanthaka and the prince fly through the air; alongside is Chandaka. Clouds drawn beneath Kanthaka's hooves replace the celestials of western representations. Perhaps these supernatural agents were not required in a culture that celebrated flying horses.[92] One curious addition is the large athletic, dark-skinned sleeping figure by the gate; presumably this is the harem guard later interrogated by the search party in the GXYJ. Next two men on horseback pursue the prince. This is somewhat odd, for in the fourth scene the search party of five is shown. The third scene has the return of Chandaka and Kanthaka, but here, for the first time, the groom rides the mount. This type of inconsistency in detail is characteristic of the banners.

An epitomized cycle of events leading up to the enlightenment fills yet another banner; these are set in the kind of mountainous backdrop commonly found in Tang depictions, like the painted plectrum guard at the Shosoin.[93] At the top the emotional farewell of the prince to his groom and mount is placed in a setting of scaly rocks and leafy trees. Siddhartha sits on a low rock on the right, on the left both Chandaka and Kanthaka kneel; the accompanying cartouche is empty. Next the prince, seated in a similar landscape, is about to crop his hair with a sword. Two figures on the right watch; may be devas who came down to collect the hair and transport it to heaven for worship. This is the first extant representation of the scene in China. The five figures kneeling in the foreground are the men sent to find the prince and bring him home, but fearful of returning without him, they remained with him in the forest. Lastly the ascetic Gautama, stripped of his worldly possessions, sits on a rock in meditation.

One banner by the hand of a lesser artist is rather typical of many examples. There have been various interpretations as to the content of the three scenes depicted.[94] At top Buddha stands on the left giving a benediction: he extends his hand to bless the head of a brahmin ascetic;

two secular figures are on the left. It has been suggested that this is the *Dipamkara jataka*, but no narrative details justify this attribution. In the background of the second scene is a large villa inside of which is a figure lying on a bed; in the foreground is a sick figure with attendant, on the right is a noble with servant, and on the far right is a figure transported by a cloud. It has been proposed that this is a representation of the three evils of life—old age, sickness, and death.[95] Here too the supporting details are lacking, hampering certain identification with the traditional representations. On another banner, really just a fragment, two of the four encounters are depicted in the traditional manner with a correct accompanying inscription in the cartouche.[96] (FIGURE 48) The third scene is clearly the dream of Maya. Asleep in her palatial quarters, the queen lies on her right side; descending on a cloud on the right is the bodhisattva riding a white elephant; two deities accompany them. The fourth scene is a puzzle—outside the palace compound are a queen and her maid.

Other scenes painted on the silk banners include the education, feats of physical superiority, and additional examples of flight and pursuit. These scenes which deal with the princely career of the bodhisattva must have been particularly charming for the devotees who, like the later Indian worshipers of Krishna, reveled in his extraordinary capacities as a youth. Significantly absent are versions of the first sermon, the miracles at Shravasti and Samkassa, and the death cycle. It is neither instructive nor necessary to catalogue the subjects painted on the banners at Dunhuang to be able to understand the persistence of the cult of Shakyamuni on a popular level, despite an apparent lack of interest elsewhere. To a large extent these popular illustrations reflect the needs of the community. Also styles of contemporary Tang court art appear—the use of landscape passages, the images of the architecture and the feminine ideal court lady.

ENDNOTES

1. Ch'en 1972: 31 considers the story possible.

2. Zurcher 1972: 27 discusses these and offers the mention of the Sanskrit terms for the Buddhist devotees *sramana* and *upasaka* in the Zhang Heng "Ode on the Western Capital" of the second century.

3. This first century Memorial of Prince Ying of Chi is often quoted; see A. Soper, *Literary Evidence for Early Buddhist Art in China* (Ascona: Artibus Asiae, 1960): 1; Ch'en 1972: 31 ff, from which this translation of Xiang Kai's memorial is taken.

4. Ch'en 1972: 31.

5. Ch'en 1972: 33ff.

6. Notably the Ma Hao caves reported by R. Edwards, "The Cave Reliefs at Ma Hao," *Artibus Asiae*, vol. XVIII, no. 1 (1954): 5-25, no. 2: 103-129. There a seated Buddha is found on the lintel of the tomb door. Wu Hung has identified and discussed the import of other such Han depictions of Buddha on mirrors, jars, and other media; see Wu Hung, "Buddhist Elements in Early Chinese Art 2nd and 3rd centuries A.D.)," *Artibus Asiae*, vol. XLVII, no. 3-4 (1986): 263-352.

7. Ch'en.

8. A series of essays dedicated to the social situation at the end of the Han is found in *State and Society in Early Medieval China,* ed. A. Dien, (Stanford Univ. Press, 1990); especially those by C. Leban, P. Ebrey and Mao Hankuang.

9. Several admirable studies have discussed the introduction of Buddhism: Ch'en 1972; E. Zurcher, *The Buddhist Conquest of China* (2 vols.) (Leiden: Brill Publ., 1959); and A.Wright, *Buddhism in Chinese History* (Stanford, 1959).

10. Soper 1960, Liang entry # 20, p. 77.

11. *Zhongguo meishu quanji: Sichuan shikou diaosu meishu,* vol. 13, Li Jijing, ed. (Beijing: Wenwu Press, 1988): 6 ff, a few isolated examples of Buddhist images from the Han are shown in the introduction. The material from Wanfosi is now in the Provincial Museum of Sichuan in Chengdu. The cache of sculpture from the temple is ascribed to the fifth to sixth centuries. One example of a narrative is an illustration from the *Lotus sutra* carved in low relief on the back of a stele dated 427.

12. L. Hurvitz, "The Wei Shu Chapters on Buddhism and Taoism," *Yun Kang* 32 vols. (Tokyo, 1952) vol. XV: 40.

13. Soper 1960: Sung entry # 27, p. 51. The *Kao seng chuan* iii records the first depiction of the *Dipamkara jataka*. Painted by a priest from Kashmir, named Chi Pin, in the early decades of the fifth century, it miraculously

emitted a light every night. Another interesting entry in the Wei Dynastic History's chapter on omens is the account of a golden image of the Dipamkara that wept. *Wei Shu*, cxii, p. 12, v; Soper 1960: Wei entry # 14, p. 105.

14. Ibid.: Wei entry # 16, p. 107; # 12, p. 104; and # 23, p. 109.

15. Y. Mino *The Great Eastern Temple* (Art Institute of Chicago, 1986): 77, fig. 2.

16. S. Moran, "The Death of the Buddha, a Painting at Koyasan," *Artibus Asiae* vol. XXXVI (1974): 111 ff. See chapter IV.

17. E. Zurcher "'Prince Moonlight' Messianism and Eschatology in Early Medieval Chinese Buddhism," *T'oung Pao* (Leiden) vol. LXVIII (1972): 1-58.

18. *Sichuansheng bowuguan* (Beijing: Wenwu Press, 1988): 20-ff.

19. LTMHJ, see Acker: 378ff.

20. C. P. Fitzgerald, *A Short History of China* (NY, 1950): 174.

21. *Zhongguo meishu quanji huihuabian, Maijishandeng shikou pihua*, vol. 17, Yan Wenru and Dong Yuxiang, eds. (Beijing: Wenwu Press, 1988): 6ff.

22. Among the sites the government has begun to repair and maintain are Dunhuang, Maijishan, Binglinsu, and others.

23. *Zhongguo meishu quanji: diaosubian, Binglingsideng shihkou diaosu*, vol. 9, Wang Ziyun, ed. (Beijing: Wenwu Press, 1988); one small stucco figure in Cave 169, attributed to the Western Chin, is an emaciated meditating Buddha which alludes to the ascetic life, but is not truly a narrative; see p. 20, pl. 13.

24. For the caves see *Chugoku sekkutsu tonko bakkotsu*. For discussion of jataka depictions, see Hsio-Yen Shih 1993: 59-88.

25. A stele dated to 698 recounts the founding of the site in 366 by Lozun, who had a vision of a golden light and a thousand Buddhas and so dedicated a statue. Also recorded is another, somewhat later dedication by the monk Fa Liang. *Tunhuang pihua* (Beijing: Wen Wu Press, 1959): 1 ff.

26. *Zhongguo meishu quanji huihuabian*, vol. 17: 24-30 for example at Qianfodong.

27. The pillar has a great iconographic significance as well. See J. Irwin, "The Axial Symbolism of the Early Stupa: An Exegesis," in Dellapiccola 1980: 12-38; and Snodgrass 1985.

28. On the opposite section of the north wall is a scene from the *Sivi jataka* treated in the same style.

29. *Chugoku sekkutsu, Tonko bakkutsu* vol. I: 231-233, pls. 26-37. The depiction of the *Mahasattva jataka* particularly recalls the "so-called" First or Indo Iranian style in Qizil's Peacock Cave. In addition the artist of Cave 254 directly portrays the animal savagery that later artists of China squeamishly obscure behind a sheaf of tall grass.

30. Ning Qiang, "The Emergence of the 'Dunhuang Style' in the Northern Wei Dynasty," *Orientations*, May 1992: 45-51.

31. For examples see the fragments of the Pelliot expedition in Qizil; this material, preserved in the Musee Guimet, shares the same blue green tonalities. The expedition of 1907-9 brought one fragment from the Maya Cave of members of the Buddha's audience inv. no. MG 4804, and an aquatic scene MG 17808.

32. *Chugoku sekkutsu, Tonko bakkutsu* vol. I: 236-237, pls. 52-57.

33. See Karetzky 1992: 23.

34. *Chugoku sekkutsu, Tonko bakkutsu*, vol. I: 237, pls. 58-61.

35. Tissot 1982: fig. 46 illustrates a stupa raised on a square base with columns in each corner, but the capitals of the columns have seated lions, in the Ashoka model, and there are no narratives on the body of the stupa.

36. The Dunhuang stupa has multiple stories, dome, *harmika* or super structure and eight-tiered spire. At the four cardinal points are columns, which are similar in appearance to the superstructure of the dome, harmika, and tiered spire. But the "Ashokan" reliquary has only two stories, lacks a dome, and has tall corner acroteria; the narratives, though housed in arches, celebrate *jataka* tales. For the Ashokan reliquary see A. Soper, "Japanese Evidence for the History of Architecture and Iconography of Chinese Buddhism," *Monumenta Serica* vol. IV. 2 (1940): 657, pl. XXXVIII. Soper translates Genkai's (a pupil of Qian Chen (Jian Chen) account of the Ashokan reliquary, written in his diary of his travels in the south. On p. 662 Soper ascribes the Ashokan reliquary to the fourth century stating that it probably came into the temple's possession in the sixth century. In Soper 1959, the history of the accounts of the reliquary, including that of Tao Xun and of Maspero, are given. The stupa is now in the Hangzhou Museum.

37. This figure has tentatively been identified as the Buddha Vairocana by A. Howard, "The Monumental 'Cosmological Buddha' in the Freer Gallery of Art: Chronology and Style," *Archives of Asian Art* vol. XIV (1984): 53 ff.

38. See later discussion of parinirvana scenes.

39. P. Karetzky, "Some Cosmological Schemes in the Early Caves at Dunhuang," *Journal of Chinese Religions*, Fall, vol. 20 (1992): 103-116.

40. Cave 285 of the Western Wei, *Chugoku sekkutsu, Tonko bakkutsu*, vol. I: pl. 131, may be included in this group. On the upper section of the southern wall in small scale are a series of paintings of the Buddha converting the five hundred robbers and their travails, but this theme is unrelated to scenes under study.

41. *Chugoku sekkutsu, Tonko bakkutsu*, vol. I: 253-254, figs. 174-182.

42. Northern Zhou is the ascribed date given in *Chugoku sekkutsu tonko bakkutsu*, vol. I: 253.

43. P. Karetzky, "A Chinese Illustration of the Guoqu xianzai yingguo jing at Dunhuang," *Journal of Chinese Religion* vol. 17 (1988): 54-72.

44. In Gandhara sometimes human agents give the bath; in Mathura it is always nagas (snakes). See Karetzky 1992: 18 ff.

45. They are a little differently portrayed, but the general configurations of intertwining dragons and the concept of duality defined through the use of color is found on the *fei-i* banner from tomb no. 1 Mawangdui Changsha; see *New Archaeological Finds in China* (Beijing, 1973): 42.

46. D. Hawkes, *Songs of the South* (Great Britain, reprint: 1985), "The Lord of the East," p. 113.

47. There are three versions of this scroll; all treat the dragon-drawn chariot in the same way. The Beijing version is in *Ku K'ai chih yenchiu tzuliao* (Beijing, 1962). The earliest versions are believed to be twelfth century copies of the lost late fourth-century original.

48. P. Karetzky, "The Engraved Designs on the Late Sixth Century-Sarcophagus of Li Ho," *Artibus Asiae,* vol. XLVII (1986): 81-106. See especially S. Bush, "Thunder Monsters, Auspicious Animals, and Floral Ornament in the Early Sixth-Century," *Ars Orientalis,* vol. X (1975): 19-35.

49. Soothill 1934: 456a says that it is a tree that produced fruit without flowers, except for once ever three thousand years.

50. That is the *Lalitavistara* chapter 7: 498.

51. XXBJ: 465c.

35. GXYJ: 630ff *The prince went out the southern gate. Indra transformed himself into a sick man by the side of the road. His body was emaciated but his stomach was distended, his body had grown soft, he coughed and vomited. The one hundred evils that produce illness had caused the nine apertures (of the body) to break down and drip. He was filthy from having leaked on himself. His eyes were no longer clear, he could no longer distinguish sounds. He groaned crying out loud. His hands and feet groped at the emptiness and he called out to his parents, while his grieving wife attended to him. The prince asked: "What kind of person is this?" His servant answered: "This is a sick man!" "Who gets sick?" "People are made of the four principal (elements) earth, water, air, and fire. There are 101 major diseases which combining with the (four elements) spontaneously develop and spread into 404 illness. This man is suffering the extremes of cold, heat, hunger, over-eating, thirst, and drinking too much. Now because of this disease he has lost his regularity and tosses about aimlessly. The prince sighed.*

(However, since ancient times, the Chinese have considered that there are five elements.)

53. J. Chaves, "A Han Painted Tomb at Luoyang," *Artibus Asiae,* vol. XXX (1968): 5. This is ascribed to the first century C.E.

54. GXYJ: 630ff.

55. See Karetzky 1992: 51 ff.

56. XXBJ: 467 b18.

57. Faccenna 1962: Swat Museum, inv. no. 3753: pl. CCXXXVI and Swat Museum inv. 1687, pl. CL; see GXYJ: 630.

58. Confusion appears in the texts as well, where the number and identity of the audience of the first sermon is inconsistent.

59. *Chugoku sekkutsu, Tonko bakkutsu* vol. I; for Cave 296, see pl. 184-195; for Cave 299, see pl. 196-197.

60. See the representations found at Yungang for example.

61. For Cave 290 see *Chugoku sekkutsu, Tonko bakkutsu,* vol. II, pls. 112 and 113; for Cave 278 see pls. 115-116; for Cave 397 see pls. 149 and 151.

62. *Chugoku sekkutsu, Tonko bakkutsu,* vol. III: pls. 2 and 3.

63. The only exceptions are a few battle scenes in the Han. Many have written about these cave carvings and their unusual subject matter; See Liu Xingzhen and Yue Fengxia, *Han Dynasty Stone Reliefs-the Wu Family Shrines in Shandong Province* (Beijing, 1991). Another later site where such themes are found carved is the funerary monument at I-nan.

64. *Zhongguo meishu quanji huihuabian,* vol. 17: 84 for example Cave 26. The earliest painting of the death scene attributed to the Northern Wei is at Maijishan; the painting is in the front room of Cave 127, *Maichishan* (Beijing, 1954): pl. 4.

65. Giles, *Six Centuries of at Dunhuang* (London, 1944): 4 of these are from the Stein expedition of 1906-7; none of 760 pieces of the sutra were dated.

66. Ch'en 1972: 88.

67. P. Pelliot, *Les Grottes de Touen houang* (Paris, 1914) vol. VI, pl. CCCXX-CCCXII. This cave is not illustrated in *Chugoku sekkutsu Tonko bakkutsu.* The main altar, on the rear wall of Cave 294 (Pelliot 126), has a stucco triad of the Buddha with bodhisattvas; bodhisattvas and flying devas are painted behind them. On the coving overhead is a depiction from the *Lotus sutra*; stucco triads occupied the sidewalls.

68. These are the same scenes of death mentioned in note 36.

69. *Chugoku sekkutsu Tonko bakkutsu,* vol. II: 72-73. This beautiful Sui dynasty cave has niches filled with Buddha groups on its sidewalls; flanking the rear wall niche in the upper corners is the Vimalakirti and Manjusri Debate.

70. For an example of the Wei dynasty mural restored by the Ming in Cave 1, see *Maijishan, 1954*: pl. 9; For the painting in the front room of Cave 127, see pl. 4. See also Sullivan 1969.

71. In the most ancient Pali version translated by Rhys Davids for example, see *Sacred Books of the East* vol. XIX chapter V, section 4:86.

72. A. Soper, "A T'ang Parinirvana Stele," *Artibus Asiae,* vol. XXII (1968): 160ff, translated a part of it. Tan Qing of the Southern Qi (Southern Ch'i) translated the text; it is reprinted in *Daizokyo,* vol. XII: 1012-1013.

73. *Chugoku sekkutsu, Tonko bakkutsu,* vol. II: pl. 42, illustrates the death scene.

74. *Chugoku sekkutsu, Tonko bakkutsu,* vol. II: pl. 114.
75. *Chugoku sekkutsu, Tonko bakkutsu,* vol. II: pl. 89.
76. *Chugoku sekkutsu, Tonko bakkutsu,* vol. IV: pl. 63-65
77. *Tangzhao minghua* credits Yan Liben (Yen Li-pen) with painting tribute bearers from foreign nations and exotic figures, see Soper 1958: 212; see also Kuo Ruosu's eleventh century account in Soper 1951: note 591, p. 187. The mid-ninth century *Lidai minghuaji* gives a description of Yan Liben. For the theme of foreigners in Tang art, see P. Karetzky, "Foreigners in Tang and pre Tang China," *Oriental Art* vol. XXX (1984): 160 ff.
78. Pelliot 1914, vol. IV: pl. CCXLV-CCCXLVU.
79. T. Kuno, *Ancient Sculpture in the Horyuji* (Tokyo, 1958): 90-7. The directional orientation is, respectively north, west, east, and south. For dating see Tokyo National Museum *Pageant of Japanese Art: Sculpture* (Tokyo, 1958): 84.
80. Pelliot 1914, vol. II: pl. CII.
81. Wu Hung, "Reborn in Paradise: A Case Study of Dunhuang Sutra Painting and its Religious, Ritual and Artistic Contexts," *Orientations,* May, 1992: 52-64, explores some illustrations of Mahayanist scriptures.
82. T. Akiyama, *Arts of China* (Tokyo: Kodansha Pub., 1972) vol. I: 9.
83. A. Waley, *A Catalogue of Paintings Recovered from Dunhuang by Sir A. Stein* (London, 1931): 117, for one example.
84. Soper 1958: 222. This sutra is not specifically related to a known work but is rather a generic title. Soper proposes the *Buddhacarita* as the most likely possibility; see note # 91.
85. R. Hayashi, *The Silk Road and the Shoso-in,* Heibonsha Survey of Japanese Art, vol. 6 (NY: Weatherhill Inc. 1975.) The articles stored in the Shosoin since the eighth century are documented in inventories of the collection. Many of the objects in the Imperial Repository (international gifts to the court, Todaiji temple ritual objects, and personal articles of the Japanese Emperor Shomu) are considered to be either of Tang manufacture or a skilled copy of Chinese art.
86. Stein 1921: pl. LXXIV, (2'2 1/2" x 7 1/2/"); Waley 1931: 127, catalogue entry XCIV.
87. See Sickman 1987: 181, pl. 125.
88. Ibid. pl. 121.
89. Stein 1921: pl. LXXIV, (measuring 1'11" x 6' 3/8"). See also Waley 1931: 294, catalogue entry CDXCII.
90. In the British Museum, see A. Waley, *Introduction to the Study of Chinese Painting* (London, 1921): l. IV.
91. Stein 1921: pl. LXXV, (measuring 1' 9 1/2" x 7 1/4"). See also Waley 1931: 284 entry number CDCXCII. Waley identifies the third scene as the restraint Suddhodana placed on his son's household after the latter's departure.

92. Such as the one found in the tomb of General Chang in Gansu from the Han dynasty; see M. Sullivan, *Arts of China* (Berkeley: Univ. of California, 1982): 65.

93. Stein 1921: pl. LXXV, Waley 1931: XCVII, (measuring 1"10 X 7 1/4"); see *Shosoin Homotsu* (Tokyo, 1962) vol. II, pl. 98-99.

94. A. Stein, *Serindia* (Oxford, 1921): pl. LXXIV, (1'11 1/2" X 66'3/8").

95. Waley 193: 125.

96. Pelliot, vol. II: pl. CII. Stein 1921: 119 catalogue entry LXXXXVIII, this is not however illustrated by Stein.

CHAPTER III

PICTORIAL BIOGRAPHY OF THE BUDDHA IN CHINA

I. CAVE SITES

1. YUNGANG

Yungang in Shanxi is only a short distance from the first capital, Pingcheng, the modern Datong, of the Northern Wei dynasty (396-535). The Northern Wei established Pingcheng after they conquered the Northern Liang dynasty in Dunhuang: at that time they forced the captive population to move east to the new capital in 396. After the Buddhist persecutions of 441-5 of Emperor Taizu, Emperor Wenchang invited the monk Tan Yao to the capital to help in the construction and building of Buddhist monuments in 453. As part of the restoration activities a series of caves were excavated at Yungang. Work began with the execution of five colossal cave-chapels. Some scholars believe these were made in honor of the previous emperors of the Wei lineage.[1] The Yungang caves manifest the phenomenon of northern Buddhism, which merged the cult of the emperor with that of the Buddha. It was in this way that Buddhism was proselytized at the highest levels of society. The origins of this kind of integration date back to before the persecution, to the priest Fa Guo.[2] Soper points out that when the emperor adopted the use of Chinese robes for official dress, in the period 481-486, both the Buddha image at Yungang and the ruler were similarly attired.[3]

Tan Yao, supervisor of monks, lived at the site as director of construction. One must see his role in the layout and iconography of the cave-chapels as being formative.[4] Although Tan Yao's origins are unknown, he is recorded as a priest under the Northern Liang who was one of the populations of monks and artisans forced to migrate east from Dunhuang. Under his direction construction began at Yungang in 460 with the colossal imperial caves (XVI-XX). The initial edict to excavate the caves is recorded in the Wei history:

> *Tan-yao petitioned the Emperor that five caves should be excavated in the stone wall hewn out of the mountain ridge of Wu chou fortress near the capital with one Buddhist statue carved in each cave. The tallest was 70 chih high and the others 60 chih. The carvings were of exceptional excellence and unparalleled throughout the world.*

In all, thirty-odd caves that range in date from 460 to 520 were cut from the living rock. The period of activity is divided into three phases. The first, which includes the five imperially sponsored caves (XVI-XX) each dominated by a colossal Buddha, ends sometime around 475.[5] The second, comprising high-level patronage of four sets of paired caves (VII and VIII, IX and X, I and II, V and VI) and single caves XI, XII, and XII, is ascribed to the last quarter of the fifth century.[6] The third phase, consisting of the many small caves carved at the western end of the site, takes place in the last decade of the fifth century, after the transfer of the capital to Luoyang in 495. In 500 Emperor Xiaowendi ordered that new caves be excavated in the new location (Longmen) on the scale of Yungang.[7] When the court moved south to set up a new capital at Luoyang they brought the artisans with them. Imperial patronage also transferred to the new site. Thus the carving of the last period at Yungang is markedly inferior. As the inscriptions at the west end reveal, the caves of the last period did not enjoy high level sponsorship but were supported by societies of monks and/or nuns and lay patrons.

Overall narratives do not play a dominant role at Yungang, yet the site has one of the earliest and most complete Buddhist biographical illustrations in central China. The three stages in the evolution of narrative are observable here—as a primary decorative theme, as an abbreviated and secondary motif, and as a diminutive or epitomized cycle that is an insignificant feature of the iconographical scheme. Among the celebrated caves with colossi of the first stage of construction (XVI-XX) there are no narratives at all. Images of the thousand Buddhas, Buddhas of the past, and other divine themes line their interior walls. Narratives first appear as an important part of the decor in the paired caves of the second period where scenes of the historic Buddha are relatively large and occupy a major role in the decorative scheme. Told in nearly complete fashion, the biographical depictions are infused with their ancient didactic function to be read in the venerable manner—during ritual circumambulation of the icons. Quite similar to the classic Gandharan style, the narratives are set in individual panels and formally separated from each other by frames. Each scene's subject is self-contained with its own set of main and supporting characters. Siddhartha, shown in normal scale, is easily identifiable by his central placement and attributes—cranial protrusion (ushnisa) and halo. The most complete extant treatment is in Cave VI. The second stage in the evolution of narrative depiction—abbreviated narratives—also appears during the second period of construction. Here the narrative characters attending the large central icon are diminutive; often the narrative elements are so atrophied that they are easily overlooked. Most commonly they are gathered at the base, with one exception—the scene of the temptation of Mara, where they form a decorative arch above the head of the Buddha. Narratives characteristic of the third stage—atrophied, small-scale, and placed in inconsequential areas—appear infrequently in the late caves.

Despite the fact that the population of Dunhuang (especially the skilled workers) was forced east to Yungang, there is little in common with the Dunhuang narratives. This may be because most of the Gansu caves belong to a later era and a further stage in the development of Chinese Buddhist art. As will be shown, the disparity in style is evident in the structure and decorative schemes of the caves, as well as the narrative techniques and details. Unlike the caves at either Qizil or Dunhuang, those at Yungang have an anteroom separated from the rear chamber by a large door wall with a large window in the upper area. Differing from the friable soft stone of the Gansu caves, the hard stone at Yungang allows for stone bas-reliefs. In general caves from the various sites share similarities, including the division of the interior walls into registers filled with niches housing icons. But at Yungang there is a less strict organization of the motifs—some registers have a few large-scale niches, others are crammed with numerous smaller ones and decorative relief carvings. For the most part, the narrative art at Yungang is largely based on the bas-reliefs of Gandhara. There is no evidence of the use of the continuous horizontal scroll format that was seen at Dunhuang in the sixth century.

I. NARRATIVES AS A MAJOR THEME

Narratives are carved on the walls of the antechamber and main rooms of the cave-chapels as well as on a new feature that dominates second period caves—a central square pier carved to resemble a multi-tiered pagoda. The square central pier was a dominant architectural form at Dunhuang, but it did not resemble a pagoda. Most commonly it was a stepped structure that alluded to Mount Sumeru; the pagoda form was absent at Qizil as well.

CAVE VI

Cave VI is unique for its complete telling of the life of the Buddha. The biography begins on the first story of the south face of the almost square central pier and following the direction of the path of circumambulation continues in sequential fashion along the west, north, and east sides of the pagoda. There are four scenes on each face of the square pier, two on the outer and two on the interior arch faces. (FIGURE 49) The story continues in the lower register of the side walls. The upper wall area has numerous niches, small and large, that house a variety of Buddhist icons. Below are the narratives, contained in rectangular panels topped by the stylized rinceau pattern of honeysuckle, and donors in procession, in imitation of the ritual circumambulation of devout worshipers.[8] All of the biographical scenes are of equal importance, sharing the same degree of detail. The chronological arrangement overrides any iconographical consideration. Thus scenes of relatively little significance are afforded the same importance, except for the temptation of Mara, which occupies a large panel on the west wall.

1. Beginning on the southeast side is a scene under a gabled roof. Two haloed divinities are seated on a long bench, two haloed figures stand behind them.

2. On the interior post is a personification of the tree divinity who appeared on the occasion of the birth of the Buddha; assuming human form, it prostrated itself. Here the tree spirit, wearing the scarves that

criss-cross the lower torso in the Sino-Wei fashion, sits under a large tree.

3. On the west interior arch post are two divinities, haloed, kneeling with their hands clasped reverently before them.

4. This scene shows five more haloed divinities.

5. On the west face the birth cycle is portrayed. (FIGURE 50) The exterior south arch post has the birth. Maya is dressed in a long robe with crossing scarves and a tall crown; she holds the tree branch in her right hand. Out of her right side the baby, with a leaf-shaped mandorla, issues forth to be caught by a kneeling figure on the left. Uniformly the newborn is shown with a leaf-shaped mandorla. On the right are two figures; above the tree, two devas carrying garlands flank a flying angel.

6. The interior south arch post has the seven steps: standing at center, with a canopy over his head; the baby is drawn as an adult Buddha, fully dressed, not semi-nude as at Dunhuang. To the right are music-making angels; one plays a round-bodied instrument, the other a woodwind.

7. The interior north arch post has the first bath. Now in natural scale, the newborn stands on a dais flanked by two kneeling bodhisattvas. Above his mandorla are arching and intertwining dragons who bathe him, but here there are only eight, one less than at Dunhuang.

8. On the north arch post is the return from Kapilavastu. Maya, seated on an elephant, holds the baby in her arms. A divine orchestra is placed on the left. Above are garland-carrying figures and a flying angel.   On the left an attendant carries the royal umbrella.   The elephant is the vehicle mentioned in the GXYJ, as opposed to the other texts that describe a naga/dragon-drawn chariot or neglect to mention the mount. (FIGURE 51)

9. On the west arch post of the north face of the pier is the reading of the lakshana by Asita. On the right the haloed half-naked ascetic is seated on a grass stool holding the baby in his arms. His hair is drawn

up into a topknot; his right leg is bent over his left. By reading the physical signs of beauty on the baby, the sage can predict his future. Kneeling before the sage and baby are Suddhodana and Maya; the king wears a high crown. Over their heads is a gabled roof, above which fly garland carrying devas and angels.

10. On the interior of the arch is the naming of Siddhartha. The haloed child is dressed as a prince; on his right Suddhodana and Maya are seated on a low bench, the former in the pose of royal ease. Above them a tiled roof indicates the palatial setting.

11. The east arch post interior has a figure housed in a single-story, tiled-roof building with a ramp. This is the setting for the entry of the prince on the royal elephant into Kapilavastu. Surrounding him are heavenly musicians, an attendant carrying a royal parasol, devas, and angels.

12. On the north arch post of the east face the divine child kneels before his parents in their palace. Behind him is another haloed figure. This scene may represent Suddhodana instructing the crown prince to visit the ancestral temple, the scene on the interior of this arch post.

13. The haloed child stands in the gateway of the temple, a tiled-roof, single-story structure with a ramp in front. These illustrations of the filial behavior of the prince, especially the visit to the temple, are not commonly represented, though there is a textual basis for them in the GXYJ. Inside the temple, on the left, is the crown prince; on the right are the temple icons, one of which is a tiny sculpture with a leaf-shaped mandorla and square base. To the extreme right are two temple attendants.

14. The last pier scene has the royal couple, haloed and seated on a low bench on the left. A messenger approaches from the right. In the background are two flying devas. Perhaps the parents are being informed of the miracle that has just taken place in the temple: all the statues fell off their pedestals to revere the child.

The story continues along the side walls of the chamber.

15. The first panel is damaged beyond recognition.

16. The athletic competitions begin with the archery contest. The two cousins and the crown prince are in three-quarter frontal view; standing in line, they hold their bows and arrows in ready position. Set on thin pedestals to the right are the round targets with plumes at top.

17. The victorious crown prince is seated in his palace on a high throne in the posture of royal ease. The palace is the standard structure with tiled roof and Chinese-style bracketing. On the right Nanda and Devadatta wrestle. Except for the fact that the figures are dressed in robes, this composition follows the Gandharan prototype rather closely. The figure on the left holds his sparring partner's leg; the one on the right takes hold of his waist; in the foreground Nanda's win is celebrated with a libation. Next Nanda pushes his brother with his hand causing him to fall; this is the coup of the meet, which previously had not been depicted. In the left foreground are two onlookers. Nanda, the victor, later concedes he is no match for the prince. In the texts, the prince has already demonstrated his physical superiority by throwing the elephant, which is not carved here, but figures prominently in Qizil and Dunhuang.

18. The crown prince asks his father's permission to leave the palace on an excursion. This exhibition of filial piety is an obvious accommodation to Chinese morality, which is carefully delineated in the GXYJ. Seated under a trabeated and curtained canopy supported by slender columettes is the king on his high back throne. On the left is the kneeling prince, identifiable by his halo.

19-23. The next four panels illustrate the four sorties from the palace. These are all shown in the same manner. The palace gate, a tiled-roof-bracketed structure, is on the left; at center is the prince on horseback, attended by a servant holding the royal parasol over his head. On the far right is the vision; first is the old man, stooped over, leaning on a cane. Flying in the air is a deva—this is an attempt to render the divine agent who created the vision. In the second exit the sick man, as described in the texts, is seated on the side of the road supported by two crutches. (FIGURE 52) The meeting with the dead man is the last scene on the east wall, but it is severely effaced and impossible to read.

It may not have illustrated a funeral chariot, like the one found in Dunhuang Cave 290, for here, on the top of Cave VI's panel, are the remains of a magic-making deva and two members of the funeral cortege, one of whom carries a standard that is animated by the wind.

24. The first depiction of the south wall is severely damaged. Judging by the extant architectural elements on the left, a curtained balcony with a trabeated arch, this was a harem scene. Beneath the balcony are two figures. This was perhaps the continuation of life in the palace during which the prince was unable to be distracted from thinking about his encounters.

25. The next panel has the last of the encounters—the brahmin ascetic dressed in a dhoti with a scarf covering one shoulder. Above is a flying divinity.

26. The sleep of the harem follows the Gandharan prototypes exactly— in front of the bed are four sleeping beauties, who have relaxed their arms but still hold the musical instruments with which they entertained the prince. (FIGURE 53) Yashodhara lies on the bed covered by clothes, leaning her head on her right arm. The prince sits at the foot of the bed. On the extreme left, a haloed divinity reminds the prince that it is time to leave. Above in a balcony topped by a trabeated arch are two standing figures. At left is a bird, perhaps a cock announcing the arrival of dawn.

27. In the great departure the prince exits the city gates on the left; he and his horse are shown in full profile. The flying figure who holds a parasol over his head must be Chandaka. In traditional fashion, four celestials uphold the feet of the Mount Kanthaka.

28. The narratives that continue across the door wall are concerned with the ascetic wanderings of the prince, who, now dressed in a long robe, walks among small conical mountains.

29. He encounters the five ascetics.

30. The bottom panel is damaged.

31. On the west wall is a large iconic treatment of the conquest of Mara. Here as elsewhere at Yungang, the demons are arranged in an arch over a seated Buddha. The lower right side of the temptation is damaged. On the interior left are the three seductive daughters; farther left they are transformed into old hags. Above them are a pig-snouted soldier carrying a mace, a jackal-headed warrior, a tree-hurler, and a pig-faced demon throwing a bowl. At the apex a fiend is about to hurl a six-humped mountain range; on the right are more evil spirits holding boulders, spitting fire, and carrying clubs and double-balled maces. (FIGURE 54, a, b) Mizuno and Nagahiro reported that once there were smaller narrative scenes related to the attack below. It is likely that these were from the enlightenment cycle: the gift of milk gruel by the shepherdess, the bath in the Nairanjana River, the gift of the grass cutter, and the homage of the Naga Muchilinda.

32. The scenes in this panel—offering of food to the Buddha and the gift of the four bowls— are treated as two iconic images. The oversize Buddha is flanked by smaller narrative figures.

33-34. The east wall has the first sermon and the conversion of the Kashyapa brothers, which are also treated in iconic format. At the bottom of the niche of the first sermon, in one-third scale, are the tiny figures of the flanking deer and representation of the Three Jewels— three discs mounted on a base. (FIGURE 55) The Buddha's hands are in the "fear not" (*abhaya mudra*) not the teaching gesture (*dharmachakra mudra*). Housed in panels flanking the architectural niche are the small-scale figures of the audience—monks and worshiping figures. Filling the rest of the wall surfaces are niched Buddhas and the thousand Buddha theme.

The scripture that demonstrates the closest textual correspondence with the representations in Cave VI is the GXYJ. This may reveal the influence of Tan Yao, who made a second translation of the text after that of the Central Asian monk Gunabhadra of the early fifth century. Literal accuracy was evident both in the completeness of the scenes illustrated, some of which have no pictorial precedents: for example, the prince's request of Suddhodana to leave home, the entry of the child into the temple when the icons all fell over, the defeat of Devadatta in the wrestling competition, and detail of the encounter with the sick man, which shows him supported by crutches. Accommodation of the

Indian story to Chinese taste is observable in the modification of the objectionable aspects of the Gandharan reliefs, the most glaring alteration of which was the unclad female body. The art of northwest India, more than that of Qizil, was formative in the Yungang carvings, as seen in such direct parallels as the presence of an elephant, and manner in which the baby was born from the flank of Maya, the attack of Mara, wrestling, and harem scenes. Some of the illustrations important at Qizil are not depicted at Dunhuang—notably the elephant contest—or are treated in a different manner.

SECOND PERIOD CONSTRUCTION CAVES

Other caves in the second period of construction have scattered representations of biographical narratives. A new story appears relating a former life of Emperor Ashoka.The third century B.C.E . Indian emperor is shown as the boy Vijayamitra, who, having nothing to give the Buddha Shakyamuni, offered him a handful of dust. The Buddha Shakyamuni, pleased with the child's pious reverence, uttered a prophetic statement that the humble child will be reborn as a great king and patron of Buddhism. The story enjoyed moderate popularity in Gandhara, when the text was purportedly written for the Kushan King Kanishka who is mentioned in the text and for whom a similar legend was created.[9] The Ashoka legend was extremely potent in early Buddhist China where he was the embodiment of the ideal sage king. There are numerous statues, reliquaries, temples, and monasteries that claim to be related to Ashoka.[10] The gift of Ashoka is frequently paired at Yungang with the Dipamkara legend, a scene not found at Dunhuang and rarely at Qizil. This jataka tells the story of a former incarnation of the historic Buddha when as a young brahmin ascetic he bartered his future lives to purchase flowers for the Dipamkara Buddha. Offering the flowers in homage he then spreads his hair out as a carpet for the Buddha to tread.[11] For these reverent acts the brahmin was reborn as Shakyamuni Buddha. Both stories exemplify the theory of karma and remind worshipers that any act of veneration to the Buddha is rewarded manifoldly. How much more then could a fifth-sixth-century patron or regent expect in his next life after supporting Buddhism by dedicating a chapel, carving a sculpture, or having a sutra copied.

Frequently illustrations of jatakas appear in the anteroom of the Yungang caves. Cave X presents an extensive treatment of the

Dipamkara jataka in several panels but the damage suffered by these is considerable; before the Japanese uncovered them, they were plastered with stucco and paint.[12]   The first panel shows a two-story gateway through which the youthful brahmin passes; townspeople pay reverence to the Buddha on the right. The Buddha, human in size, has a large oval mandorla. In the second panel the girl sells her flowers and extracts, as part of the bargain, the promise of future lives together. (FIGURE 56) Lastly, having bought the flowers, the brahmin offers them to the Buddha, kneeling on the ground with his hair spread out. Attending the Buddha are worshipping figures and a yaksha. The cartouche between the panels are blank.[13] Jatakas such as these are consistently placed in the fore hall, as they were at Dunhuang. This positioning of jatakas may have iconographical significance in that it provides a prelude to the scenes of the life of the Buddha portrayed in the main room. A favored story at Yungang, the Dipamkara appears several times representing the same reverential acts carved in Gandharan bas-reliefs. Although uniquely popular in Afghanistan, it was rare at Qizil.[14] A more condensed version was carved in the lower register of the wall of the anterooms of Caves VII, VIII, and XII. In Cave IX, it is carved with the *Syama jataka*, another frequently illustrated narrative of the filial Syama, which was translated by Tan Yao in 472.[15] It is also carved in the main room on the east wall of Cave I; on the south wall is a carving of the Buddha's encounter with the ascetics.

There are but isolated examples of biographical scenes found in the paired caves. These include a very damaged rendering of the sleep of the harem on the east wall of the main room of Cave VIII. The prince is seated in pensive posture[16] (chin resting in his right hand, right leg bent with the foot resting on the left knee) under a gabled, tiled roof, with curtains drawn aside. Beside the prince is a kneeling figure; on the right lying in bed, obscured by blankets is his wife. Above, in a balcony are a series of heads with remarkably strange faces; they recall a similarly odd sculpture from Swat.[17] At the bottom of the first register of the east wall, the vague remnants of the great departure can be made out. Although the horse and rider have been effaced, the celestials that supported the hoofs of the escaping horse are still visible. Cave II has several reliefs from the youthful period of the prince in the main chamber; the east wall has the archery contest. Three contenders stand in profile facing the right, aiming their arrows at the targets—

round shapes on slender pedestals decorated with ribbons that flutter in the breeze. This is the only scene that remains of what must have been a continuous frieze like that of Cave VI.

II. SECOND PHASE OF NARRATIVES—ICONIC STYLE

Of the scenes shown in the iconic format the most important is the temptation by and conquest of Mara. Such representations are fairly familiar and uniformly portrayed at the site. Mara's army forms an arch over the meditating figure. The Western prototype is somewhat altered—figures form the arch frame.[18] The scene of the temptation appears on the first register of the main wall of Cave VIII: the Buddha, seated in a deep niche, has a canopy over his head. His right hand is in *abhaya-mudra*, the left rests in his lap. On the right side is the damaged image of Mara, dressed like a Parthian warrior; to his left is his son. Overhead are his horde—one aims an arrow at the Buddha's head; to the right is a reptilian-headed creature; above is a one-eyed, half-naked demon threatening with his ax. Interspersed among these are other soldiers. Despite the considerable damage, the interior right side of the niche shows two of Mara's daughters and at the top a round-faced creature wields a club. The temptation is also carved on the south wall of Cave X.[19] Here the attacking demons are three figures deep. On the right Mara, now dressed in tunic, trousers, and boots, reaches out to two of his fallen soldiers. Sumati, his son, tries to restrain him on the right and Mara's daughters in long gowns with high crowns approach from the left. Above them flame haired monsters threaten with clubs and pitchforks; at the apex one ghoul holds a stylized three-humped mountain over his head, ready to hurl it. On the right are an archer, an elephant-headed creature, and defeated warriors who stand in a subdued fashion with their hands clasped. At the feet of the latter are two vanquished warriors—one supine, the other prone. This figural disposition of the defeated warriors is greatly indebted to the bas-relief carvings of Gandhara. The attack of Mara also appears on the east wall of the anteroom of Cave XII and on the north face of the central pier of Cave II. It is noteworthy that both this type of composition and its placement on the north wall were present at Qizil. This orientation identifying Mara with the north is not unrelated to the cult of Vaisravana, Guardian King of the North, reflecting the fact that it was the most dangerous direction in India, Central Asia and China.[20]

A rare theme seen in China is the emaciated Buddha performing his austerities but it is represented as one of the three seated Buddhas on the south wall of the anteroom of Cave XII. The skeletal structure is visible, the face gaunt; he has a leaf-shaped aureole. The five ascetics who rejected him when he gave up the practice of austerities are shown in small scale on either side of the seated figure. The theme appears only once at Dunhuang;[21] the avoidance of depicting human suffering is consistent with Chinese preferences. The emaciated bodhisattva is found in several examples in Gandhara, though the scene was never popular.

Another scene commonly set in the iconic mode is the representation of the offering of food by the two merchants Trapusa and Bhallika who flank the oversize standing Buddha. The theme relates the first gift of laymen, who encountering the Buddha after enlightenment give him his first meal.[22] The two merchants became important in China—one indication of their appeal is revealed in the sutra *Tiwei boli jing* by the Northern Wei monk Dan Jing, which describes the duties of a layperson.[23] The scene is found among the four stories of niches in the main rooms of Caves VII, VIII and XII (FIGURE 57).

Cave XII is unusual in that in the coving of the anteroom ceiling are iconic-style narratives including the *Dipamkara jataka*, gift of food by the four Guardian Kings, and the first sermon. It should be noted how rare images of the first sermon are in early Chinese Buddhist art. This may reflect the late date of the evolution of the scene in India—it was not until the Guptan era that the image was standardized.[24] The attack of Mara also appears on the east wall of the anteroom of Cave XII.

III. THIRD PHASE—ABBREVIATED NARRATIVES

Narrative scenes in this last phase are small-scale, atrophied, and appear in minor areas of the decor. Though for the most part third-phase scenes are found in the later caves of the west end, some appear in the earlier caves of the second era. One manifestation of the third phase is the pairing of highly abbreviated and small-scale narrative images on either side of large icons. One formulaic set features the bodhisattva riding an elephant and Siddhartha on his horse. The pairing of these condensed images of conception and the great departure appears contrived and is not justified by iconographical concerns. Such adaptations are accomplished during a period when

Chinese artistic preferences override iconographic dictates. These decorative motifs of paired depictions are familiar later at Dunhuang, Longmen, and on freestanding steles. Another combination of truncated images consists of the *Dipamkara jataka* and gift of Ashoka. Both sets are carved in the identical caves Va and Vb. Caves XXIV, XXXV, and XXIX, executed during the first two decades of the sixth century, also have symmetrically placed depictions of the Dipamkara and Ashoka legends. Cave XXXIIE, a small cave decorated with mostly Mahayanist themes, has the set of the bodhisattva on an elephant and Shakyamuni on a horse; placed symmetrically below is another pair—the birth and first meditation—framed by trees.

Several other abbreviated scenes seem to be distributed in a random way among the caves of the second and third eras. One very popular example is the farewell of the mount Kanthaka, represented in small scale in the third niche of the second story of the west face of the pier of Cave II and on the south wall of Cave XXIX. There the bodhisattva, in pensive prince posture, bids farewell to the kneeling horse. The temptation scene carved on the south wall of Cave XXIX, though damaged, still retains the figures of Sumati restraining his father, quelled demons who piously clasp their hands, and two fallen warriors before the base of the Buddha, in addition to the earth spirit emerging from the ground. The appearance of such new details as the depiction of the vanquished offering worship and the rendering of the earth spirit should be noted. Abridged treatment of the *Dipamkara jataka* is found on the doorwall of Cave XI and the image of Ashoka appears in Niche XIIIF outside of Cave XIV and Cave XXVIII. Cave XXXXV is unique in the number of historic scenes pictured on its walls. In its version of the attack on the south wall, the seated Buddha has his hands in meditation (*dhyana mudra*) not *bhumisparsa mudra*; on the right Sumati restrains his father, and on the left are Mara's voluptuous daughters. The upper register of the south wall has a representation of the conversion of the Kashyapa brothers and on the east and west walls are the *Dipamkara jataka* and Ashoka legend. Lastly is a rare and highly abbreviated treatment of the parinirvana on the west wall. Also unusual is the inscription that provides the names of the donors but not their dates:

> *The Buddha's disciple Wang I, for the benefit of (my) younger brother made a stone image. . . . The Buddha's disciple Chang . . .*

*.O! O! On the fourteenth day of the fifth month of Yen-ch'ang of the (Great) T'ai (Wei) Heng Yung. . . Cheng. . . . Wei T'u-tung. . . Hua T'ang-Chiu Kung. . . Ch'ang Chu-chang for the benefit of the late brother An Feng-han made a Maitreya and seven Buddhas. . . .Bhiksu Tao.*25

A rendering of the parinirvana scene, which is extremely rare at Yungang, is done in minute scale and occupies an insignificant area on the pedestal of a statue of Cave XI (FIGURE 58, a); it is easily overlooked.[26] The scene is reproduced with a minimum of narrative detail; the small scale demands a severe reduction in the number of accessory figures so that the reclining Buddha has but a few mourners. Although representations of the parinirvana were prevalent at Dunhuang, they belong to a later period—the Northern Zhou through the Tang dynasties. Indeed this is one of the few small-scale depictions of the death scene at the site; two others are found among the later caves of the west end.

The minuscule scene of the conception of Cave 48 is typical of this late phase in its extreme condensation and sinification of the image. Maya lies on her side, her body totally obscured by drapery. In the upper left is the elephant with a celestial rider holding a representation of a small Buddha with leaf-shape mandorla. The elephant is in flying gallop—four legs splayed beneath him. In front of the bed are four seated figures who bear little resemblance to women, let alone to the voluptuous beauties of Gandhara. (FIGURE 59) In addition there is a parinirvana scene. Cave XLI also has scenes from the nativity cycle carved in horizontal registers on either side of the large canopied niche decorating its north wall. On the right at top is the birth; Maya stands frontally, lifting her left arm; now the baby emerges from her sleeve. The Chinese artist has adopted the convention of using the sleeve rather than the naked flank for the birth and reduced the attendant characters to one kneeling figure ready to catch the child. In the second register are the seven steps and proclamation. In contrast to the Gandharan technique of showing the path the child has trod with lotus flowers, the Yungang artist shows the child seven times; in the last image he has a leaf-shaped mandorla and there is a worshiping figure kneeling at his feet. The contests of physical strength—the dragging, lifting, and hurling of the elephant—are carved on the facade of Cave XXXVII. This is the first representation of the elephant contest at Yungang.

In summation, the narratives at Yungang during the last stage appear as isolated scenes and seem almost to be randomly selected. It is apparent that a model different from the earlier eras was used for these biographical scenes. Differences exist in the depiction of Maya giving birth through her sleeve, the multiple images of the boy child taking his seven steps, the representation of the dragging of the elephant and the image of the parinirvana. Later in date than the imperial caves, the western end caves were based on popular sources of Buddhist art. Like the Tang silk banners of Dunhuang, these efforts mark the popularization of the doctrine. Here too the patrons, no longer imperial or important members of the social hierarchy, either individually or in groups had an image or inscription carved. Certain events, of seemingly secondary importance, are repeatedly seen in these caves, suggesting that it was personal favorite or that a particular aspect of the doctrine was being presented; one such theme is the tangible rewards of patronage. Increasing secularization and absorption of Chinese elements are also apparent.

The treatment of these scenes marks both the late period of carving at Yungang and the second stage of Buddhism in China. As was elsewhere evident, expanded narratives of Shakyamuni's life are related to the relatively early stage when Buddhism was first brought into China—they were used to introduce the strange, new, and varied tenets of Buddhism. By the second stage, with its more widespread dissemination of the doctrine, the scenes were no longer as important. By the third period of construction, images of events in the life of the historic Buddha are severely diminished in size and infrequently seen. Interest in Mahayanist doctrines and their icons increased.

OTHER CAVE SITES

Several other caves carved into the mountains yield examples of scenes from the life of the Buddha. Two caves, Xiawangmu Miao and Wangzhia Cave, located on a mountain bluff along the Qing River, are near to Yungang and close in date of execution. Ascribed to the Northern Wei era, the style of cave and decorative programs affirm the attribution. At the new capital of Luoyang excavation of the Longmen caves began at the end of the fifth century. Construction of the caves spans the era from the Northern Wei through the Tang era.

2. CAVES ON THE QING RIVER

The caves of the Qing Valley, located on the Gansu side of the border, were explored by the Fogg Museum expedition in the early twentieth century. Among these caves are two extensive examples of biographical narratives. These, it has been observed, were based on the Yungang prototypes, notably Cave VI, though they have been attributed to a later date, the first decade of the sixth century.[27] The influence of the Yungang style is apparent—narratives are still important in the decorative scheme, they are carved on the central square pier and surrounding side walls to be read during circumambulation. Although rather damaged now, the episodes were told in a complete way, with special attention to detail. Emphasis is on the rendering of the themes of the early life, like the athletic competitions. Of all the scenes to be selected for illustration, these youthful events are somewhat curious for they present no clear doctrinal theme, as the first meditation or four exits might. They reflect a desire of the patron to see heroic martial events rather than points of doctrine, characteristic of a culture that celebrated the military arts and depended on those skills for survival. In this way the scenes of the caves of the Qing River manifest the second stage of Buddhist art, when native values and artistic preferences are prominent.

A. XIAWANGMU MIAO (HSIA WANG MU MIAO)

At the site of Xiawangmu miao, scenes of the physical superiority of the crown prince decorate the central core of the cave. The throwing of the elephant, for example, has Nanda trying to drag the beast away from the city gate: Nanda stands facing it with both of his hands on its trunk; the elephant has its mouth wide open. To the right is Devadatta, on the left is the climax of the story—the prince holds the elephant in his right hand, all four feet are balanced in his palm, as at Dunhuang. The second event is the sword contest, which though not found at Yungang or at Dunhuang, was present at Qizil. Here, too, the three contestants stand in the same posture—the sword in right hand, left hand resting on thigh. But the targets for the sword competition are shown—two balls mounted on slender stands. Third, is the archery meet: the three cousins hold their weapons aimed at the targets, round disks mounted on tall poles with cresting plumes at top. Two angels fly above.

B. WANGZHAI CAVE

The Wangzhia Caves of the Qing Valley also have scenes from the life of Shakyamuni. These are somewhat later in date and representative of a more degenerate stage of narrative carving than those at Xiawangmu miao. Like the last period of carving at Yungang, the biographical scenes are relegated to the minor areas of the cave, like the space between the aureoles of the Buddhas and bodhisattvas that terminate at the top of the side walls or in the interstices between the icons. These images have been ascribed to the early decades of the sixth century, slightly later than the central pier narrative carvings of the preceding site.

Although in a ruinous state, some of the narratives that decorated the central core are preserved. In general they appear to conform to the Northern Wei style, but the narratives have unusual attributes. For example, on the south wall is a rather interesting addition to the nativity cycle: Maya holds the baby in her arms; she is seated on a four-legged stool; two figures kneel before her. More traditional treatment is afforded two scenes on the north wall where the sleep of the harem is combined with the great departure. Among the sleeping women in the pavilion only Siddhartha is awake; on the left he and his groom leave the palace on horseback, the feet of Kanthaka are supported by divine agents. On the west wall the farewell is preserved; the horse kneels to lick his master's feet. These are all that remain of what may have been a fairly complete cycle. Here, as at Xiawangmu miao, only scenes of the early life remain.

2. LONGMEN, HONAN

The Northern Wei rulers established Longmen, located near the capital of Luoyang, at the end of the fifth century. It, like Yungang, was the recipient of imperial patronage. Narratives do not appear in the early caves. When they become part of the decorative program, they are characteristic of the last phase of carving at Yungang. The scenes are highly abbreviated, in small-scale, and placed as decorative themes subordinate to the iconic images. Thus among the dozens of caves at Longmen, narratives appear only in the upper register of the door wall of the Binyang Cave where the Mahasattva and Visvantara *jatakas* are carved, in companion with the Vimilarkirti and Manjusri Debate.[28] Some extremely small-scale biographical scenes occur in minor areas of the decorative scheme, like the areas between the niches or aureoles of the icons. Several, being small scale, inaccessibly placed, and executed in extremely low relief, are known primarily from rubbings.

Among the hundreds of niches that fill the Guyang cave dated by inscription to 523 is a niche along a narrow section at the top of the south wall that has two rectangular panels.[29] The upper register of the panels has a minuscule representation of the Vimalakirti debate. Below are two exceptionally small narrative panels each with scenes of the nativity. In the birth, Maya wears a long Chinese robe. For the seven steps, the child, naked but for a loincloth, stands on two lotus blossoms, and in the bath two figures flank the standing child. (FIGURE 60) All narrative details are neglected; only the central figure is represented. Similarly treated are the biographical scenes carved on the corresponding lower section of the opposite wall—an unidentified scene and the reading of the signs of beauty by Asita. The sage is seated in his hut, holding the baby in his hands; four figures, two seated, two standing, listen to the prophecy. (FIGURE 60a)

A number of minuscule and simplified similar examples at Longmen can be cited. Four scenes from the life of the Buddha adorn the upper wall of the Northern Wei Weizi Cave.[30] Two illustrations of the first meditation are framed in trabeated arches. In each the bodhisattva sits in pensive prince posture under a gingko tree. Kneeling before him is his father with two attendants holding parasols. On the lower section of west side of the north wall is another view of a meditating figure under a tree; damage to the right side of the scene obscures identification, but on the opposite side is a highly condensed rendering of the parinirvana. The reclining Buddha is placed on a bed behind which are six figures. (FIGURE 61) This exact configuration is also found in the Putai Cave.[31] Lastly is the minute scene of the miracle of the shade and symmetrically placed offering of the milkmaid carved on either side of the aureole of the Buddha of Cave XIV. In the former the young prince is seated on a grass stool under a tree; his father kneels before him; four attendants wait on the left.[32] In the second, the prince is similarly seated and the girl offers up the bowl with two hands, two attendants are behind her.

4. XIANGTANGSHAN, HONAN

At Xiangtangshan there are almost no scenes of the biography of Shakyamuni; in their place are carved icons, inscriptions, and excerpts of the scriptures. One rather remarkable small-scale depiction of the parinirvana is reproduced in Cave 5 among the southern group. The whole scene is enframed by two sala trees and contained within an architectural niche topped with a curtain.[33] Nine mourners surround the bed, one at the head; another at the foot. In addition, for the first time, there are two guardian figures. In front of the bed Maya weeps over her son's body. It has been suggested that this representation is a reference to Lady Li, ex-empress of the Northern Qi, the possible donor, mourning her son.[34]

CONCLUSIONS

In conclusion the evidence gleaned from a survey of biographical narratives in the cave-chapels of China reveals that the worship of Shakyamuni climaxed during the Northern Wei era. This is supported by epigraphical evidence tabulated by the number of inscriptions dedicated to the historic Buddha found in the caves. The period of greatest flourishing of faith in the historic Buddha occurs during the Northern Wei dynasty (386-535). This increase in the later half of the period corresponds to the second phase of construction and decoration at Yungang.[35] The peak of narrative carvings at Yungang took place during the Northern Wei, especially important were caves I, II, VI. During this phase the narratives had a close correlation with the biographical sutras, especially the GXYJ. The relationship is manifested in the order of the occurrence of the events, completeness and literalness of the illustrations and emphasis on filial piety. The most influential artistic source was Gandharan bas-relief sculptures that provided the general composition of the scenes, settings, figural dispositions and narrative details. Contemporary narratives at caves of the Qing River Valley provide clear parallels in the selection of events portrayed, style of representation and content.

Within decades, this climax of narrative expression peaks. Biographical scenes of the third phase at Yungang, ascribed to the end of the fifth century, are reduced in size, importance, and quantity. There is an expressed preference for the representation of scenes of the nativity, youth, great departure and temptation, with a near total absence of illustrations of the death cycle. The unimportance of narratives at other sites of the Northern dynasties—Gongxian, Longmen, and Xiangtangxiang—is significant in establishing the falling off of interest in scenes of the life of the Buddha.

II. PICTORIAL BIOGRAPHY OF THE BUDDHA IN OTHER MEDIA IN CHINA

1. FREE-STANDING STELES WITH SCENES FROM NARRATIVE CYCLES

Since the Han dynasty freestanding steles were traditionally used to preserve the calligraphic styles of famous artists and historical inscriptions. With the introduction and adaptation of Buddhism, the format of the large stone slabs incised with literary inscriptions was appropriated for Buddhist icons. As early as the Six Dynasties period motifs and icons on steles were organized in the same hierarchical arrangement employed in cave interiors. The main icon is placed at center on the front face and the surrounding sculptural images, like those on the cave walls, are placed in flanking horizontal registers. On the rear face are secondary images, along with the occasional narrative theme, images of donors, and their names. All available surfaces— between the niches on either face or on the sides of the stele—are also filled with images, like seated meditating Buddhas (sometimes recalling the Thousand-Buddha theme) atrophied narratives, celestials and auspicious emblems.

Of the several dated freestanding steles housed in public collections but a handful have biographical illustrations. The scarcity of material may be due in part to the destructive rage of the three great persecutions of Buddhism (445, 574 and 845). Judging by the extant material, it appears that carving narrative themes on steles was never widespread. This may be because the format of the stele, with its limited amount of space for carving, was not the best for narrative depiction. Yet there are several fine examples. In general the style of carving and the iconographical patterns on the steles conform to that observed in the monuments of China, though several examples are quite atypical. Parallel to the appearance of biographical scenes in the caves, they were prevalent only during certain periods: they flourished during the Northern Wei, although some examples from later periods are found. The most popular narratives are, as at the cave sites, the nativity, great departure, and to a lesser extent, the farewell of Kanthaka. Here too, with one notable exception from the Tang era, the death cycle is ignored.

Stylistic conformity among the steles is readily visible. On the front face is an icon of Shakyamuni, seated in lotus position, with his hands in *Dhyana mudra* (meditation posture). He is dressed in monastic garments that are wound around one shoulder, the other being bare; his hair carved into a mass of snail-shell curls. Usually flanked by two princely figures, the Buddha has a halo comprising zones alternately filled with seated Buddhas or patterned flames. The narratives appear on the rear face, often accompanied by an inscription in the lowest zone; sometimes images of donors and their names are also incised. Frequently the nativity is at the very top; a condensed version of the cycle of events may include the birth, proclamation, seven steps, and first bath. These compositions more or less correspond to the conventional standards of Gandharan bas-reliefs. For example the scenes from the nativity cycle on a stele inscribed to the first year of Taian, 455, which is now in Beijing, has the birth with the child issuing from the left flank, the first steps and arrival of Asita.[36] Though badly damaged, the names of the donors, the Zhang brothers, and the record of their dedication are still legible on the lowest zone on the rear face. Another example with two narratives of the nativity cycle, now in the Bahr Collection, shows the birth amidst a hilly landscape. The depiction of the first bath has the child, with leaf-shaped mandorla, standing on a Chinese-style dais (replacing the Gandharan tri-legged stool) bathed by snake-like dragons. This Sinicized treatment seems at odds with the stone's early inscription of the third year of Taian, 457:

> *Third day of the ninth month of the third year of Taian (457), the devoted Sung Dexing in memory of his deceased wife, Zong Xiang, had a statue of Shakyamuni made, with the wish that all of his relatives and ancestors for seven generations attain complete knowledge, and that his wife Zong Xiang, and all living creatures have the good fortune to encounter the various Buddhas and forever be far away from pain and that they obtain these wishes soon, and achieve bodhisattvahood.*[37]

A most extraordinary example, dated 471, has several events from the early life of the Buddha, and is now in the Shaanxi Provincial Historical Museum.[38] The scenes appear in horizontal registers on the rear face; each is contained in a rectangular frame. Extensively told in several episodes is the *Dipamkara jataka,* which occupies the middle zone. In one panel the youth enters the city; the next shows him bargaining for the flowers, and offering homage to the Buddha—presenting the flowers and performing the ritual kowtow. (FIGURE 62) There is also a representation of the Seven Treasures of the Chakravartin. Six scenes from the nativity cycle are carved at the top. In both style and iconography these are treated in the traditional manner. There is the conception which shows Maya sleeping in a Chinese-style house with the disc ensconced elephant above her; the interpretation of the dream; the birth with the child emerging from the capacious sleeve of Maya's Chinese robe; the first steps and proclamation combined into one scene, and the first bath. Finally is a pensive figure of the prince seated under the tree during his first meditation. The arrangement of the scenes sacrifices chronological order to design. Despite the skewered sequence of some events, there is an attempt to render the narrative stories at length, and all of the nativity scenes are at the top, and the *Dipamkara jataka* scenes in the mid section. A more abbreviated treatment of two nativity scenes—the birth and first bath—is carved on the rear face of a stele from Nailiang dated 472.[39] Dedicated by the devotee An Zhang in memory of his parents, this stele is carved in an awkward style. Inscribed by Guo Yuanqing in the Taihe period, 492, another stele has the farewell of the horse Kanthaka. With the passage of time narrative depictions on steles all but disappear, with one notable exception of a portrayal of the bath dated to the Northern Zhou dynasty.[40] But this is a highly abbreviated treatment characteristic of the phase in which interest in the biographical scenes has already waned. All accessory figures have been eliminated—only the centrally placed semi-naked child with corona of snakes above his head is portrayed.

Another popular theme involves the mount Kanthaka. Several steles dated to the Wei dynasties are carved with the sole scene of the farewell to Kanthaka. (FIGURE 63) Curiously this episode of little iconographic importance enjoyed favor at other sites in China as well. Surely this reflects the high esteem of the horse in Chinese culture in general and during the period of Northern Dynasties period in particular. It may also be noted here that the dedicatory part of many steles often shows high-ranking donors with their mounts. One of the several steles with the farewell carved on its rear face is dated by inscription to the sixteenth year of Taihe (492) by a devotee of Yangmi prefecture and another, dated 526, has the Twin Buddha miracle on its front face.⁴¹ The theme appears on a third stele dated to the Northern Wei as well.⁴² The last example, ascribed to the Eastern Wei, has a damaged inscription that reads: *"The second year of Xai Chang. . . in memory of the parents and relatives. . . of all living creatures. . . achieve Buddhahood."*

Mention might also be made of a stele also ascribed to the Eastern Wei period that shows the gift of Ashoka.⁴³ This unique example of the theme is contemporary with the appearance of the subject during the second period of construction at Yungang.

These steles, like the banners of Dunhuang, reveal the popular interests of the patrons. Singly or in a group, members of the laity or sangha commissioned the stones in honor of their family as well as all living creatures. This deep concern for parents and family members may seem out of place in philosophical Buddhism but is characteristic of the second phase of the development of Buddhism in China. Such attempts to accommodate the ancient ethical teachings of filial piety are consistent with the Mahayanist doctrine of universal compassion. The seemingly idiosyncratic selection of illustrated themes must reveal the preferences of the patrons, but may also be the result of the capabilities of the craftsmen and the models in their ateliers.

Although there are many steles with one or more depictions of the life of the Buddha housed in Asian and Western collections, they are not included here because they neither offer a new source of information nor add significantly to what has already been presented. Discussing such works of art also introduces matters of connoisseurship and authenticity that are extraneous to this study, which relies only on primary sources.

2. EPITOMIZED VERSIONS OF THE PICTORIAL BIOGRAPHY

By the time of the Northern Qi dynasty (550-570), the continuous traffic along the Silk Route brought new developments in Indian Buddhism and its art to China. The influence of Guptan era (fourth-sixth century) icons makes itself apparent in the image of the Buddha as well as in a new iconographical theme—the epitomized cycle. This condensed biography of eight scenes of the life of the Buddha appears at various sites, but is nowhere more clearly stated than on the steles from Sarnath.   Each of the eight selections represents a different chronological stage of the life, is associated with a special location, and carries a unique symbolic content as well.   Naturally the four most important scenes are the birth, enlightenment, first sermon, and death; the second set is concerned with the devotion of animals (taming the elephant at Nilgiri, and the gift of the monkey at Vaisali) and the performance of miracles such as those displayed at Shravasti and Samkassa.

The influence of the epitomized set can be seen as early as the Northern Qi period in China.   Two long horizontal stones have the eight great events in the life of the Buddha and a long inscription, dated to 557, naming the tens of monks who joined together to commission the piece which is now in the Tokyo National Museum.[44] Large leafy trees set and separate the scenes on the first stone, which includes the birth, first steps, first bath, and reading of the lakshana by Asita.   The back face has the enlightenment cycle, beginning with the bath in the Nairanjana River, first meal, and four stages of meditation rendered by the repetition of the seated Buddha four times.   The second stone has the first sermon with deer flanking the wheel in front of the Buddha and the monks seated beside him, and a parinirvana scene that shows the Buddha flat on his back, an unusual feature, with mourning figures surrounding the bed.   These mourning figures are quite discrete in their grief when compared to the murals of Dunhuang and Xinjiang.[45] Though clearly the Guptan narrative sets of eight events were the model for these stones, the choice of scenes differs.   Naturally the most important episodes appear in both the Indian and Chinese examples. But on the Northern Qi stones the nativity is expanded to include several scenes.   There is an apparent concordance between the choice of scenes depicted on the Northern Qi stones and Chinese translations of scriptures that offer an abridged life of the Buddha as an introduction to the subsequent Mahayanist sermon.   In particular, the selection is similar to those presented in the *Mahayana Shradaddhotpada Shastra*, (attributed by some to Asvaghosa of the Kushan era under King Kanishka) which was first translated into Chinese by Paramartha in 553.   This scripture has a similar emphasis on the birth cycle which includes the descent from Tushita Heavens, entering the womb, dwelling in the womb, birth, as well as four other events—the great departure, enlightenment, first sermon, and parinirvana.[46]

Such condensed cycles become a decorative feature in Sui dynasty pagoda decor. This burst of creative life breathed into the narrative depictions was owing to the patronage of Sui Emperor Wendi who, in imitation of Ashoka, commissioned and dedicated 83 pagodas. The epitomized cycle is particularly appropriate adornment for this structure, for the pagoda is a native interpretation of the stupa reliquary for the historic Buddha's remains and such adornment was consistent with its long history. A Sui pagoda with this motif remains in Zhangde, Honan, founded, according to the inscription, in the first year of Sui Ren Shou (601), but it is also recorded that the structure suffered and was much restored.[47] The Tianningsi pagoda has scenes of the life of the Buddha adorning the upper part of the entrance and windows. Better preserved is the set of eight episodes found on the base of the Sarira pagoda.

Established during the second year of Sui Renshou (602), the Sarira pagoda stands on the grounds of Chixiasi, is believed to be one of the 83 recorded and erected by Sui Emperor Wendi.[48] Although the pagoda was later restored during the Southern Tang dynasty, the designs are thought to be Sui in origin. The five-story pagoda, octagonal in plan, has eight panels each with one of the great episodes in the life of the historic Buddha—conception, birth, four exits, great departure, temptation, enlightenment, gift of the four bowls, and parinirvana. (1) The conception shows the magical event in truly Indian style—the bodhisattva actually rides a six-tusked elephant. (2) The representation of the birth is also in keeping with Indian tradition—the child issues forth from Maya's right side, not from her left sleeve, and the proclamation and first bath are conflated. (3) The four exits are given prominence here. The prince is on horseback with a group of attendants, among them Chandaka. To the left the four visions are merged into one. At bottom is the old man supported by two figures, in the upper corner is a sick man in a hut, further left are a dead man surrounded by mourners, and lastly two ascetics, one of whom holds a begging bowl, confront the prince. Unlike the Indian prototypes, the sick man is in a hut, and there are two monks not one. (4) As in the Dunhuang banners, the great departure takes place among clouds and the celestials are omitted. Also similar to the banners is the landscape setting of the exchange of clothes with the hunter: set in the mountains, the seated ascetic prince is flanked by two stags and a few trees. (5) The temptation of Mara is remarkable for its lack both of the god of death and desire and his daughters, only the demonic army is portrayed. Now dragons are incorporated into the army, and the detail of hurled rocks being transformed into lotus flowers, found in the textual description of the GXYJ, is illustrated. (6) The enlightenment cycle comprises the bath in the Nairanjana River, meditation, and offering of food. To the left, the ascetic bodhisattva reaches for the branch of a tree to get out of the water, his garment lies on a nearby rock. This rarely illustrated scene is an episode found in the GXYJ: after Enlightenment the bodhisattva takes a bath, but is so enfeebled by his ascetic practices he is unable to get out of the river and reaches for a branch of a nearby tree. At center is the meditative figure, on the right is the milk maiden joined by additional maidens and cows. (7) The presentation of the four bowls is shown in traditional fashion, the four Guardian Kings on either side of the seated Buddha hold their bowls. (8) The rendering of the parinirvana is extraordinary: in addition to the ten monks surrounding the funeral couch, there are two guardian figures and lions; the kings are posed symmetrically around an incense burner, as they would be in a conventional iconic group, but they are grieving. On the left is the burning of the coffin—here five monks mourn, clouds carved above produce the rain that puts out the fire.

These narrative panels of the Saira pagoda are unusual in that they represent a rather expansive and literal treatment of the biographical narratives. Chinese secular details are employed whenever possible for architecture, clothing, figure type, furnishings, the presence of dragons, etc. Yet in the process of sinicizing, the India prototypes have not been forgotten. These scenes reflect the brief spasm of interest in the life of the historic Buddha in the Sui era. This concern is no doubt due to the impact of new forms of Buddhist art recently introduced into China. This renewed influence of Indian Buddhist art intensifies with the growing desire to know Buddhism in its original expression in the country in which it developed and leads to an ever-increasing westernization of iconography and style in the Tang period. It was also at this time that new developments in Buddhism were introduced into China and gradually overwhelmed interest in Shakyamuni.

3. SCENES OF THE DEATH AND THE PARINIRVANA STELE

Scenes of the death of the Buddha were treated elsewhere in this study as a separate theme because of the atypical character of the depictions. Here among the extant evidence of the Buddhist monuments of central China, such portrayals are even more rare. The iconic image of the reclining Buddha was probably a creation of the early Guptan era, one such example of the fifth century being cited in the literature. The image of the oversize recumbent Buddha was probably introduced into China soon after—the earliest extant representation is found in Dunhuang during the Northern Zhou period. But it is not until the Tang that such large-scale sculptures are common. The introduction of this new format accompanies other late Six Dynasties period innovations inspired by Guptan art, like the set of eight scenes, which resulted in a brief revival of interest in the pictorial biography.

Reviewing the depictions of the death among the monuments of central China discussed above, it has been shown that they were few, small scale, abbreviated, and unimportantly placed renditions. These were found at Yungang in the late period of construction in Cave XI, Cave XXXXV, and Cave XXXVIII; at Longmen's Northern Wei Weizi and Putai caves; as well as at Xiangtangshan in Northern Qi Cave V. The death also appeared among the sets of eight scenes on the Northern Qi dynasty stone dated 557 and Sui dynasty pagodas.

There is little evidence of interest in the parinirvana found in the pre-Tang literature aside from two small references in the biography of Buddhist nuns, *Piqiuni juan*, written as a companion to the history of eminent monks. First is the reference to Tan Lo who had a recumbent image of Shakyamuni (entering parinirvana) made.[49] It also recorded that Dao Qiong (active mid-fifth century) commissioned images for a convent in Nanjing, the Qianfosi, among which was a Shakyamuni entering nirvana and a hall to house it.[50] The details of size and material unfortunately are not preserved.

According to literary evidence Nirvana scenes continued to be painted in the Tang dynasty. There is the reference to Yang Tingguang 's (active 713-41) mural of a nirvana scene on the north east wall of Anguosi.[51] At Baoisi, Lu Lengjia painted a nirvana on the west wall of the Buddha hall and wrote an accompanying inscription as well.[52] Though these works of art are long gone, an important treatment of the death cycle may still be seen on an extraordinary dragon-topped stele dated to 692 that is found in Datong, Shanxi.

The dragon-topped stele's inscription reads:

> *Great Zhou, Great Cloud Temple on behalf of the sacred and divine Imperial majesty one stele with scene of the Nirvana has been made.*[53]

The lower zone of the rear face carries the inscription: "*Stele for the two story Maitreya Pavilion of the great Cloud Temple (Dayunsi).* The dynastic name Zhou as well as the great Cloud Temple have been identified with the Dowager Empress Wu who reigned from 690-705.[54] The front face of the stele is remarkable for its narrative zones which contain rarely represented scenes such as the last supper and funeral procession in addition to the more common, farewell, parinirvana, and burning of the coffin. (FIGURE 65) Since this piece has already been exhaustively analyzed, only the salient points will be summarized here. The last supper in the house of Cunda has the seated Buddha with flanking divine attendants, a pair of monks, bodhisattvas and their attendants. Before them is the banquet table spread with various dishes; in front of the table, seen from the rear, is Cunda. Eleven monks are placed at either end of the table. This is the earliest extant example of this very rare scene. The parinirvana appears in the second register: Buddha, lies on his right side, supporting his head with his right arm, in the traditional manner. In front of the bed are three mourning monks, a fourth is prostrate. Among the numerous readily identifiable grieving figures surrounding the bed are Kasyapa, Subhadra, and the Mallas; new characters include the bearded deity Vajrapani who holds a thunderbolt and a lion.

Rather unusual scenes are found below. For example in the third register is a funeral procession of a group of pallbearers who carry the coffin in a manner recalling the *Admonitions* scroll scene of an imperial lady being borne in a litter painted by Gu Kaizhi. Second, to the right, the Buddha miraculously sits up in his coffin to bid farewell to his mother. In the fourth register is Maya's farewell to her son, as described in the *Maha Maya Sutra*, translated around the last quarter of the fifth century.[55] Maya also figured in the parinirvana scenes at Dunhuang, as in Cave 295 for one, and elsewhere; but there she does not swoon over the coffin, but sits by the head. The last scene is the burning of the coffin, the whole is ablaze while figures look on with clasped hands. Of the three zones beneath the coiling dragons of the rear face of the stele, only the top one has a narrative. The division of the relics consists of a centrally placed large coffer flanked by six monks, kings with their retinue, and attendant monks.

This Tang stele is truly extraordinary in its format and the details of the narrative scenes. Many aspects of these representations are unique. The theme of the last supper, procession to the crematory grounds, and Maya's farewell seem without parallel. The inclusion of the Vajrapani and a lion in the death scene may be the earliest expression of a convention that has great longevity in the representations of the parinirvana scene in Japan.

III. TANG LITERARY EVIDENCE

The innovations seen in the 692 stele may be born from the developments in pictorial narratives of the Tang dynasty that are now known through copies or descriptions in contemporary art historical documents. The following list of efforts only partially preserves what was lost in the destruction caused by time and human events. Some are clearly related to sutra illustrations, like the record of Yang Qidan 's illustrations of the *Sutra of Former Actions* on all four sides of the pagoda at Dayunsi, originally erected by Sui Wendi (r. 589-604).[56] Cheng Xun painted the same subject on the walls of the northwest Dhyana precinct at Shengzesi in the eastern capital of Luoyang, as did Yang Tingguang (active 713-41) on the wall of Huadusi.[57]

Wei-chi Yiseng, a foreigner who was active at the Chinese court at the outset of the 627-650 era, painted a subjugation of Mara with its grotesque army and seductive goddesses on the rear facade of the Seven Treasures Terrace of Guangzhesi.[58] Ju Jingxuan, in his *Tangzhao minghualu* of the middle of the ninth century said the work was "truly original, full of countless monstrosities." Duang Zhengshi writing around the middle of the ninth century discussed the work in his *Sidaji* (Vacation Glimpse of the Tang Temples of Chang-an). Duang places the scenes in the Samanthabhadra Hall adding "Wei-chi shows the three daughters of Mara in the process of transformation (into hags) giving them bodies that seem to come right out of the wall."[59] The most famous Tang artist, Wu Daozu, also portrayed a "Subjugation" on the western corridor of the pagoda at Zuensi in the eighth century that had "coiling dragons and the like on the walls."[60] Two noteworthy references to Buddhist narratives appear in Guo Ruoxu 's *Tu hua jianwen zhi* of the later half of the eleventh century.[61] The first concerns the monk Zhi Yun, a painter of the Five Dynasties Period and native of Honan, who painted a Dipamkara Buddha at Guangaisi. The second records an artist of the early Sung period, Gao Wenjin who created a "Subjugation of Mara" for the west wall of the great hall of Xiangguosi.[62]

ENDNOTES

1. The major bibliographical source for the study of the Yungang caves is the seminal work done by Nagahiro and Mizuno, 1951. A more recent publication is the volume of the *Zhongguo meishu quanji: Diaosubian, Yungang shiku diaoke*, ed. Su Bai and Li Zhiguo vol. 10, (Beijing: Wenwu, 1988). A. Soper, "Imperial Cave-chapels of the Northern Dynasties," *Artibus Asiae*, vol. XXVIII (1966); and J. Caswell, *Written and Unwritten* (Univ. of Vancouver, 1988) and "'The Thousand Buddha Pattern' in Caves XIX and XVI at Yun-Kang," *Ars Orientalis*, vol. X (1975): 35-54. Both Mizuno 1951, vol. XII: 91; and Soper 1966: 241 identified the honorees for the large caves.
2. Mizuno 1951, vol. III: 91. Soon after Taizu proclaimed himself emperor in 396, he invited Fa Guo to come to the capital, appointing him Superintendent of Monks, a post he held until his death during the Taichang era (416-23) Fa Guo reportedly said: "Taitsu is enlightened and a lover of the way. He is in his very person the "Thus-Having-Come-One". Sramanas should pay him all homage." Thus he would do obeisance. Fa Guo would say to others: "He who protects the teaching of the Buddha is lord of men, I am not doing obeisance to the Emperor I am merely worshipping the Buddha." See Hurvitz 1951: 53, entry #53. See also Ch'en 1972 and 1975.
3. Ibid. vol. III: 481-6; A. Soper, "South Chinese Influence on the Buddhist Art of the Six Dynasties," *Bulletin of the Museum of Far Eastern Antiquities* vol. XXXII (1960): 57, attributes the change in dress code to an influence from the southern courts.
4. There are four major biographies of Tan Yao: Z. Tsukamoto, "The Sramana Superintendent Tan yao and his Time," *Monumenta Serica*, (1957) vol. XVI: 363 ff; S. Mizuno and T.Nagahiro, *Yun Kang*, vol. XIII: 91 ff; L. Hurvitz, "Chapter of the *Wei Shu* on Buddhism and Taoism," *Yun Kang*, vol. XVI: 72; and Ch'en 1972: 152-158. Mizuno 1951, vol. XIII: 96, reports during the 445 persecution of Buddhism, Tan Yao did not abandon his faith but sought refuge in the mountains and noted Tan Yao's translation of the *Tsa-pao tsang ching (Zaobao zang jing)* which narrates the jatakas. Mizuno, 1951: vol. II: 58 translated and recorded an entry of the *Xugao seng juan* of Tao Xuan that stated the founder of the cave temples, Tan Yao lived in a temple called Donglosi.
5. Scholars have sought to identify the imperial donors for the paired caves. See Soper "Imperial Cave-chapels" 1966: 244 ff.
6. Dating of the caves is given in Mizuno, 1951, vol. XVI: 13 ff.; *Zhongguo meishu quanji,Yungang:* 5ff ascribed the early period to emperor Xiaowendi, but does not discuss the other imperial patrons. Soper 1966: 243, offers that Cave I and II were perhaps opened by the boy emperor Xiaowendi (r 471-499)

who commissioned the caves in memory of his father Wenchengdi and his wife, soon after his father's death in 465. Mizuno 1951, vol. III: 117 also attributed it to Emperor Xiaowendi who visited the site in 480, 482, and 483. Soper 1966: 243 also proposed an early date for construction of caves VII and VIII; that Cave IX and X were dedicated by Xiaowendi for his father Xianwendi and his Empress mother, and completed after his father's death in 476; and that the paired Caves V and VI were constructed in memory of the Dowager Empress Wenming's father and in honor of herself, as regent during her grandson's minority, in the last quarter of the sixth century. Caswell 1988 is largely at odds with these attributions.

7. Soper 1966: 243.

8. Mizuno 1951, vol. III: 113.

9. S. Beal, *The Fo Sho Hing Tsan King*, (*Wisdom of the East*, vol. XIX, London, 1883): XXIX, Kaniska's dates are highly disputed.

10. Soper 1959: xiv discusses the importance of Ashoka and many of the Chinese sculptures that claim to have been related to Ashoka or his daughters; these are noted under the historical periods, see for example p. 8. Zurcher 1972: 278 also devoted some attention to Ashoka, and has a less complete, but similar list of structures.

11. Mizuno 1951, vol. VII-IX plate discussion of entry 41 gives a reference to the *Hsien Yu Ching* (Xian yu-jing) in *Daizokyo* (Taisho edition) vol. IV: 368-9 for the story.

12. Ibid.: 86.

13. An inscription was found in the cartouche of panel two, but it is no longer legible. A third panel is unidentified: on the right side is the seated prince; at the top is a balustrade with four empty arches, and the left has four kneeling figures facing the prince.

14. For Hadda see Meunie 1942: pl. X, fig. 36, pl. IX, fig. 37-41. It also appeared at Shotorak; see Degens, 1964: pl. I, no. 1 from area MK 74; pl. II, no. 2, from area MK. In Beal, *Buddhist Records:* xxxi.

15. Mizuno 1951: vol. VI: 126, pls. 21-26.

16. Ibid. vol. V: 67. D. Leidy, "The Ssu-wei Figure in Sixth Century A.D. Chinese Buddhist Sculpture," *Archives of Asian Art,* XLIII (1990): 21-37, considers the importance of this figure in various sculptures in China, Korea, and Japan as well as many of the possible iconographic interpretations, this example is however not mentioned. The pose was seen in Qizil as well.

17. Faccenna 1962: 17, from Butkara, inv. no. 3945.

18. On the rear wall of the Steppenhohlen, see Grunwedel 1912: 117-9.

19. Mizuno 1951, vol. VII: pl. 55.

20. Soper 1959: 238 points out that Vaisravana was among the gods whose statue fell to earth during the visit to the temple by the child as narrated in the *Lalitavistara.*

21. A skeletal emaciated Buddha found in Dunhuang Cave 428 in the central pier's second story; see illustration in Pelliot 1914: pl. CCLXXI.
22. Mizuno 1951, vol. IV: pl. 4.
23. Ch'en 1972: 181-2, says it is a forged sutra.
24. P. Karetzky, "The Origins of the Myth of the First Sermon," *East and West* vol. 45, no. 1-4 (1995): 127-147.
25. Mizuno 1951, vol. XV: 176.
26. Ibid. vol. VIII: pl. 45.
27. H. Jaymes, "The Buddhist Caves of the Ching Ho Valley," *The Eastern Buddhist*, 1923: 65ff.
28. S. Mizuno and T. Nagahiro, *The Buddhist Cave Temples of Lung-men in Honan* (Tokyo, 1941): fig. 18, 119.
29. *Zhongguo meishu qianji: Diaosubian, Longmen shihkou diaoke*, ed. Su Bai and Wen Yucheng, vol. 11, (Beijing: Wenwu Press, 1988): 25, pl. 26, plate discussion p. 9. See also E. Chavannes, *Mission Archeologique dans la Chine Septentionale* (Paris, 1915) part II, pl. DLXXXV, fig. 384, no. 1734, 1735.
30. Ibid. 80-81, pls. 82-83, plate notes p. 28.
31. Ibid. 90-91, pls. 92, plate notes p. 31; the authors identify one of the kneeling figures as the king, the other as the queen, though the latter is never included in this episode. Similarly, the kneeling figure by the head of the Buddha in the parinirvana scene is identified as Kashyapa. As the older monk usually stands by the feet, this is more likely Ananda in his traditional place, at the head.
32. *Pei wei shih k'u fou-t'iao p'ien hsuan* (Peking, 1958): pl. 28-30.
33. S. Mizuno, *Hsiang T'ang Ssu* (Tokyo, 1937) and Tokiwa and T. Sekino, *Buddhist Monuments of China* (Tokyo, 1931) vol. I: 4. See also *Zhongguo meishu qianji diaosubian, Gongxian Tianlongshan, Xiangtangshan, Anyang, shiku diaoke*, eds. Chen Mingda and Ding Mingshi, vol. 13, (Beijing: Wenwu Press, 1989): 132, pl. 151.
34. A. Soper, "A T'ang Parinirvana Stele," *Artibus Asiae,* vol. XXII (1959): 167.
35. Soper *Literary Evidence* 1960: 125.
36. S. Matsubara, *Chugoku bukkyo chokokushi kenyu* (Tokyo, 1966): pl. 161 and inscription p. 231. The base of the sculpture has the Twin Buddha theme in an arched niche at center flanked by seated niched Buddhas; and at either end are two seated lions. On the rear are simplified representations of the Mahasattva jataka and Syama jataka.
37. Ibid. pl. 14, 15, discussion p. 38.
38. *Shensi sheng po-wu-kuan ts'ang shih-k'e hsuan-chi* (Shensi, 1957): pl. 14, 15.
39. Matsubara 1966: pl. 19, p. 232.
40. Mizuno 1937: pl. 186.

41. Matsubara 1966: pl. 90, inscription on p. 248.
42. *Shifoxuancui,* Li Jingjie, ed. (Beijing: Renmin jiaoyu chuban she, 1995): fig 34, p. 54. But there are several confusing details: the Buddha, not the bodhisattva, is seated with the right leg over the left, the horse kneels on the left to say goodbye, Chandaka kneels on the right.
43. S. Omura, *Shina bijutsu shi chosohen* (Tokyo, 1915): 249, pl. 597
44. Matsubara 1966: 262, pl. 142-3.
45. *Shifoxuancui:* fig 34, p. 54. A second example donated by Cui Yingxian and others was found in Yijingpu, Yanshi County. At the top of the rear face are the conception, with a large elephant being ridden by the deity, and on the right side is the first bath with a nine dragon shower.
46. Mochizuki 1960, vol. V: 4215. This sutra was attributed to Ashvaghosa, according to Soothill 1934: 84b, without sufficient evidence. Paramartha made a Chinese translation in 553, and Siksananda made one in 679-700.
47. Tokiwa and Sekino 1931: vol. III: 90
48. Ibid. vol. IV: 8 ff. Pl. 7.
49. Soper *Early Evidence*, part II, Chin entry #17, p. 29, a disciple of the eminent Tan Pei (324-396) favored by Emperor Wu (r. 345-361). Tan Lo who gained her position by imperial order, fashioned in addition to a four-story pagoda, a lecture hall, dormitories, and a hall with shrines for the Seven Buddhas of the Past.
50. Ibid. part II, Sung entry #8, p. 40
51. Acker 1954: 272
52. Ibid. 298.
53. Soper "A T'ang Parinirvana Stele": 159.
54. Ibid. 160.
55. Soper "A T'ang Parinirvana Stele": 160, Soper has translated a part of it Tan Qing of the Southern Qi translated the text, it is reprinted in *Daizokyo*, vol. XII, p. 1012-1013.
56. In the third chapter of the *LTMHC* on "Wall Paintings of the Buddhist and Taoist Monasteries of the Western Capital Chang-an," see translation by Acker 1954: 300.
57. Acker 1954: 340 and 180 respectively.
58. TCMHL *t*ranslated by Soper 1958: 213.
59. A. Soper, "Vacation Glimpses of the T'ang Temples of Ch'ang an," *Artibus Asiae,* vol. XXIII (1960): 31.
60. TCMHL Soper 1958: 210.
61. *Kuo Jo-Hsu's Experiences in Painting* Soper 1951: 39.
62. Ibid. 51.

CHAPTER IV
NARRATIVES OF THE LIFE OF
THE BUDDHA IN KOREA AND
EARLY JAPAN

KOREA

When Buddhism was introduced into Korea, the country was divided up into three kingdoms: Koguryo, Silla and Paekche. Buddhist art from China entered each of the kingdoms at a different time. Koguryo, the first native Korean kingdom, began with the conquest of Chinese forces occupying Lolang. In 372 monks and travelers from the Toba kingdom of Northern China introduced Buddhism. Paekche, the kingdom in southwest Korea, had trade relations with south China. A Chinese monk brought Buddhism to Paekche in 384, after which time it was court sponsored. Paekche, in turn, had relations with Japan, sending them their first embassy in 552. Silla, located in the southeastern region, was the last to be subjected in the sixth century to Chinese influence and by 528 Buddhism became the state religion. Thus it was the Buddhist art of the Six Dynasties period that was introduced to Korea. By the seventh century Korean cultural preferences affected the appearance of the images which developed Korean facial features. In this early era the Buddha of the Future was most frequently portrayed.

When in the later part of the seventh century Korea was unified under Silla leadership, the influence of Tang China was manifest. Two magnificent monuments remain from the United Silla period (668-918), the Pulguksa monastery and Sokkuram grotto near Kyongju. Beginning in the seventh century the paradisiacal doctrine of Amida Buddha was dominant. Near the end of the Silla period Korea endured extreme hardship that led to the persecution of Buddhism in the mid-ninth century. With the establishment of the Koryo dynasty (918-1392), Buddhism truly flourished. King Wan Kon (King T'aejo), its founder, was a devout patron who supported the building of monasteries and temples. He commissioned the wood block printing of the Buddhist canon and the blocks are still preserved at Mt. Kaya.[1] During the Yi dynasty (1392-1910) Confucianism became the state ideology and Buddhism suffered its final decline.

Korean history from the later Yi dynasty onward is a record of warfare and invasions by the Chinese Mongol and Manchu peoples as well as the Japanese. In 1592 there was a Japanese invasion that was repulsed in 1627. The Manchu-Sino-Japanese war lasted for but one year 1894-5. Finally from 1910 –1945 Japan annexed Korea.

KOREAN BUDDHIST ART

As a consequence of this dramatic history of military confrontations and conquests, little is left of Korean Buddhist art. Narratives of the life of Shakyamuni are particularly rare. Since Mahayana Buddhism entered Korea during the early phase, little interest was directed to the historic Buddha. One rare example of art is an eighth-to-ninth century small bronze sculpture of the baby Shakyamuni standing with his right hand raised.[2] This kind of icon was used in celebrations of the Buddha's birthday when it was washed with sweet tea in ritual reenactment of the first bath. The birthday, one of the most important holidays in Korea, was also marked by the display of paintings of the event. The survival of such celebrations suggests what kind of ritual observances might have been practiced in China, which would account for the prevalence of nativity scenes there. Extant Korean paintings are exceptional. It is commonly said that of the 100 Buddhist paintings that survived from the Koryo period, ten remain in Korea and eighty have been taken to Japan.[3] Most of these are celebrations of Amida's paradise. One set of scrolls from the eighteenth century shows several scenes from the early life of Shakyamuni, but these are very late in date and thus beyond the scope of this study. It can be said that the iconographical considerations are closely executed, though the paintings are overwhelmed by the plethora of details of the ornate architectural settings and complex figural groups.[4]

The Korean role in the evolution of Buddhism in the Far East can be seen in the importance it had in the transmission of the doctrine to Japan. It was the Korean King of Paekche who in 522 sent an envoy to

Japan with Buddhist scriptures, icons and other gifts. In 577 monks, nuns and craftsmen were sent to make images and build temples. Again in 584 more statues were sent.[5]

JAPAN

After a period of resistance, Buddhism found imperial support in Japan. With the royal sponsorship of the regent Shotoku Taishi and the Empress Suiko (r. 592-628) several temples were built, like Wakakusa-dera and Horyuji. Buddhism began to spread among the aristocracy. In the Nara Period (710-784) Chinese models were imitated—Emperor Shomu tried to outdo the sovereigns on the mainland in the planning of his new capital and establishment of the great temple, Todaiji. As a result Nara style art and monumental architectural characteristically resemble Chinese grandeur and replicate its international style.

I. ILLUSTRATED SCRIPTURES
A. *KAKO GENZAI INGA-KYO*
The earliest extant illustrated Buddhist scriptures are the Japanese eighth-century versions of the *Sutra of Cause and Effect*, the *Kako genzai inga-kyo*.[6] Today numerous copies of the scripture are housed in both private and public collections in Japan. Their survival is no doubt due to the 1400 years of uninterrupted reverence of the Buddha in Japan. The oldest of the scrolls is ascribed to the Nara period (710-784) specifically the Tempyo era (729-748) under Emperor Shomu. Once owned by the Joborendai temple, they are now dispersed among the Nara National Museum, the Hoon-in Daigo temple, Tokyo University of Arts, the Atama Museum (Shizuoka ex. Masuda collections) and the personal collection of Prince Kuni.

Japanese scholars have used historical documents like the 737-dated inventory of scriptures in the Shosoin, the *Zushoryo Kyo Mokuroku*, to ascribe the eighth-century date to the scrolls. One list itemizes two sets of sixteen scrolls; and another dated 756 mentions a 13 scroll set.[7] The *Sanetaka koki,* or Diary of the Courtier Sanjoinishi Sanetaka, dated March 16, 1528 reports a scroll dated 735.[8] The copy that belonged to the Joborendai temple, which is judged to be the oldest, has an inscription that gives only the day, name, and rank of the scribe, Shoshasei, Junior eighth rank of the sutra copying office.[9] Okudaira found a similar inscription on the roller of the scroll that belongs to the Hoon Temple that he translated as: *"Seventh day of the fourth month, scribe of the lower eighth rank."* Beginning in the Tempyo era the scribes who copied the sutras in the Official Bureau were ranked and so the inscriptions can be used to affirm the eighth-century date of the scrolls. A large enterprise, the sutra copying office had two to three hundred workers including scribes, "proof readers," and binders.[10] The scrolls belonging to the Tokyo University of Art and the Atami Art Museum may be a century later as both bear the seal of the Dempo-in of Kofuku temple, a building constructed for Prince Shuei in the second decade of the ninth century.[11]

After the eighth century, illustrations of the *Inga-kyo* subsided until the Kamakura era (1185-1333) when there was revival of interest in the Nara period and its art. At this time several versions of the scroll were made. One signed by the artists Keiin and Shogumara of the thirteenth century is housed in the Nezu Art Museum. A similar signature is found on the work formerly in the Daitoku Memorial Library and currently in the Goto Art Museum in Tokyo. A second Kamakura example, ascribed to the later half of the thirteenth century, once part of the Matsunaga collection, is now in the Burke Collection. Another section, made into a hanging scroll, is in the Power's collection.[12] Structural and stylistic differences distinguish these later versions. In contrast to the early ones, in which landscape elements act as both a stage setting and divider between the scenes, the Kamakura era scrolls have no interruption in the continuous flow of narration. Secondly, the quick hand of the draftsman in the later works reveals a vitality of line lacking in the earlier Nara period examples.[13] Lastly, the depiction of Mara's monstrous army and deformed daughters in the Power's scroll resemble the depictions of the ghoulish creatures of the Hell scenes in the twelfth century Buddhist scrolls—the *Jigoku Zoshi* and *Gaki Zoshi*.[14]

1. JOBORENDAIJI VERSION

The Joborendaiji scrolls are the earliest, most complete, continuous illustration with the pictures above and text written below in a one-to-one relationship. (FIGURE 66) The events are read in sequential fashion from right to left, as the scroll unrolls. Despite the lack of an accompanying written text for the illustrations at Dunhuang's Cave 290 and Yungang's Cave VI, these two sites provide the best comparative material, for they were closely based on the same scripture—the GXYJ. Since, in the early centuries of Japan's national development, Chinese art played a formative role, the Buddhist architecture, sculpture, and painting greatly resemble religious developments and styles of art on the mainland. In the case of the *Inga-kyo* such influences are easily seen. The details of costume, architecture, landscape, figural type and disposition reflect direct borrowing from mainland prototypes. Naturally the Japanese made changes and these become evident when the illustrated scripture is compared with the Chinese examples from Yungang or Dunhuang.

The Joborendaiji scroll begins with the events of the first half of the second chapter—the archery contest that has counterparts at both Dunhuang and Yungang. The text informs the reader that when the prince arrived at his tenth year, his father Suddhodana summoned well-known archers to instruct him. They began by requesting the prince to demonstrate what skills he had. Finding that a single bow was of insufficient strength, he joined seven bows together and shot an arrow, which pierced seven targets. All were taken aback at this display of awesome strength and accuracy. The scene takes place in a garden setting with a background file of trees, some decorative rocks, and a pavilion in which the bodhisattva and his attendants are housed. Holding the bow and arrow ready, the prince has shot one arrow, which pierced the first target; another passes through the seventh. Twelve youthful onlookers on the left and five figures on the right surround the pavilion. The architecture is Chinese style—the gabled, tiled roof and bracketing resemble the structures in the biographical compositions at Dunhuang and Yungang. The targets—with spherical drums supported by pillars, surmounted by decorative plumes, and shown in three-quarter view—also duplicate the Chinese prototypes, but here more targets are depicted.

Next the prince's spectacular performance is related to the king. Seated in a pavilion in the posture of royal ease, the king listens to the report of the archery instructor kneeling before him; courtiers stand in attendance on the left.

The throwing of the elephant takes place outside the city gates where the thick defensive walls are made of brick; there is a Chinese watchtower placed on a diagonal. Villagers whose egress is blocked by the elephant's carcass stand to the left. Devadatta holds the beast's nose, about to smash it with his fist—in a fit of temper he will paralyze it. The groups of large and small boulders and scattered trees that fill the foreground set the scene as well as separate it from the next event.

Standing by the city gate, which is nestled among rocks and trees, the townspeople explain to Nanda the reason for their inability to get through the gate. Three figures are on the right; the beast lies unconscious in the center. Entering from the left, attended by his retinue, the crown prince wears princely long white robes with flowing sleeves and a youthful double knot hairdo. Another rocky landscape acts as scene divider. The prince hurls the elephant over the city gate, holding it in that memorable pose—the four feet of the animal rest in his hand, his right arm is extended for balance. Attendants, on the left watch the extraordinary feat described in the text above.

Suddhodana, seated in his pavilion with two attendants, watches the archery competitions. The three cousins, Siddhartha, Nanda, and Devadatta, stand in the pavilion: one still holds the bow and arrow; his shot, already discharged, has pierced the first drum. Five onlookers surround the pavilion. The decorated target drums are lined up in three-quarter-profile view. In the foreground a group of rocks gradually builds up into a slope that divides the scene. The rendering of the archery contest here seems repetitious, for shortly before the demonstration of Siddhartha's skills at archery were depicted.

Ananda and Devadatta, the prince's two cousins, engage in a wrestling contest. As the text relates they were evenly matched, and in this version the bodhisattva interferes—standing between them. His strength is so great that they both fall to the ground. But because of his compassionate spirit, the text explains, neither suffers any injury or pain. The two wrestlers wear only loincloths in true Gandharan style, but the third wears tunic and trousers. On the right are three figures, at left there are five; this distribution of attendants is a conventional grouping that is commonly employed when a crowd of onlookers is called for in the text below. Although the scene of breaking up the wrestling bout has not been found in China, there are depictions of the match at both Yungang Cave VI and Dunhuang Cave 290.

A unique representation in the *E-Inga-kyo* is the ritual coming of age, marked by the lustration ceremony. In the text the king summoned the petty kings of the neighboring realms for the ceremony:

> *Then Suddhodana sent for his ministers to consult them about the prince's having come of age. [They agreed] that he was*

*knowledgeable and courteous, performing satisfactorily in all
matters. "Now is the time for the ritual of lustration with water
drawn from the four great seas." All of the petty kingdoms were
invited to the ceremony to be held on the eighth day of the second
month. On that day all the people, sages, and sramanas from the
[surrounding] kingdoms gathered like clouds. Banners and
canopies were hung, incense burned, flowers scattered, bells rung,
and drums struck. Music was made with all kinds of instruments
fashioned from precious materials. Sages arrived carrying pots on
their heads filled with water drawn from the four seas. Sramanas
came doing the same. Then the ministers approached the king in
turn, carrying (ewers filled with water) on their heads. They
poured [them] over the prince. Next the official seal fashioned
from the seven precious (materials) was handed over to the prince.
At the strike of the great drum a loud voice announced: "Now here
is Siddhartha, the heir apparent." That night dragons appeared
lined up in rows in the sky. Celestials made unearthly music, with
their contrasting voices they harmoniously sang "Oh excellent! To
be in Kapilavastu when the prince is named heir. On this day he is
installed as crown prince of the eight kingdoms."*[15]

The artist has pictured many of these details. In the foreground two
large gongs are suspended from wooden frames, nearby two men each
hold a stick ready to strike. Two officials upturn the ewers over the
head of the prince. Banners animated by the wind flutter and the eight
classes of beings—dragons, devas, guardians and others—together
praise the newly named heir.

In the first meditation the restless prince, having requested
permission, leaves the precincts of the palace and comes to the border
of the realm. There he dismounts to sit beneath a shady tree and watch
the farmer and oxen plow the earth. As the text describes, moved to
compassion by the toil of beast and man and the plight of earthworms
upturned by the plow being eaten by birds that swoop down, he enters
meditation. The shade of the tree becomes immobilized to protect the
meditating prince. In the scroll the prince is seated beneath the tree at
the center. On the right, contained within the broad contours of the
hill, are the farmer and his ox. Witness to the miracle of the shade are
his groom Chandaka, his horse Kanthanka, and the king, who,
informed of the strange occurrence, has just arrived. On the right two
grooms attend to his tethered horse. Further left the king kneels before
his seated son and, in unique version of the event, extends his hand to

the prince. Accompanying the text, which offers a long discussion about the prince's meditative thoughts, is an extensive rocky landscape.

The prince is in his palace surrounded by members of his harem who unsuccessfully attempt to divert him. The landscape emerges again—tall scaly mountains, vegetative grasses, and a few leafy trees. The wedding follows. Suddhodana is seated out-of-doors on a low dais, he has a writing table before him. Behind him are three attendants; in front are five kneeling advisors. A tall hill with flowering and leafy trees occupies the background. This setting is absent at Yungang and Dunhuang where most scenes of the king and his courtiers are placed within the palace walls, and often the advisors are in adjacent halls.

The setting is repeated with the notable addition of Yashodhara who is seen from the rear and dressed in typical Sui-early Tang fashion. A slender girl, she wears a long dress with flaring hem, low slung scarf around her shoulders, and hair piled in a low chignon.[16] While the sutra describes the nuptial preparations, the marriage cortege is depicted making its way through a landscape. A mountain slope gradually builds up to the top of the scroll. These are not the low rolling hills of Japan later popularized in native style painting but the steep cliffs of China's topography. At left are city gates through which the wedding party passes. Three ox-drawn carriages proceed: one is in the gate; another, in profile, is on the road, and a third, in rear view, disappears behind the mountains that loom on the left. The cortege travels on a road that curves and recedes on a diagonal. The carriages differ from those pictured at Dunhuang, they are not open-topped, but rectangular boxes with overhanging roofs and black walls. The rear of the carriage is open, but curtains conceal the passengers. Two servants walk alongside guiding the oxen.

The newlyweds are in their palace seated on a low dais, entertained by five female musicians. The bodhisattva's lack of interest in his bride described in the text is pictorially expressed in this garden scene by the large-scale rock that separates the married couple, stressing their alienation. Flowers, decorative rocks, and trickling streams are deftly drawn and delicately colored. (FIGURE 66, right side)

The four exists are a repetitive cycle of events that begins with the prince approaching his father, who is seated in the open air on a low dais. Uniquely in this text, the youth requests permission to leave the palace precinct for a short excursion. Attending the king are four members of his retinue, drawn behind them is a hill, sparsely populated by a few flowering trees. In the first sortie the city gate is on the left, the prince rides his mount with five attendants beside him; on the far right beneath the craggy mountain is the stooped old man; flowering trees are placed on the right and in the background. Following a mountainous passage, the prince is in his palace seated on a low dais surrounded by female attendants. Despondent, he meditates on the suffering of old age. The king holds court in open air and receives the unhappy news that his son is even more depressed after his encounter. The cycle begins anew with the prince kneeling before his father requesting permission to go out for another excursion.

The composition of the second exit is reversed; now the gate is on the right and the party is facing to the left. The sick man is seated on a mat; two women nurse him. The artist seeks variety through the reversal of the compositional elements as well as the addition of the women, who are not described in the text. This presents the possibility that the copyist and illustrator were different people, and that the latter was not necessarily able to read the text which he was illuminating. The scene of the prince's return to the palace is also somewhat altered, the prince is alone in his palace, and on the right the groom Chandaka leads the horses back to the stable. Suddhodana receives the report of the failure of the second excursion. There is a brief interlude with the prince and his retinue. The scripture tells of the second exit, but the illustrations have the seated bodhisattva with one of the women combing his hair; two stand nearby, and two more approach from the right. This is the king's attempt to distract his son by adding more young women to his harem.

Yudani, the Brahman ascetic who wandered into Kapilavastu and who under protest obeyed the king's order to become the prince's constant companion, is now included in the royal retinue as it nears the city gate. He wears a loincloth and scarf, is barefoot, and has his hair in a tall topknot. It is his job to report on the prince to the king, which he does in the following scenes.

The city gates indicate the third exit (the text describes the preparations made to clean the roads, scatter flowers, and hide unfortunates). Accompanying the prince on horseback is his entourage, which now includes Yudani. The ascetic has usurped Chandaka's role as mediator between the prince and the vision encountered—the dead man, covered by a shroud, borne on a pallet by four pallbearers. On the right the bereaved widow kneels. Details depicted at Dunhuang, such as the crying children sharing their mother's tears and members of the funeral cortege who burn incense, throw flowers, and carry banners and streamers, are omitted. As the text continues with a vivid description of the suffering caused by death, the artist illustrates the retinue of the deceased, followed by the bodhisattva and Yudani. Increasingly depressed, the prince turns his horse around, and the entourage follows his lead. A spacious landscape of trickling brook, flowering trees, and rocks fills the area above as the philosophical discussion on the nature of death continues. The intervening spaces between the monotonous sequences of the exit cycle are accompanied by similar landscape scenery.

On the way back to his palace the prince happens upon a park where there are music making maidens, decorative streamers, banners, and flowering trees, all of which heighten his sadness. The youthful entertainers are dressed in typical Tang style, recalling those courtly parties painted on musical instruments housed in the eighth-century Japanese imperial repository, the Shosoin.[17] Following a brief passage of verdant hills is an image of the meditating prince. The text relates he has attained the fourth stage of meditation. Yudani kneels before the bodhisattva who is seated in pensive posture under a leafy tree. On the left are two servants. The party returns home. Yudani reports the calamitous results of the third exit to the king, who, as usual, holds court out of doors.

The fourth exit begins with the prince seated in his palace surrounded by his music-making harem. A landscape with the city gates accompanies the text's description of his melancholy. Once again, the princely party departs the city. After dismounting, the prince sits beneath a tree when an ascetic, dressed as a monk with shaven head and carrying a begging bowl, appears. The scroll seems to be patched here. Soon after is the prince's vision of a monk flying through the air; the monk is on the left. Finally, the prince orders his carriage to turn about and they return home along the banks of the river with its leafy trees and rocks. Yudani again informs the king of the prince's state of mind. Another scene of the prince in a garden attended by several girls takes the place of the sleep of the harem.

The prince having reached his twenty-ninth year, kneels in front of his father and requests permission to leave the world. Surrounding Suddhodana, in his open-air court, are courtiers and servants who hold the regal paraphernalia. Next the king weeps copiously at the request of his son. Amidst some patching the scroll ends.

In the Joborendai scrolls the copyist's hand reproduces narrative details—fashionable woman's garb, chariots, musical parties, and garden settings—which reflect contemporary court life in China. Large areas present landscapes, which were of great interest in Tang China. Ninth century art historical texts extol the beauty of landscape efforts by such artists as the Li family, Wang Wei, and Wu Daozu. In addition to the typical scenic space cell that frames the figural disposition (reminiscent of the Gu Kaizhi scrolls and more contemporary examples at Dunhuang) extensive landscape passages act as a divider between the scenes. Some are mountainscapes with distant views of valleys. Often such landscape sections are the pictorial counterpart to the non-narrative sections of the texts. Unlike the artists of the Chinese cave-chapels who were not attempting a one-to-one relationship in the illustration of a scripture and could therefore be more selective, these illustrators had to cover the space above the text with appropriate imagery even when the text was philosophically abstract, repetitive, or monotonous. Also the presence of the text required the illustrators to be more literal in their visualizations. As a result, their efforts seem, at times, swollen with repetitive figural and landscape scenes.

2. HOON-IN COLLECTION SCROLL OF THE INGA-KYO

The third chapter of the *Inga-kyo* from the Hoon-in collection ascribed to the Nara period shares several characteristics with the Joborendaiji version. The scroll begins with the royal family's unhappy reception of Chandaka and Kanthanka who has returned home with the crown jewels but no heir. Suddhodana, seated on a low dais, receives the groom who holds the prince's jewels in his hands. When the women of the court are notified of the prince's departure, Yashodhara swoons as she did both in the text and in the bas-relief from Amaravati.

The rest of the scroll is occupied with the events of six years of ascetic wandering in the forest that culminate in the enlightenment cycle. The prince visits with a brahmin ascetic seated in a rocky grotto in the forest. The bodhisattva is dressed as a prince though the text has already told how he has cut his hair and exchanged clothes with a hunter. It must have seemed problematic to the illustrators to change the identity of the main character. He next encounters the leader of an ascetic colony who wears a fur cap; some of his followers ride horses through the countryside. The prince explains his reasons for leaving home. The search party of five dispatched by his father rides through the landscape in pursuit. On the left the bodhisattva continues his wandering.

Reaching Rajagriha the prince enters the city gate and is met by a throng of people. One member of the group, attracted by the beauty of the prince, reports his arrival to King Bimbisara. The king sits in his pavilion with three messengers on the right, he sends one of them to find this extraordinary stranger. The messenger nears the rocky enclosure in which the prince is meditating; flanking the scene are two ginkgo trees on the banks of the river. These landscape elements are sketchily drawn. But the mountains are not convincingly portrayed and seem papery and the trees are only defined as crude trunks with leaves that individually sprout from the branches.

King Bimbisara, informed of the prince's location, sets out with a few of his retinue; they ride off in search of the prince. Having found him, they dismount and approach the contemplative. In answer to Bimbisara's questions, the bodhisattva explains his quest and before taking his leave is forced to promise to return after enlightenment. They bid him farewell and he walks away to the left.

For a second time the five-man search party is shown—one lifts his hand to his mouth to call out, another shades his eyes to improve his sight; a third extends his hands pointing, while the fourth holds the reins of his horse. The bodhisattva continues his travels in search of the mountain sages of whom he has heard. A short section of hills and trees introduces the mountainous setting in which he encounters Alara Kalama and Udraka Ramaputra, two eminent mountain ascetics. The two ascetics are portrayed as described in the text: wearing animal skins, barefoot, with their long locks tied on top of their heads. They engage in long discussion on the nature of pain and suffering, but the bodhisattva is disappointed with their lack of insight and prepares to depart. The philosophical debates take place in a mountainous setting with scattered trees and rocks. These characters are his last encounter with the world; they represent the highest level of conventional wisdom. Subsequently, the bodhisattva cuts himself off from external events to seek inner wisdom. These extremely long pictorial passages are rather unimaginative and repetitious. In the seventh and final scene the ascetics bid him farewell; he goes off to the left, they stand to the right.

Seated by the bank of a river, the bodhisattva has resolved to restrict his daily intake of food to only two grains and to practice self-mortification. As witness to his vow two devas fly down; dressed as Sui-Tang angels, in dhotis and fluttering scarves. Cloud puffs beneath them indicate their heavenly descent. The eventual success of the search party results in an encounter with the now emaciated bodhisattva, though he is still shown wearing his court costume. Four of the party remain in the forest, the fifth returns to the city. Having passed through the city gate, he reports to Suddhodana seated in his pavilion. The king again summons his court advisors and they resolve to dispatch another party. The groom Chandaka, who in the text takes responsibility for leaving the prince alone in the forest in the first place, leads this search party. These events are unique to this sutra. A brief composition of rocks and ginkgo trees follow. Chandaka receiving his orders makes his preparations and departs. Ox-drawn carriages form the caravan of the search party. Informed that the prince is extremely thin, they bring food supplies to him. Finally Chandaka finds the prince, prostrates himself, and begs him to return home. Rejected Chandaka returns alone.

The enlightenment cycle begins with the gods descending on a cloud to beg the prince to cease fasting. Convinced of the error of the path of self-mortification, he strips himself to bathe in the Nairanjana River. But the banks are too steep and slippery and, as the texts state, he is so enfeebled a divine agent must assist the prince to get out of the water. Now, for the first time the prince is dressed as a bodhisattva in dhoti and fluttering scarves. A divine messenger begs him to eat, and the milkmaid Nandapala, dressed as a court beauty, prepares a meal of milk gruel. Kneeling before him, she offers it with both hands. The five men of the search party, afraid to return home without the prince, remained in the forest practicing austerities with him. But when they witness his eating, they believe he has abandoned the spiritual path and reject him.

After the meal the bodhisattva begins his walk to the bodhi tree, during which he experiences many miraculous signs that augur his imminent enlightenment—earthquakes, loud noises, restoration of the sight to the blind nagas, singing blue birds, thunder, and fragrant winds. Most of these omens are rendered. The dragon, with his sight restored, nears the bodhisattva and praises him. Birds fly in circular formation above his head, and on the left the dragon and his wife, in human form, kneel reverently. The gift of grass-cutter shows the two men walking together; one offers the grass; the other extends his hand to accept it. At the end the bodhisattva sits in a rocky setting on top of the grass under the bodhi tree.

The multiple scenes of the temptation of Mara are all pictured. Seated in his palace, Mara confers with his son who has inquired why he is so sad. He converses with his daughters who stand before him. Curiously they are drawn in ancient garb of the Six Dynasties—the easy flowing robes and windswept ribbons as worn by the women on the Datong screen of 484.[18] The girls escort their father to the place where the bodhisattva is seated; he is now shown as an early Tang-style seated Buddha with his left shoulder covered and the right one bare. Aiming his bow and arrow, Mara threatens the meditative. Behind him Sumati dissuades his father from attacking. The attempted seduction by the three daughters follows; the daughters are on the left of the Buddha; further left they are transformed into old hags: stooped over, leaning on canes, with untailored garments that suggest their bloated figures. Mara, in a landscape of hills and trees plans the next phase of his attack—the seduction of soft words. But the bodhisattva responds by calling the earth to witness to his countless incarnations. Emerging from behind a rocky escarpment, the earth spirit holds a vase of precious materials filled with lotus flowers, offers them to the Buddha-to-be, and prostrates himself.

Mara in his garden is in an increasingly foul mood and schemes an attack by his demon army. In the following onslaught a close correspondence with the text is evident. Among the horrific creatures threatening the Buddha are armed naked figures, who wearing loincloths, carry sticks and swords. (FIGURE 66a) Monsters—one-eyed, dragon-headed, horned, or winged with fire—march in file amid the rolling hills. Attending Mara on the left of the bodhisattva is his horrific entourage—some in fur garments, others elephant-headed, boar-headed, or falcon-headed. Disembodied animal heads snarl and grimace on the right; some are reptilian, others canine, all are grotesque. According to the text below, the two figures in long robes and flowing scarves, one of which holds a skull in her hands, are Mara's sisters. A steep, craggy cliff with vegetative grasses provides the setting for the defeat. Weapons hurled by the demons are suspended in mid air—bows, pitchforks, and swords. In the sky is the god of thunder, encircled by his drums.   To the left one soldier unsuccessfully attempts to lift a rock.

A brief landscape sets the scene for the victory. Buddha's head is in the sky, the defeated Mara kneels, sword in hand. Cowed Mara returns to his dominion. A long landscape section ends with the victorious seated Buddha. Mara is in his palace, another landscape follows, and the Hoon-in scroll ends with the seated Buddha worshiped by two angelic beings.

3. OTHER SCROLLS OF THE INGA-KYO

The Matsuda Collection's scrolls illustrate the post-enlightenment events, relating the miraculous conversions, preaching scenes, and donations, which formed a minor role in the narrative art of India and China. These Kamakura scrolls reproduce the narrative details of the earlier series with remarkable fidelity.   Not being substantially different, they do not warrant describing.

CONCLUSIONS

This analysis of the *E Inga-kyo* has revealed the difficulties of sutra illustration. The artist at times strained to keep up with the text written below. Employing the emerging art of Tang landscape painting, the artist was able to provide narrative filler as well as a setting. These Nara-era scrolls differ from the continuous narrative art so favored in later Japanese scroll painting, in that the scenes are separate from one other in the Gandharan fashion, though the formal architectural dividers have been replaced with rolling hills. The dependence on Chinese prototypes is particularly evident in costume, furnishings, architectural and landscape elements. Even the high mountains of China are delineated.

But there is some variety in the treatment of scenes that gives an indication of intervention on the part of the Japanese artist. For example the conventional Chinese archery scene is rather different here. It may be the artists, familiar with the archery and wresting sports, felt free to change the composition slightly. These quotidian scenes of palace life and the heroic martial contests were as much an entertainment as a didactic tool. Careful comparison of the texts and images has shown that there may have been two sets of copyists—a scribe for the text, an illustrator for the pictures since there are occasional, though relatively minor, discrepancies.

Considering the slight degree of difference between these Japanese copies of Chinese scrolls and the illustrations found in mainland China, the extraordinary conservative nature of the pictorial biography must be acknowledged. For the most part, the narratives are homogenous with but small alterations in the details. These scrolls are basically uniform in content, mode of narration, figural disposition, and use of architecture.

II. OTHER EXAMPLES OF BIOGRAPHICAL NARRATIVES

Recently the Japanese scholar Kajitani Ryoji identified three kinds of biographical illustrations of the life of the Buddha in later painting in Japan: those based on the ancient tradition which focus on the four great events; those illustrating independent scenes; and the iconographical format of the eight great events.[19] These categories follow, in a more general way, the stages of narrative development outlined in this study. Yet another type of format for biographical scenes in Japan is the panel painting; on these selected scenes are presented in very complex narrative settings.[20] The latter demonstrate a late phase in the evolution of the biographical narratives as they have been deeply altered to suit native tastes in both style and iconography.

One example recently discussed by Masao Watanabe from the early Muromachi Period (fourteenth century) now in the Metropolitan Museum has several episodes from the biography of the Buddha. The scenes, painted on paper and pasted to panels, illustrate the birth, four exits, subjugation of Mara, and conversion of King Bimbisara; however it may be that they originally were eight in total and would have included the conception, temptation, enlightenment, and death.[21] According to Watanabe, the events are based on episodes from various sutras. Watanabe has demonstrated that these renderings are quite similar to a Kamakura-period scroll from Daifukuden-ji. Here the scenes such as the birth and bath preserve the Indo-Chinese tradition of Maya extending her arm and the baby issuing from the sleeve. But though she stands beneath a tall tree, she no longer grasps its branches for support. Female Japanese attendants in court dress surrounded her. For the bath, except for having but two dragons in the sky that hover over the standing child, the scene is similar to its predecessors. It is, as usual, conflated with the scene of the first steps which portrays the baby in the same way—raising his arm and taking seven steps marked out by lotus flowers. However, several important changes have taken place in the depiction of the four exits. Outside of a complex architectural compound, a Japanese palanquin draws the prince. Now there are two old men; the sick man is housed in a lean-to shelter; the dead man is in a coffin; and most interestingly, the fourth encounter with a monk is replaced by the image of a woman giving birth. As Watanabe points out these alterations reveal a new grouping representing the four sufferings—old age, sickness, death, and childbirth that was known in Japan since the Heian era, and may have been brought from ninth-century China.[22]

III. PARINIRVANA SCENES

The earliest scene of the death in Japan is the one preserved on the platform of the Horyuji pagoda dated in the temple inventory entry to 710. With the Distribution of the Relics, the paradise of Maitreya, and a hell scene, the four sculptural panoramas fill each quadrant of the central altar in the pagoda. Both the choice of themes and the use of the interior of the pagoda as a ritual space are extraordinary and nearly unknown elsewhere. Kuno found evidence in the record of the *Kokon mokuroko-sho* that the scenes of the distribution of the relics once had a pile of incense wood on the coffin emitting flames of fire and two figures of men carrying firewood to the cremation site.[23] At that time the damage and incompleteness of the scenes were also recorded.[24] Current opinion is that the sculptures have been moved from one scene to another. Extensive restoration and replacement of the sculptures hamper formal analysis and stylistic observations. The pagoda is heavily screened in now and nothing is observable in the darkened interior. However, it is important to note that the biographical narratives were included with the more conventional Mahayana themes. Their presence is probably due to the popularity of the Mahayanist version of the *Mahaparinirvana sutra*.

The great number of paintings of the death of the Buddha in Japan is remarkable contrast to the dearth of scenes elsewhere, save Xinjiang. Its popularity is in part due to the annual ritual commemoration of the death in Japan with the display of a *nehan* or parinirvana scene on February 15th.[25] Should a temple be bereft of a depiction, one is commissioned. Thus numerous examples can be found throughout Japan. One of the earliest is at Kongobu-ji at Koyasan. Colossal in size measuring over 100 inches square, the painting has a dated inscription: *"The seventh day of the fourth month of Otoku (1086)."* The huge Buddha is shown lying flat on his back, dead, a different version of the more common posture of bidding farewell—lying on his right side, propping his head with his right hand, and his legs placed one above each other. This variant position was noticed at Yungang, though these are small in scale, lack detail, are relatively unimportant in the overall scheme, making these representations poor comparisons.[26]   Adaptation to Japanese taste is easy to appreciate, though the Chinese prototypes are still remembered.

The painting is clearly Mahayanist in theme, as the numerous bodhisattvas and Buddhas in the audience attest; in fact each is named in an accompanying cartouche. As for bodhisattvas, there are Manjusri, Avalokitesvara, Samanthabhadra, and Maitreya. In the case of the latter his role is considerable: seated at the head of the dying Buddha, he is shown in full body pose (as opposed to the more crowded representations of figures standing behind the bed) with his hand resting on the funeral couch. Thus his role as future Buddha is anticipated. Although bodhisattvas as well as Buddhas were present in Chinese parinirvana scenes, Maitreya was not this prominent nor so clearly labeled; although some examples did include a standing Buddha among the mourners who might be identified as Maitreya.   In comparison to the bodhisattvas, the monks are diminished in size. The ten disciples (who include the Buddha's son Rahula) are drawn, but Kashyapa is not present, perhaps following the ancient but sometimes neglected tradition of his late arrival. In the upper left Maya descends on a cloud, a paragon of Heian court beauty. At Dunhuang she sits by the head of the bed, while in the Tang stele of Dayunsi she weeps over the coffin.   Among the numerous other figures may be counted Vimalakirti, Vajrapani, the householder Cunda, and his family.

Japanese preferences are also seen in secondary motifs. In these the number of representatives of the animal world increase dramatically, with a growing variety of creatures in postures of extreme mourning. For example, in the Koyasan representation a lion rolls on the ground in anguish. Stylistic adaptations in the painting of the mourners, the garments, brocade designs, hairdo, and heavy make-up as well as applied gold reflect Heian secular tastes. Perhaps most revealing of the native taste is the Japanese landscape of low rolling hills, rocky boulders, flowering trees, and deer grazing in the upper right corner.

Late medieval paintings of the death demonstrate a continuity of style despite the passage of time and artistic innovation. Carolyn Wheelwright's study of several medieval painting—one by Mincho in the early fifteenth century, another by Hasegawa Tohaku in the early seventeenth, and others— found a fairly strict concordance between the representations and the scriptural sources.[27] The slight variety in the depictions she traced to the affiliation of the artists and patrons with Buddhist sects and the texts that were important to them.

In conclusion the Japanese material demonstrates an early dependence on mainland style, iconography, and techniques. Thus the illustrated *Inga-kyo,* with its continuous narrative format in conjunction with the text written below and the style of architecture, dress, and other narrative details, shows a great indebtedness to China. Gradually, however new forms of presentation evolve that are the result of the evolution of Japanese Buddhism. In contrast to the didactic treatment of the biography in China, Japanese pictorial narratives demonstrate a freer hand in adopting certain scenes and placing them in a native landscape setting. Here too scenes are chosen for a variety of reasons that are the result of characteristic popular practice. Over the centuries such choices increasingly affect the appearance of the narratives. Because Buddhism is still a living religion in Japan, there is a wealth of material. When Mahayanism Buddhism became dominant early, the narratives were quickly marginalized, except for the scene of the Nehan which were mainstream. This annual celebration of the death of the Buddha stands out as distinct from mainland practices.

In conclusion the continuous support of Japanese Buddhist institutions for over more than a thousand years afforded a continuous evolution of art and iconography. Here the ancient material was hallowed and preserved. Thus we can see that scenes of the life of the Buddha were an important theme in early Japan and that the main characteristics of the narrative were not lost despite the great distance and centuries of its transmission east.

ENDNOTES

1. Pal 1988: 262. These were made in imitation of the Song dynasty set sent by the Chinese to Korea.

2. Pal, *Light of Asia,* 1984: cat. no. 27, p. 85.

3 . Yi Ki-baek (Catalogue of the) National Museum of Korea (Seoul, 1993):156.

4 . Pal, *Light of Asia,* cat. no. 10, p. 78 with the Maya's dream and conception, cat. no. 37, p. 93 with the great departure. The scrolls are in the Dongkuk University Museum, Seoul.

5 . S. Mizuno, *Asuka Buddhist Art: Horyuj*i (Tokyo: Heibonsha Press, 1974):14.

6 . Although a cache of scrolls was found at Dunhuang by the Stein expedition, the earliest dated scrolls are from the ninth century and are not pictorial narratives but illuminated front pieces and chapter divisions of the *Lotus sutra.* See H. Giles, *Six Centuries at Tun Huang* (London, 1944): 43.

7 . T. Kameda, *E Inga Kyo: Nihon Emakimono Zenshu*, vol. XVI (Tokyo: Kadokawa Publ. Co.,1969): 2; see also D. Seckel, *Emakimono,* trans. J. M. Brownjohn (NY: Pantheon Books, Inc., 1959).

8. Kameda 1969: 2.

9. Kameda 1969: 2.

10. H. Okudaira, *Narrative Picture Scrolls* trans. E. ten Grotenhuis (Tokyo: Weatherhill Inc.1966): 46 ff.

11. Kameda 1969: 2.

12. M. Murase, *Japanese Art, the Collection of Mary and Jackson Burke* (NY: Metropolitan Museum of Art, 1975): 44-46, entry #12; measuring 156.4 x 27.7 cm; ex collection Setsuda; Matsunaga Yasuzaemon, Tokyo; once a set of Shoriji, Nagoya. See J. Rosenfield, *Tradition of Japanese Art, the J. Powers' Collection* (Cambridge: Fogg Museum, 1970) p. 107ff; entry # 42, 43 measuring 26.7 x 40 cm; 27.6 x 22.9 cm.

13. Murase 1975: 45

14. Okudaira 1969: 179 One scroll of the *Gigoku Zoshi* attributed to Mit-sunaga of the early twelfth century is in the Nara National Museum. Another is in the Tokyo National Museum. One scroll of the *Gaki Zoshi* with a similar attribution is the Tokyo National Museum and another is in the Kyoto National Museum.

15 . GXYJ: 629.

16. This fashion has been observed in the recent early Tang (seventh to early eighth century) archaeological finds unearthed in Xian, the Tang capital; notably the tomb from the first decade of the eighth century of Princess Yong-tai in Xian, illustrated in Akiyama 1972: 131.

17. *Shosoin Gomotsu Zuroku* (Tokyo, 1969) vol. I: 51; vol. II: pl. 4.

18. *Historical Relics Unearthed in New China* (Beijing, 1972): pl. 135.

19. R. Kajitani, "Butsusen-zu no tenkai: bukkyo setsuwa-e no hyogen to tokuhitsu," *Nihon no bijitsu*, vol. 9, (Tokyo: Kodansha, 1991): 158-167. Ryoji maintains the set of eight was introduced from the Song dynasty; in this study they have been shown to derive from the Tang era.

20. Q. Phillips, "The Price Shuten Doji Screens: A Study of Visual Narrative," *Ars Orientalis*, vol. XXVI (1996): 1-22.This author demonstrated the very complicated narrative structure for later biographical depictions, unique to Japan, which has been adapted to screens.

21. M. Watanabe, "A Preliminary Study of 'Life of the Buddha' in Medieval Japan: The Metropolitan Museum Paintings," *Orientations*, September, 1996: 46-56.

22 . Watanabe mentions the Hojo-ji commissioned in 1022 displaying the four sufferings. Though he cites a text found in Dunhuang Cave 17 describing them, no illustration has been found. (see p. 48.)

23. Kuno 1958: 18.

24. Kuno 1958: 84.

25. Akiyama 1977: 48.

26. S. Moran, "The Death of the Buddha, a Painting at Koyasan," *Artibus Asiae,* vol. XXXVI (1974): 111.

27. Carolyn Wheelwright, "Late Medieval Nirvana Painting," *Archives of Asian Art,* vol. 38 (1985): 67-94.

CONCLUSION

In summary, the extant pictures of the life of the Buddha at the various sites in Central Asia, China, Korea and Japan reveal the initial importance of the pictorial life of the Buddha in Asia. Images of the historic Buddha and the remarkable events that shaped his life were a primary interest to believers. From the analysis of the material drawn from various cultures several dramatic transformations become apparent. Foremost is the role that the historic Buddha played in the development of Buddhism and its art as it was brought east. At first the historic Buddha was the focus of the doctrine. The events in his life encapsulated the major tenets of his teaching. The four exits illuminated the miseries of human existence, the great departure and meditation represented the difficult solution to end suffering. As Buddhism evolved into a religion whose concerns were increasingly that of universal salvation, concern for the historic Buddha and his personal path to enlightenment diminished. In the light of the new Mahayanist deities who promised salvation in an eternal paradise, Shakyamuni was eclipsed. However, the historic Buddha remained the source of the doctrine and reference to him was constant. Thus, in the early period the spiritual environments that comprised the cave-chapels of Xinjiang, Gansu, and China, images of the historic Buddha and the events in his life begin as a dominant iconographical theme. Gradually they become secondary, and then tertiary motifs.

An analysis of the formal characteristics of narrative technique in the portrayals of the pictorial biography indicates that the narrative evolution underwent several contrasting stages. Three major formats were identified. Stylistic changes gradually evolved as the result of the transformation of the doctrine as it adapted to the new cultures and the artistic milieu in which it was adopted.

In the first format narrative is a major element of the iconography. In this early phase the role of Shakyamuni is paramount. Biographical narratives function as an important theme of the decoration covering the walls of the main room in cave temples. The scenes are contained in individual rectangular panels set off from one another by formal architectural dividers. For the most part the panels are laid out in horizontal courses on the side walls of the cave. Read during ritual circumambulation of the cave, the images have a clearly didactic function—to familiarize the worshiper with the events in the life of the Buddha. Nearly the complete biography is told in chronological order, and narrative details are rendered with care. The Buddha is shown in normal scale in contrast to the other members of the narrative scene.

The story is told in a continuous linear manner, being based on Indian Gandharan compositions (whether the preserved stone bas-reliefs from stupas or the purported existence of illustrated scriptures). Early caves utilizing this format include the Stepped Cave at Qizil. In contrast to these the earliest biographical narratives at Dunhuang comprise single scenes like the four exits of Cave 275, or the more popular scene of the temptation in Cave 254. Set against a red background, white-skinned figures are shown with a bare minimum of setting in rectangular compositions (Caves 254, 275).

For the most part these early caves rely on western themes, colors, appearance of the figures, and style of rendering their bodies and draperies. At Yungang the complete biography carved on the walls of caves, as in Cave VI, is based on western compositions, iconography and narrative details; however, Chinese preferences are clearly incorporated. Figures are no longer western in appearance nor are their naked bodies exposed to view. By the end of the sixth century such changes are also seen in the pictorial narratives at Dunhuang, as in Cave 290, but by this time the narratives, though complete, no longer occupy a primary area in the decor. Eighth-century examples of illustrated sutras are found in Japan, based on Chinese prototypes of the late sixth to the seventh century. Told in continuous fashion with the text written below, these horizontal scrolls demonstrate the one to one relationship between the written scripture and its pictorial illustration. Moreover, these scrolls suggest what might have existed in an earlier period and served as the basis for the illustrations of the life of the Buddha in Central Asia and China.

In the second phase of narrative evolution there is a reduction in the number of scenes portrayed, a decline in the amount of detail included in the individual scenes, and secondary placement of the scenes in the decorative decor of the ritual space. There are three subtypes of this phase—the epitomized cycle, the abbreviated grouping, and the iconic format. The prototype for an abbreviated group of scenes may be associated with Gandharan traveling shrines and perhaps lost portable paintings. At Qizil, the scenes may be contained in lunette-shaped frames over the door wall as in Cave 99, or more frequently placed on the rear wall.

Usually the epitomized cycle of the life includes a set of four of the most important scenes or a set of eight. This technique, characteristic of a later phase of narrative development in India, was first seen during the mature period of Gandhara and Amaravati. Later it was brought to a climax by the Sarnath sculptors of the Guptan era. At Qizil, it is utilized in Cave 19 of the Maya Cave in the illustration of the story of King Ajatasatru. This story within a story is the earliest painted example of the four great events in the life of the Buddha in this region. Epitomized cycles are seen later in China proper. By the late sixth century, as a result of a wave of influence from Guptan India, the set of eight scenes is appropriated for pagoda decor, as well as independent freestanding steles. Silk banner paintings from the early Tang at Dunhuang sometimes display epitomized cycles as well. However, the scenes on the banners often appear be personal favorites of the donors or randomly selected rather than part of the canonical set. Later this format was also transmitted from China to Japan, where the epitomized cycle emerges as a format for screen paintings in the late medieval period.

The iconic format of the second stage employs small narrative figures to flank the large central icon of the Buddha. Indian precedent can easily be found. Among the most familiar examples are Guptan caves I or II at Ajanta. Typically treated in this mode are representations of the temptation, first sermon, and gift of food by the merchants. It is notable that this format in which narrative elements are clearly subordinate to the iconic image can be seen in a variety of locations including the caves of Qizil, Dunhuang, Yungang, and elsewhere. Despite the reduction of the narrative elements of the life of the Buddha in this second phase, it is important to note that Shakyamuni is still important. One reflection of this status is the significant locations of these types of icons in the sacred chapels.

In the last phase isolated scenes in small-scale act as a decorative element in places of secondary or tertiary import in the cave. These do not represent an epitomized biography but are randomly chosen. This is the last phase of narrative illustration. Such representations, nearly miniature in scale, combine to form a decorative pattern in the ceilings at Qizil where a lozenge design incorporates small seated Buddha images with attendant figures. At Dunhuang, Yungang and Longmen, decorative pairings of certain scenes as the conception and great departure act as a minor theme among the myriad decoration of the caves. These narratives are reduced to a single compressed image.

PARINIRVANA

In this study the scenes of the death have been treated as an independent subject. Formulated later than the pictorial cycle, the death scene is portrayed quite differently. Similar to the evolution of other illustrations from the biography, two formats are appropriated for the parinirvana—the narrative and iconic. The former derives from Gandharan India where the secondary scenes dealing with the activities of the cremation and division of the relics are shown in detail. The iconic scenes, which portray a large Buddha surrounded by mourners, undergo several transformations. Representations are increasingly emotional in their expression of the grief of the mourners. The participants grow in number and diversity to include not only the historical characters but also all manner of divine creatures and members of the animal world; and the size of the reclining Buddha reaches colossal proportions in contrast to the scale of the mourners. Precedent for the colossal dying Buddha is found in Guptan India.

Qizil artists introduced many modifications in the format, presentation, and details of the parinirvana. Innovative architectural organization of the interior ritual space results in the placement of the important image of the dying Buddha in a rear chamber with flanking aisles that allow for circumambulation. The death image appears in most of the caves; its primacy is evident in its prominent placement and its large size. In China, however, due to indigenous distaste for scenes of human suffering, the death scene appears infrequently. Caves 294 and 420 at Dunhuang have narrative illustrations of the death cycle in accordance with the scriptures. There in small scale are the farewell, Kashyapa's late arrival, the wrapping of the coffin, the burning of the coffin, and the battle of the relics. Prototypes for these kinds of scenes are present among the Gandhara bas-reliefs and the caves of Qizil. Some other Dunhuang caves importantly display the iconic form on the rear wall of the cave-chapel. These icons reflect Mahayanist doctrine in their inclusion of multiple deities, the Buddha of the future, as well an international set of mourners. However, among the caves of China proper, representation of the death is even more rare. In Japan parinirvana scenes achieve a new importance: they are the chief focus of annual celebrations of the event. Ritually displayed large-scale paintings offer an ever-increasing complexity in the number and diversity of the mourning figures drawn from the supernatural as well as the animal world. These parinirvana paintings are clearly associated with Mahayanist teachings.

Looking at the body of evidence, it can be said that native artists, once introduced to the biographical depictions, gradually adapted them to accommodate indigenous preferences. Thus changes in figure type, clothing, and architecture reveal regional styles. Alterations in the details of scenes like the marriage, athletic competitions and death evince local artists adapting the scenes to their cultural melieu. The narratives are also a vehicle by which to see currents of contemporary artistic movements such as the emerging art of landscape painting in China, Korea and Japan.

In conclusion, changes in the representation of the pictorial biography gradually evolved over centuries. Adaptations emerged as the result of the transformation of the doctrine in its accommodation to the new cultures in which it was adopted. Despite these alterations in style and expression, images from the life of the Buddha are easily identifiable, attesting to the essential homogeneity of the pictorial tradition in Indian, Central Asia, China, and Japan.

GLOSSARY
CAST OF CHARACTERS

Ananda youthful disciple and personal attendant of the Buddha

Asita bramin sage and seer

King Bimbisara of Magdha , king encountered during years as an ascetic in the forest

Chandaka personal attendant and groom to the young prince Siddhartha

Dipamkara Buddha Buddha of the past during whose life Shakyamuni incarnated as young ascetic paid him homage *Indra* ancient Vedic sky deity

Drona brahmin sage who divides the relic of the Buddha among his followers

Kanthaka Siddhartha's horse

Kashyapa Aged and learned disciple of the Buddha

Indra Vedic sky god

Mahaprajapati step mother of Siddhartha

Malla--Indian princes, lay followers of the Buddha responsible for funeral of the Buddha

Mara--God of death and desire

Maya Mother of the Buddha

nagas--snake deities

rishi--ascetic

Shakyamuni name of the historic Buddha

Siddhartha--first name of the prince who becomes the Buddha.

Subhadra, the last disciple to be personally admitted by the Buddha.

Suddhodana Father of the Buddha

Yaksha earth deities

Yashodhara wife of the Buddha

TERMS

abhaya mudra--hand gesture indicating "Fear Not" with right hand raised, finger up, palm facing out.

arhat--the monk ideal, goal of religious practice of self-discipline and meditation

atman-- soul

bhakti--devotion

Bhumisparsa-mudra--hand gesture representing enlightenment, with right hand pointing to ground.

bodhisattvas--divine beings who have evolved to the highest spiritual stage and are ready to enter *nirvana* but postpone their own salvation to help others achieve it.

chaitya--long narrow hall with rounded end housing a stupa at the rear and ambulatory path

deva-- celestial being

dharma--teachings of the Buddha

dharmacakra-mudra--hand gesture indicating teaching/ preaching the law, with fingers of right hand in gesture of counting fingers on left.

dhoti--a piece of cloth wound around the body like a skirt

dhyana mudra--hand gesture of the Buddha indicating meditation, with both hands in lap, palms facing up, the right hand placed on top of the left

Dipamkara jataka-- tells the story of a former incarnation of the historic Buddha, when as a young brahmin ascetic, he bartered his future lives to purchase flowers to offer in homage to the Dipamkara Buddha

Hinayana--derogatory term applied to earlier form of Buddhism by later sects.

jatakas--stories of life experiences of the previous incarnations of the Buddha.

kakemon-- hanging scroll painting

karma-- the belief in reincarnation conditioned by the quality of life and actions of one's *atman* or soul as it transposes through eternal rebirths

lakshana--32 distinguishing characteristics or marks of beauty seen on the baby Siddhartha

mandorla--oval shape body halo

Mahayana--later development of Buddhism in which numerous Buddhas and divinities offer the faithful a path to salvation

Maitreya--Buddha of the Future

mithuna--loving couple representing fertility

mudra--hand gesture of the Buddha imbued with symbolic meaning

Nehan enlightenment of the Buddha (Japanese)

nirvana-- enlightenment of the Buddha

parinirvana--death of the Buddha

sangha--monastic institution

Shakyamuni Buddha--Historic Buddha

sramana--Buddhist monk

stupa--a reliquary containing the remains of the Buddha buried in the ground and covered with a mound of earth.

sutra--religious scripture

Theravada--"way of the Elders", early form of Buddhism, orthodox sect.

Three Jewels-- (*triratna*): respecting the person of the Buddha (Buddha), revering his words (*Dharma*), and supporting the monastic community (*Sangha*).

ushnisna--a small, discrete protrusion covered with wavy hair on the Buddha

Vedic religion ancient proto Hindu religion in ancient India

BIBLIOGRAPHY

SCRIPTURES

Abhinishkramana sutra, trans. into Chinese by Djanakuta, *Foben jing*, ca. sixth century, trans. into English by Samuel Beal, *The Romantic Legend of Sakya Buddha*, 1875, reprint Delhi: Motilal Banarsidass, 1985.

Buddhacarita, trans. from Sanskrit by E. B. Cowell, *Buddhist Mahayana Texts*, Sacred Books of the East, vol. XLIX, 1894, reprint NY, 1969.

Foshuo puyaojing, trans. in 308 C.E. by Dharmaraksha, Bunjio Nanjio, *Daizokyo*, Tokyo: Taisho edition 1912-1926, vol. IV, no. 186: 491ff.

Foshuo taizu ruying benqi jing, (TRBJ) trans. by Zhi Qian, third century, Bunjio Nanjio, *Daizokyo*, Tokyo: Taisho edition 1912-1926, vol. III, no. 186: 461ff.

Foshuo xingzan jing, trans. from the Sanskrit attributed to Ashvaghosa ca. common era, into Chinese by Dharmaraksha in 414-421 C.E., into English by S. Beal, in the Sacred Books of the East, Oxford, 1883.

Guozhu xianzai yinguo jing (GXYJ) trans. in 443-443 C.E., by Gunabhadra, in Bunjio Nanjio, *Daizokyo*, Tokyo: Taisho edition 1912-1926, vol. IV, no. 189: 622ff.

Lalitavistara, Tibetan version, trans. by Edouard Foucaux into French, Paris, 1880.

The Lotus Sutra, trans. into Chinese by Dharmaraksha C.E. 414-421, into English by E.B. Cowell, E. *Buddhist Mahayana Texts: Lotus Sutra*, Sacred Books of the East, vol. XLIX, London, 1888.

The Lotus Sutra, trans. by H. Kern, Sacred Books of the East, vol. XXI, London, 1883 reprinted under the title, *Saddharma Pundarika or The Lotus of the True Law*, NY, 1963.

The Lotus Sutra, trans. by Leon Hurvitz, *Scripture of the Lotus Blossom of the Fine Dharma*, NY: Columbia Univ. 1976.

Madhyama-ityukta-sutra, trans. in 207 C.E. into Chinese, *Zhongbenqi jing*, by the Western monks Tanguo and Kang Mengxian, Bunjio Nanjio, *Daizokyo* Tokyo: Taisho edition 1912-1926, vol. IV, no. 196: 147-163.

Mahaparinirvana sutra, trans. from the Pali to English by T. W. Rhys Davids, in the Sacred Books of the East, vol. XI, London, 1881, rpt. in *Buddhist Suttas*, NY, 1969.

Mahavastu, trans. from the Sanskrit by Edouard Foucaux, Paris, 1914.
Xuxingbenqi jing (XXBJ) trans. in C.E. 197 by Ku Dali and Kang
Mengzeng, *Daizokyo*, Tokyo: Taisho edition, 1912-1926, vol. III,
no.185: 471ff.

WESTERN LANGUAGE SOURCES

Acker, William, *Some T'ang and pre T'ang Texts on Chinese Painting*,
Leiden: Brill Publ., 1954.
Adams, Edward, *Korea's Golden Age,* Seoul: Seoul International
Publishing House, 1991.
Akiyama, Terukazu, *Arts of China, Buddhist Cave Temples*, vol. I,
Tokyo: Heibonsha, 1972.
Alchin, F.R. "A Cruciform Reliquary from Shaikan Dheri," in Pal, ed.,
Aspects of Indian Art, Leiden, 1972.
Anesaki, Masaharu, *A History of Japanese Religions*, Vermont: Charles
Tuttle & Co. 1963.
Andrews, F., *Wall Paintings from Ancient Shrines in Central Asia*,
London, 1948.
-------------, "Central Asian Wall Paintings," *Indian Arts and Letters*
vol. VII. 4 (1934): 14.
Auboyer, Jennine, *Art of Afghanistan*, Czechoslovakia: Paul
Hamlyn, 1968.
-----------, *La Route de la Soie*, Paris, 1976.
-----------, *Rarities of the Musee Guimet,* NY: Asia Society, 1987.
Banerjee, P. *A New Light on Central Asian Art and Iconography* New
Delhi: Abha Prakshan, 1992.
Bareau, Andrea, *Les Sects du Petit Vehicle,* Saigon: École
        Francaise d'Extrême Oriente, 1955.
--------, *Recherches sur la Biographie du Buddha dans les
Sutrapitaka et les Vinayapitaka Anciens*, 3 vols., Paris: 1963.
--------, "La Legende de la Jeunesse du Buddha dans les Vinayapitaka
anciens," *Oriens* vol. 9 (1962): 16 ff.
Barthoux, Jules, *Les Fouilles de Hadda*, Paris: Delegation francaise
dans L'Afghanistan, 1933.
Barua, Dipak, *Buddhist Art in Central Asia,* Calcutta: Bhoomitter
Parashar, 1981.
Beal, Samuel, *Buddhist Records of the Western World*, London, 1882,
reprint, NY, 1968.

----------------, *The Fo Sho Hing Tsan King*, Wisdom of the East Series, vol. XIX, London, 1883.

Bhattacharya, Chhaya, "A Stylistic Study of the Wooden Buddha Figures from Kizil in the Berlin Turfan Collection, Museum fur Indische Kunst, Berlin," *New Delhi National Museum Bulletin* no. 4-6 (1983): 95-107.

Blunt, Wilfred, *The Golden Road to Samarkand*, NY: Viking Press, 1973.

Brinker, H. and Fischer, E., *Treasures from the Rietberg Museum*, NY: Metropolitan Museum of Art , 1980.

Buckley, Patria E. and Gregory, Peter, *Religion and Society in T'ang and Sung China*, Univ. of Hawaii Press, 1993.

Bush, Susan, "Thunder Monsters, Auspicious Animals, and Floral Ornament in the Early Sixth-Century," *Ars Orientalis* vol. X (1975): 19-35.

Bunsaku, Kurata, *The Art of the Lotus Sutra,* Tokyo: Kosei Publ., 1987.

Bussagli, M., *The Painting of Central Asia*, Geneva: Skira Publ., 1963.

Caswell, James, *Written and Unwritten*, Vancouver, 1988.

-------, "'The Thousand Buddha Pattern' in Caves XIX and XVI at Yun-Kang," *Ars Orientalis*, X (1975): 35-54.

Chang Yangmo, *Arts of Korea,* NY: Metropolitan Museum of Art, 1998.

Chappell, David, ed., *Buddhist and Taoist Practice in Medieval Chinese Society: Buddhist and Taoist Studies II*, Univ. of Hawaii, 1987.

Chaves, James, "A Han Painted Tomb at Luoyang," *Artibus Asiae,* vol. XXX (1968): p. 5ff.

Chavannes, Edouard, *Mission Archeologique dans la Chine Septentionale*, 2 vols., Paris, 1915

Ch'en, Kenneth, *Buddhism in China*, Princeton Univ. Press, 1972.

-------, *The Chinese Tradition* Princeton Univ. Press, 1975.

Chujina, N. et al., *The Museum of Oriental Art Moscow*, trans. A. Mikoyan, Leningrad: Aurora Publ., 1988.

Chung Yangmo, et. al, *Arts of Korea,* NY:- Metropolitan Museum of Art, 1998.

Coomaraswamy, Ananda, *La Sculpture du Bharhut*, Paris, 1956.

Curtin, Philip, *Cross Cultural Trade in World History* Cambridge Univ. Press, 1984.

Czuma, Stan, *Kushan Sculpture,* Cleveland: Cleveland Museum of Art,

1950.

de Bary, Wm. ed, *Sources of Chinese Tradition*, vol. I, NY: Columbia Univ. Press, 1970.

---------, ed. *The Buddhist Tradition,* NY: Columbia Univ. Press, 1972.

Degens, B., *Monuments pre-Islamique d'Afghanistan*, Paris: Delegation francaise dans L'Afghanistan, 1964.

Dehejia, Vidya, "On the Modes of Visual Narration in Early Buddhist Art," *Art Bulletin* vol. 73.3 (1990): 111-115.

--------,"Aniconism and the Multivalence of Emblems," *Ars Orientalis* vol. 21 (1991): 45-66.

--------,"*Rejoinder" Ars Orientalis* vol. 22 (1992): 157.

--------, *Discourse in Early Budhist Art:Visual Narratives of India,* New Delhi: Munshiram Manoharlal Publ. 1997.

Dellapiccola, A. ed., *The Stupa and its Religious and Historical Architectural Significance,* Wiesbaden: Franz Steiner Verlag,1980.

Dien, Albert, ed. *State and Society in Early Medieval China,* Stanford Univ. Press, 1990.

Duan Wenjie, *Dunhuang Art,* New Delhi: Indira Gandhi National Center for the Arts, 1994

Dupree, Louis, *Afghanistan*, Princeton Univ. Press, 1973.

Dutt, N., *Mahayana Buddhism*, Delhi, 1977.

Dutt, Sukmar, *Buddhist Monks and Monasteries of India,* London: G. Allen & Unwin, 1962.

Dye, Joe, "Two Fragmentary Gandharan Narrative Reliefs in the Peshawar Museum," *Artibus Asiae,* vol. XXXVIII (1976): 219-245.

Edwards, Michael, *A Life of the Buddha From a Burmese Manuscript,* London: The Folio Society, 1959.

Edwards, Richard, "The Cave Reliefs at Ma Hao," *Artibus Asia,* vol. XVIII, 1(1954): 5-25, 2: 103-129.

Eliade, M. *The Sacred and Profane*, trans. W. Trask, NY, 1958.

Eliot, Charles, *Hinduism and Buddhism*, 3 vols., London: G. Unwin & Allen Ltd, 1921.

------, *Japanese Buddhism*, London: G. Unwin & Allen Ltd, 1921.

Faccenna, Domenico, *Reports on the Campaigns of 1956-8 at Swat,* 3 vols., Rome: IsMeo Publ., 1962.

Farrer, A. and Whitfield, R., *Caves of the Thousand Buddhas: Chinese Art from the Silk Route,* NY: G. Braziller, Inc., 1990.

Fitzgerald, C. P., *A Short History of China*, NY, 1950.

Foucher, A., *La Vie du Bouddha*, Paris: 1949.

-----------,*Les Bas-Reliefs du Stupa de Sikri*, Paris, 1914.

----------, *L'Art Greco-Bouddhique du Gandhara,* 3 vols. Paris, 1905.

Frank, Irene, and Brownstone, D., *The Silk Road*, NY: Facts on File, 1986.

Frumkin, G., *Archaeology in Soviet Central Asia*, Leiden, 1970.

Gail, Adalbert, "The Four Principal Events in the Life of the Buddha--New Light on the Freer Panels," *East West,* vol. 42 (1992) 467-472.

Gies, J. ed. *The Arts of Central Asia: The Pelliot Collection in the Musee Guimet,* London: Serindia Pub. 1996

Giles, H. *Six Centuries of at Dunhuang,* London, 1944.

Godard, A. *The Art of Iran,* trans. by M. Heron, M. Rogers, ed., London: G. Allen and Unwin Ltd. 1962.

Godard and J. Hackin, *Les Antiquities bouddhique de Bamiyan* (Memoires de la Delegation Archeologique Francaise en Afghanistan, Paris: Les Editions G. van Oest, 1928.

Goepper, Roger and Whitfield, Roderick, *Treasures from Korea,* London: British Museum, 1984.

Gray, Basil*, Buddhist Cave Painting at Tun Huang*, Chicago, 1957.

Griswold, Alexander, *The Art of Burma Korea, and Tibet*, NY: Crown Publ. 1989.

Grunwedel, Albert, *Altbuddhistiche Kulstatten in Chinesisch Turkistan*, Berlin, 1912.

Hackin, J.*, Recherche Archeologique en Asie Centrale*, Paris, 1936.

Hambis and Hallade, *Toumchouq*, Paris: Delegation francaise dans L'Afghanistan, 1964.

Harper, Prudence, *The Royal Hunter: Art of the Sasanian Empire* NY: Asia Society, 1978.

Hartel, Herbert, *Along the Silk Routes: Central Asian Art from West Berlin State Museums,* Berlin, 1982.

Hawkes, David, *Songs of the South*, reprint Great Britain, 1985.

Hayashi, R. *The Silk Road and the Shoso-in,* Heibonsha Survey of Japanese Art, vol. 6, NY: Weatherhill Inc. 1975.

Historical Relics Unearthed in China, Beijing, 1972.

Howard, Angela, "The Monumental 'Cosmological Buddha' in the Freer Gallery of Art: Chronology and Style," *Archives of Asian Art,* vol. XIV(1984): 53 ff.

--------, "In Support of a New Chronology for the Kizil Mural
   Paintings," *Archives of Asian Art,* vol. XLVI (1991): 8-83
Hsio-Yen Shih, "Readings and Re-readings of Narrative in
   Dunhuang Murals," *Artibus Asiae,* vol. LIII. 1-2 (1993): 59-88.
Huntington, Susan, "Early Buddhist Art and the Theory of
   Aniconism," *Art Journal,* vol. 49, Winter 1990, no. 4: 401-8.
-------------"Aniconism and the Multivalence of Emblems: Another
   Look," *Ars Orientalis,* vol. 22 (1992): 111-156.
Hurvitz, Leon, "Chapter of the *Wei Shu* on Buddhism and Taoism,"
   Yun Kang, vol. XVI, Tokyo, 1951: 72ff.
Ikeda, Daisaku, *The Flower of Chinese Buddhism,* trans. by B.
   Watson, NY: Weatherhill Pub., 1986.
Ingholt, H. and Lyons, I., *Gandharan Art in Pakistan*, Connecticut,
   1957.
Irwin, J. "The Axial Symbolism of the Early Stupa: An Exegesis," in
   Dellapiccola 1980: 12-38
Jaymes, H., "The Buddhist Caves of the Ching Ho Valley," *The
   Eastern Buddhist* (1923): 65ff.
Karetzky, P. E., "The Recently Discovered Chin Dynasty
   Murals Illustrating the Life of the Buddha at Yen-Shang-ssu, Shansi,"
   Artibus Asiae, vol. XLII.4 (1980): 245-259.
--------"Mara Buddhist Deity of Death and Desire," *East-West,* vol.
   XXXII (1982): 75.
--------, "Foreigners in Tang and pre Tang China,"*Oriental Art,* vol.
   XXX (1984): 160ff.
--------,"An Illustration of the *Guo Zhu Xian Zai Yin Guo Jing,* Sutra of
   Cause and Effect in China," *Journal of Chinese Religions,* vol. 16
   (1988): 54-72.
--------, "A Scene of the Parinirvana on a Recently Excavated
   Stone Reliquary of the Tang Dynasty," *East and West,* (Ismeo
   Rome) vol. 38 (1988): 215-229.
--------, "The Post-Enlightenment Miracles of the Buddha;
   Texts and Illustrations," *Orientations* (Hong Kong) Jan. 1990: 71-77.
--------, "Some Cosmological Schemes in the Early Caves at
   Dunhuang," *Journal of Chinese Religions,* vol. 20 (1992): 103-116.
--------, *Life of the Buddha: Ancient Pictorial and Literary
   Sources* Lathan: Univ. Press, 1992.
--------,*Court Art of the Tang Dynasty*, Univ. Press: Latham, 1996.
Klimburg, Deborah, et. al *The Silk Route and the Diamond*

Path, LA, UCLA Art Council, 1982.

-----------, "The Life of the Buddha in Western Himalayan Monastic Art: Act One", *East-West* vol. 42 (1992): 189-213.

Kinnard, Jaocb, "Reevaluating the Eight-Ninth Century Pala Milieu: Icono–Conservatism and the Persistence of Sakyamuni," *Journal of the Association of Buddhist Studies,* vol. 19.2 (1996): 281-300.

Komayashi, Takeshi, *Nara Buddhism Art: Todai-ji* Tokyo: Heibonsha, 1975.

Kurata Bunsakau,*Horyuji-Temple of the Exhalted Law*, NY: Japan Society, 1981.

-------, *Art of the Lotus Sutra* Tokyo: Kosei Publ. 1987.

Lahiri, Latika, *Chinese Monks in India*, Delhi: Motilal Banarsidass, 1981.

Leidy, Denise, "The Ssu-wei Figure in Sixth Century A.D. Chinese Buddhist Sculpture," *Archives of Asian Art,* vol. XLIII (1990): 21-37.

Lippe, Ashwin, *The Freer Indian Sculptures,* Washington, DC: 1970.

Liu, Xinru, *Silk and Religion,* Delhi: Oxford Univ. Press, 1996.

Liu Xing-zhen and Yue Feng-xia, *Han Dynasty Stone Reliefs the Wu Family Shrines in Shandong Province,* Beijing, 1991.

Loewe, Michael, *Early Imperial China*, London, 1968.

Mair, Victor, *Painting and Performance,* Honolulu: Univ. of Hawaii Press, 1988.

Mason, Penelope, *The History of Japanese Art,* NY: Abrams Inc. 1993.

Mather, Richard, "The Life of the Buddha and the Buddhist Life: Wang Jung's 'Songs of Religious Joy,'" *Journal of the Association of Oriental Studies,* vol. 107.1 (1987): ff.

Meunie, J., *Shotorak*, Paris: Delegation francaise dans L'Afghanistan, 1942.

Mino, Yukata, *The Great Eastern Temple, Todaiji,* Art Institute of Chicago, 1986.

Mizuno, S., and Nagahiro, *Yun Kang,* 20 vols., Tokyo, 1951.

-------------, *The Buddhist Cave Temples of Lung-men in Honan*, Tokyo, 1941.

Mizuno, Seiichi, *Hsiang T'ang Ssu*, Tokyo, 1937.

---------- *Asuka Buddhist Art: Horyu-ji* Tokyo: Heibonsha Press 1974

Moran, Sherman, "The Death of the Buddha, a Painting at Koyasan," *Artibus Asiae,* vol. (1974) XXXVI: 111 ff.

Murray, Julia, "Buddhism and Early Narrative Illustration in China," *Archives of Asia Art,* vol. 48 (1995): 17-31

----------"What is 'Chinese Narrative Illustration'?" *Art Bulletin,* vol. 80.4 (1998): 603-615.

Nath, Amrath, *Buddhist Images and Narratives*, New Delhi:Books and Books, 1986.

Nagahiro, T., *The Representation Art of the Six Dynasties,*Tokyo: Bijutsu chupansha, 1969.

Nehru, Lolita, *The Origins of the Gandharan Style*, Delhi, 1989.

New Archaeological Finds in China, Beijing, 1973

Ning Qiang, "The Emergence of the 'Dunhuang Style' in the Northern Wei Dynasty," *Orientations*, May 1992: 45-51.

Okudaira, H. *Narrative Picture Scrolls* trans. E. ten Grotenhuis, Tokyo: Weatherhill Inc., 1966.

Pal, Pratapaditya, *Light of Asia*, LA County Museum, 1984.

---, *Aspects of Indian Art*, Leiden, 1974.

---, *Buddhist Book Illuminations* NY: Ravi Kumar Publ. 1988.

Pas, Julian, *Visions of Sukhavati*, NY: SUNY Press, 1995.

Pelliot, Paul *Les Grottes de Touen houang*, 6 vols., Paris, 1914.

Percheron, Maurice, *Buddha and Buddhism,* NY: Overlook Press, 1982.

Phillips, Q. "The Price Shuten Doji Screens: A Study of Visual Narrative," *Ars Orientalis,* vol. XXVI (1996): 1-22.

Piotrovsky, Mikhail, *Lost Empire of the Silk Road,* Milan: Thyssen Bornemisza Foundation, 1993.

Przyluski, J., "Le nord-ouest de l'Inde dans le Vinayana des Mula-sarvastivadin et les textes apparentes", *Journal Asiatique,* 11th seires, Vol. IV, (1914).

Pugachenkove, G., and Khakimov, A., *The Art of Central Asia*, trans. S. Gitman, Aurora Art Publ.: Leningrad, 1988.

Rahula, W., "L'Ideal du Bodhisattva dans le Theravad et le Mahayana", *Journal Asiatique*, vol. 259, (1971): 65 ff.

Rhie, Marilyn, *Early Buddhist Art of China and Central Asia,* Leiden: Brill Publ., 1999.

Rice, Tamara Talbot, *Ancient Arts of Central Asia*, London, 1965.

Rockhill, W. W. *Life of the Buddha,* rpt. Chinese Materials Center, Inc. no. 41, San Francisco, 1976

Rosenfield, John, *Dynastic Art of the Kushans,* LA: Univ. of California Press, 1967.

Rowan, D. "A Reconsideration of an Unusual Ivory Diptych," *Artibus Asiae,* vol. XLVI.4 (1985): 251ff.

Rowland, Benjamin, "Review Articles: Art Among the Silk
    Roads, A Reappraisal of Central Asian Art," *Harvard Journal of
    Asian Studies*, vol. XXV (1964): 257-60.
----------, *Art and Architecture of India*, Great Britain, 1973.
----------, *Zentral Asien*, Germany, 1970.
----------, *Art in Afghanistan: Objects from the Khabul Museum*,
    London: Penguin Press, 1971.
Saha, Kshanika, *Buddhism and Buddhist Literature in Central Asia*,
    Calcutta: Firma K.L. Mukhopadhay, 1970.
Salomon, Richard, *Ancient Buddhist Scrolls From Gandhara*, Univ. of
    Washington, Press, 1999
Saunders, E. Dale, *Buddhism in Japan*, Univ. of Philadelphia Press,
    1964.
Seckel, Deitrich, *The Art of Buddhism*, NY, 1964.
Schopen, Gregory, *Bones, Stones and Buddhist Monks*, Univ. of
    Hawaii Press, 1997.
Sha, Kshannika, *Buddhist Literature in Central Asia*, Calcutta, 1970.
Shih, Hsio-Yen, "Readings and Re-readings of Narrative in Dunhuang
    Murals," *Artibus Asiae*, vol. LIII (1993): 59-88.
Sircar, D.C. *Asokan Studies*, Calcutta: Indian Musuem, 1979.
Sivaramamurti, C., *Amaravati Sculptures in the Madras Museum*,
    Madras, 1956.
Snodgrass, A. *The Symbolism of the Stupa* Ithaca: *Cornell Southeast
    Asia Program*, 1985.
Soothill, William, *Dictionary of Chinese Buddhist Terms* London,
    1934.
Soper, Alexander, "Japanese Evidence for the History of Architecture
    and Iconography of Chinese Buddhism," *Monumenta Serica*, vol.
    IV. 2 (1940).
------, "Northern Liang and Northern Wei in Kansu," *Artibus Asiae*,
    vol. XXI. 2 (1948): 146.
------,"Aspects of Light Symbolism in Gandharan Sculpture," *Artibus
    Asiae*, in three parts vol. XII (1949): 252-283, 314-330, and vol.
    XXII (1950): 63-82.
------, *Kuo Jo hsu's Experiences in Painting*, Washington DC, 1951.
------,"T'ang Ch'ao Ming Hua Lu, Celebrated Painters of the T'ang
    Dynasty," *Artibus Asiae*, vol. XXI (1958): 210ff.
------,"A T'ang Parinirvana Stele," *Artibus Asiae*, vol. XXII (1959):
    167ff.

-----, *Literary Evidence for Early Buddhist Art in China*, Ascona: Artibus Asiae, Publ.1960.

------,"South Chinese Influence on the Buddhist Art of the Six Dynasties," *Bulletin of the Museum of Far Eastern Antiquities,* vol. XXXII (1960): 57ff.

------"Vacation Glimpses of the T'ang Temples of Ch'ang an," *Artibus Asiae*, vol. XXIII (1960): 31.

------,"Imperial Cave-chapels of the Northern Dynasties, " *Artibus Asiae,* vol. XXVIII (1966): 241 ff.

Soymie, Michel, *Contributions aux Etudes sur Toung-Houang,* Paris: Librairie Droz, 1979.

State Hermitage Museum, *Lost Empire of the Silk Road, Buddhist Art from Kharakhoto*, ed. Mikhail Piotrovsky, Milan, 1993.

Staviskij, B., *La Bactriane sous les Kushans,* Paris: Librarie D'Amerique et D'Orient, 1986.

Stein, Marcus Aurel, *Serindia,* 4 vols., Oxford, 1921.

------, *Innermost Asia,* 4 vols., Oxford, 1926.

------, *Ruins of Desert Cathay*, 2 vols., London, 1912, reprint NY: Dover, 1987.

Strong, John, *The Legend of King Asoka,* Princeton Univ. Press, 1983.

Subrahmanyam, Savitri, "Dinna, The Mathuran Gupta Artist," *The Golden Age*, Karl Khandalavala, Bombay: Marg, publ.1991: 125 ff.

Sullivan, Michael, *The Cave Temples of Machishan,* Berkeley: Univ. of California Press, 1969.

----------, *The Arts of China*, Berkeley: Univ. of California Press, 1982

Sun Dawei, ed. *The Art in the Caves of Xinjiang*, Xinjiang, 1989.

Takeshi Kuno, *Ancient Sculpture in the Horyuji*, Tokyo, 1958.

Thomas, E., *The Life of the Buddha* , London, 1927.

Tissot, Francine, *Gandhara*, Paris, 1985.

--------, *Les Arts Anciens Du Pakistan et de L'Afghanistan*, Paris: Ecole du Louvre, 1987.

Tokiwa and Sekino, *Buddhist Monuments of China*, 8 vols., Tokyo, 1931.

Tokyo National Museum, *Pageant of Japanese Art: Sculpture*, Tokyo, 1958.

-------, *Scythian, Persian, and Central Asian Art from the Hermitage Collection, Leningrad,* Tokyo, 1969.

Tsukamoto, Z. "The Sramana Superintendent Tan yao and his Time," *Monumenta Serica,* vol. XVI (1957): 363 ff.

Turin Gallerie dell'Arte, *L'Afghanistan Preistoria all'Islam Capolavori del Museo di Khabul,* Turin, 1961.

Waldschmidt, "Beschreibender Text", in Le Coq, *Die Buddhistische Spantantike Mittelasiens,* Berlin, 1928, vol. VII, p. 27.

Whitfield, R. and Farrer, A. *Caves of the Thousand Buddhas,* NY: G. Braziller, Inc.1990.

Varma, K. M. *Technique of Gandharan And Indo-Afghan Stucco Images,* Calcutta, 1987.

Vollmer, John, Keall, and Nagai-Berthrong, *Silk Roads–China Ships,* Toronto: ROM: 1983.

von Le Coq, A. *Die Buddhistische Spantantike Mittelasiens,* 7 vols. Berlin: Verlag Deitrich Reimer Ernst Vohsen, 1928.

-------------. *Buried Treasures of Chinese Turkestan*, Oxford Univ. Press: 1985.

Waley, Arthur, *Introduction to the Study of Chinese Painting,* NY: Grove Press, 1921.

--------, *A Catalogue of Paintings Recovered from Dunhuang by Sir A. Stein,* London, 1931.

Watanabe, M. "A Preliminary Study of 'Life of the Buddha' in Medieval Japan: The Metropolitan Museum Paintings," *Orientations,* September, 1996: 46-56.

Weiner, S. *Ajanta: Its Place in Buddhist Art,* Berkeley: Univ. of California Press 1980.

Wheelwright, Carolyn, "Late Medieval Nirvana Painting," *Archives of Asian Art,* vol. 38 (1985): 67-94.

Williams, Joanna, *The Art of Guptan India,* Princeton Univ., Press 1982.

Wright, Arthur*, Buddhism in Chinese History*, Stanford Univ. Press, 1959, reprint 1970.

Wu Hung, "Buddhist Elements in Early Chinese Art 2nd and 3rd centuries A.D.)," *Artibus Asiae,* vol. XLVII, 3-4 (1986): 263-352.

-------,"Reborn in Paradise: A Case Study of Dunhuang Sutra Painting and its Religious, Ritual and Artistic Contexts," *Orientations,* May, 1992: 52-64.

Yamato Bunkakan, Korean Buddhist Paintings of Koryo Dynasty Nara, 1978.

Yi Ki-baek (Catalogue of) The National Museum of Korea, Seoul, 1993.

Zhang Ting-hao, *The Famen Temple*, Xian, 1990.

Zurcher, Heinrich, *The Buddhist Conquest of China*, 2 vols., Leiden, 1972.

--------, *Buddhism*, London, 1962.

--------, "'Prince Moonlight' Messianism and Eschatology in Early Medieval Chinese Buddhism," *T'oung Pao* (Leiden) vol. LXVIII (1972): 1-58.

Zwalf, W., *Buddhism*, London, 1985.

CHINESE SOURCES

Cheng Mingchi, "Lingtai sheli shih guan, *Wenwu*, 1983.2.

Ding Mingyi, Ma Shichang," Qiziru shiku de fufu bihua (Kiziru Sekuttsu no Butsuten Hekiga)," *Chugoku sekkutsu kiziru sekkutsu*, Vol. III: 170-227.

Dunhuang Yanjiu, Dunhuang chubansha, 1944-1994.

Fojyau Yishu, Chen Chuanjian, ed. Beijing: Yishujya chupansha, 1994.

Foxue tatzu dian, Beijing: Wenwu chubansha, 1991.

Gansusheng wenwu kaogu yanjiu suobian,, *Hexi Shiku,* Beijing: Wenwu chubansha, 1987.

Gansusheng wenwu gongsuo, *Longdong shiku,* 1987.

Gansusheng wenwu gongsuo, *Qingyang Beishikusi* Beijing: Wenwu chubansha, 1985.

Guizi shiku, Han Xiang, ed. Xinjiang, 1990.

Ku K'ai chih Yenchiu Tzuliao, Beijing, 1962.

Liuchao yishu, Yao Qian, ed., Beijing: Wenwu chubansha, 1981.

Luoyang Beiwei shisu shike xiahuaji Huang Minglan, ed. Renmin yishu chubansha, 1987.

Ma Shichang,"Kizil shiku zhongxin zhuku de zhushi kuding de hou shi de bihua" (Kiziru sekkutsu chushin chukutsu no shushitsu kutsu cho no koshitsu no hekiga), *Chugoku sekkutsu,* vol. II, p. 170-236.

Maijishan, Beijing: Wenwu Press, 1954.

Pei Wei Shih K'u Fou-t'iao P'ien Hsuan, Peking, 1958.

Shanxi Sheng Wenwu gongsuo, "Shanxi Zhangtai Faxien Tang Sheli," Kaogu, 1961.5.

Shensi Sheng Po-wu-kuan Ts'ang Shih-k'e Hsuan-chi, Shensi, 1957.

Shifoxuancui, Li Jingjie, ed. Beijing: Renmin jiaoyu chuban she, 1995.

Su Bai "Kiziru sekkutsu no keishiki kuwa to so no niendai, "*Chugoku sekkutsu, Kiziru sekkutsu*, vol. I: 162ff.

Tunhuang Pi Hua, Peking, 1959.

Yungangshiku,, Beijing: Shaanxi bowuguan gongzuo 1977.

Yunglo kung Pihuu Chienchieh , Shanghai, 1959.

*Xumishan Shiku,*Beijing: Wenwu chubansha, 1988.

Zhang Yaping, Shanxisheng xinxian wenwu gongsuo, "Fanshi
 Yanshangsi Chindaide bihua," *Wenwu.*1979.2.

Zhongguo Lidaijinyan foxiang tudian, Beijing: Wenwu chubansha,
 1992.

Zhongguo meishu quanji Sui Tang diaoke, Li Pao, ed. vol. V Beijing :
 Wenwu chubansha, 1988.

Zhongguo meishu quanji: Diaosubian, Pinglingsi deng shihkou diaosu,
 vol. 9, Wang Ziyun, ed. Beijing: Wenwu chubansha, 1988.

Zhongguo meishu quanji: Diaosubian, Yungang shiku diaoke, vol. 10,
 Su Bai and Li Zhiguo, eds. Beijing: Wenwu chubansha, 1988.

Zhongguo meishu qianji: Diaosubian: Longmen shiku diaoke, vol. 11,
 Su Bai and Wen Yucheng, eds. Beijing: Wenwu chubansha , 1988.

Zhongguo meishu qianji:Diaosubian, Gongxian, Tianlongshan,
 Xiangtangshan, Anyang, shiku diaoke, vol. 13, eds. Chen Mingda
 and Ding Mingshi, Beijing: Wenwu chubansha , 1989.

Zhongguo meishu quanji: Huihuabian: Xinjiang Tulepan, vol. 6,
 Beijing: Wenwu Press, 1989.

Zhongguo meishu quanji: Huihuabiian: Maijishan deng shikou pihua,
 vol. 17, eds. Yan Wenru Dong Yuxiang, Beijing: Wenwu Press,
 1988.

Zhongguo Shiku: Yongjing binglingsi, Beijing: Wenwu chubansha,,
 1989.

JAPANESE SOURCES

Chugoku Sekkutsu: Tonko Bakkotsu Beijing: Dunhuang Institute and
 Heibonsha shupansha, 5 vols., 1980-1982.

Chugoku Sekkutsu: Kiziru Sekkutsu 3 vols. Beijing: Wen Wu and
 Heibonsha shupansha, 1983.

Kajitani, R. "Butsusen-zu no tenkai: bukkyo setsuwa-e no hyogen to
 tokuhitsu," *Nihon no bijitsu,* vol. 9, Tokyo: Kodansha Press, 1991:
 158-167.

Kojima, Tomoko, "Tunhuang Hekiga ni Okeru Beichou Suidai no
 Sangaku Hyogen," *Bijitsushi* vol. 41.1 (1992): 131 ff.

Ide Seinosuke, "Rokushin Chuko Nehan Hyogen no Henyo," *Bijitsu
 Kenkyu,* no. 355 (1993), part I: 77-92; part II 146-158.

Matsubara, S., *Chugoku Bukkyo Chokokushi Kenyu*, Tokyo, 1966.
Nihon Emakimono Zenshu, vol. XVI, Tokyo, 1969.
Mochizuki, S., *Bukkyodaijiten*, 10 vols., Tokyo, 1960.
Omura, S., *Shina Bijutsu Shi Chosohen*, Tokyo, 1915.
Omura, S., *Shina Bijitsu Zuroku* , Tokyo, 1925.
Ryukoku Daigaku Toshoguan, *Otani kentia shorai, Kyoto, 1983.*
Shosoin Homotsu, 3 vols., Tokyo, 1962.
Tokiwa, Daijo and Sekino, T. *Shina Bukkyo Shiseki*, 8 vols., Tokyo, 1951.
Tokyo Kokoritsu Bijitsukan zuhanmokuroku: Otani kentai shohinhen, Tokyo Kokoritsu Bijitsukan, 1971.

Index

FIGURE 1. Bas-relief of the conception from the Bharhut Stupa railing now preserved in the National Museum of Delhi. ca. 2nd B.C.E.
FIGURE 2. Bas-relief of the defeat of Mara, Sanchi Stupa, horizontal lintel ca. 1st century.

FIGURE 3. Bas-relief of the conception and return from Kapilavastu Sanchi stupa pillar ca.1st century.
FIGURE 4. Sikri Stupa base frieze, Lahore Museum ca. 2nd to 4th century.

FIGURE 5. Guptan Stele with set of eight scenes of the life of the Buddha, Sarnath ca 5th century.
FIGURE 6. Qizil Peacock Cave, Xinjiang, murals main room, ca 5th century.

FIGURE 6a. Qizil Peacock Cave murals birth detail
FIGURE 6b. Qizil Peacock Cave mural four exits

FIGURE 6c. Qizil Peacock Cave mural temptation of Mara's daughters
FIGURE 6d. Qizil Peacock Cave mural attack of Mara.

FIGURE 7.   Qizil Peacock Cave parinirvana line drawing after Grunwedel
1912: 87
FIGURE 8.   Qizil Peacock Cave parinirvana line drawing after Grunwedel
1912: 87

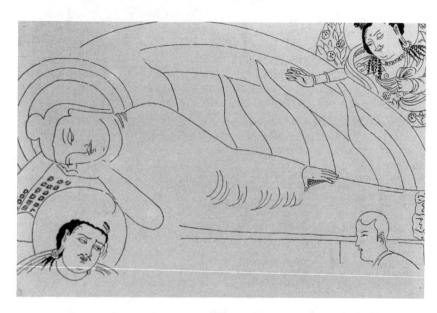

FIGURE 9.   Qizil Stepped Cave mural temptation of Mara, detail
FIGURE 9a. Qizil Stepped Cave mural temptation of Mara, detail

FIGURE 10.   Qizil Stepped Cave mural top: nativity cycle; bottom: scenes from pre-enlightenment
FIGURE 10a.   Qizil Stepped Cave mural nativity cycle: birth, detail

FIGURE 11. Qizil Stepped Cave mural nativity cycle: top: nativity cycle; bottom: scenes from pre-enlightenment
FIGURE 11a. Qizil Stepped Cave mural nativity cycle--first bath and seven steps, detail

FIGURE 12. Qizil Stepped Cave mural top: youthful activities bottom: scenes
from pre-enlightenment
FIGURE 12a Qizil Stepped Cave mural top: youthful activities bottom: scenes
from pre-enlightenment-- throwing of the elephant, detail

FIGURE. 13 Qizil Stepped Cave mural top: athletic contests; bottom: scenes
from the pre-enlightenment cycle
FIGURE 13a Qizil Stepped Cave mural athletic contests--archery contest,
detail

FIGURE 14.   Qizil Stepped Cave mural four exits
FIGURE 14a. Qizil Stepped Cave mural four exits-- sick man and old man, detail

FIGURE 14b Qizil Stepped Cave mural four exits--dead man and monk, detail
FIGURE 15. Qizil Stepped Cave mural great departure

FIGURE 16. Qizil Stepped Cave mural Gift of food by Sugata, detail
FIGURE 17. Qizil Cave 205 mural breaking the news to King Ajatasatru

FIGURE 17a. Qizil Cave 205 mural breaking the news to King Ajatasatru detail
FIGURE 18. Qizil Cave 99 lunette mural with nativity scenes

FIGURE 18a. Qizil Cave 99 lunette mural with nativity scenes
FIGURE 19. Qizil Cave 38 ceiling mural with biographical scenes

FIGURE 20. Qizil Cave 17 ceiling mural with biographical scenes
FIGURE 21. Qizil Cave 80 ceiling mural with biographical scenes

FIGURE 22.   Qizil Cave 38 mural death of the Buddha
FIGURE 22a. Qizil Cave 38 mural death of the Buddha, detail

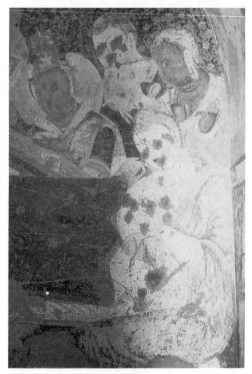

FIGURE 23. Qizil Cave 48 mural death of the Buddha
FIGURE 24 Qizil Cave 205 mural cremation of the Buddha

FIGURE 24a Qizil Cave 205 mural cremation of the Buddha, detail
FIGURE 24b Qizil Cave 205 mural cremation of the Buddha, line drawing
after Grunwedel, 1912 fig. 415

FIGURE 25   Qizil Cave 205 mural division of the relics cremation of the
Buddha, detail
FIGURE 26 Qizil Cave 224 cremation of the Buddha.

FIGURE 27. Qizil Cave 1 sculpture death of the Buddha.
FIGURE 28. Qizil Cave 80 mural scenes of Buddha preaching

FIGURE 29. Qizil Cave 129 mural scenes of Buddha preaching
FIGURE 30.   Dunhuang, Gansu Cave 275 mural four exits: detail

FIGURE 31.   Dunhuang Cave 254 mural temptation of Mara
FIGURE 31a.   Dunhuang Cave 254 mural temptation of Mara, detail

FIGURE 32.   Dunhuang Cave 428 mural stupa with scene of the birth
FIGURE 33.   Dunhuang Cave 428 mural jataka narratives

FIGURE 33a. Dunhuang Cave 428 central pier
FIGURE 34.   Dunhuang Cave 290 ceiling mural scenes from the life of the
Buddha

FIGURE 35.   Dunhuang Cave 290 ceiling mural scenes from the life of the Buddha
FIGURE 36.   Dunhuang Cave 290 ceiling mural scenes from the life of the Buddha

FIGURE 37.   Dunhuang Cave 290 ceiling mural scenes from the life of the Buddha
FIGURE 38.   Dunhuang Cave 290 ceiling mural scenes from the life of the Buddha

FIGURE 39.   Dunhuang Cave 290 ceiling mural scenes from the life of the
Buddha
FIGURE 40.   Dunhuang Cave 290 mural encounter with Yudani, first
meditation

FIGURE 41.   Dunhuang Cave 290 ceiling mural scenes from the life of the Buddha

FIGURE 42.   Dunhuang Cave 280 ceiling mural first sermon

FIGURE 42a. Dunhuang Cave 280 ceiling mural conception
FIGURE 43.   Dunhuang Cave 420 ceiling mural death scenes

FIGURE 43a. Dunhuang Cave 420 ceiling mural death scene
FIGURE 44. Dunhuang Cave 280 mural death scene

FIGURE 45.   Dunhuang Cave 157 mural death scene
FIGURE 45a . Dunhuang Cave 157 mural death scene, detail

FIGURE 46. Silk banner from Dunhuang-Tang dynasty nativity scenes
FIGURE 47. Silk banner from Dunhuang Tang dynasty four exits

FIGURE 48. Silk banner from Dunhuang four exits.
FIGURE 48a. Silk banner from Dunhuang four exits.

FIGURE 49. Yungang Shanxi, Cave VI interior view
FIGURE 50. Yungang Cave VI bas-relief birth

FIGURE 51. Yungang Cave VI bas-relief return to Kapilavatu
FIGURE 52. Yungang Cave VI bas-relief four exits

FIGURE 53. Yungang Cave VI bas-relief sleep of the harem
FIGURE 54. Yungang Cave VI bas-relief temptation of Mara, details

FIGURE 55. Yungang Cave VI bas-relief first sermon
FIGURE 56. Yungang Cave X bas-relief *Dipamkara jataka*

FIGURE 57. Yungang Cave XI bas-relief offering of the four bowls
FIGURE 58. Yungang Cave XI bas-relief death

FIGURE 58a. Yungang Cave XI bas-relief detail
FIGURE 59. Yungang Cave 48 bas relief carving conception

FIGURE 60.   Guyang Cave, Longmen, Honan, relief carving birth and seven steps.
FIGURE 60a.   Guyang Cave, Longmen, bas relief carving, reading of the special signs.

FIGURE 61. Weizidong Cave, Longmen bas relief carving, miracle of the shade and parinirvana.
FIGURE 62. Stone stele dated 471 in the Shaanxi Provincial Historical Museum.

FIGURE 62a.   Stone stele dated 471 in the Shaanxi Provincial Historical Museum, rear face.
FIGURE 62b.   Stone stele dated 471 in the Shaanxi Provincial Historical Museum, narrative scenes on rear face.

FIGURE 63. Stone stele from Northern Wei Period with farewell of Kanthaka at top, lower left birth.
FIGURE 64. Northern Qi marble support stone with bas-relief scenes of the life of the Buddha, Tokyo National Museum.

FIGURE 65. Stele from Tang dynasty dated 692 with death scenes.
FIGURE 65a Stele from Tang dynasty dated 692 with death scenes

FIGURE 66. E Ingakyo Joborendaiji painted scrolls—life in the palace.
FIGURE 66a. E Ingakyo Joborendaiji painted scrolls-temptation of Mara.

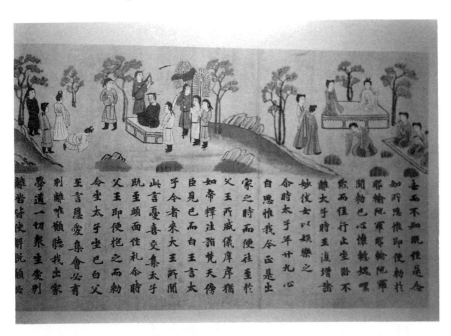